JELLICOE

Edited by A. Temple Patterson

JELLICOE PAPERS
(*2 volumes*)

JELLICOE

A BIOGRAPHY

A. Temple Patterson

Emeritus Professor in the University of Southampton

MACMILLAN

ST MARTIN'S PRESS

First published 1969 *by*
MACMILLAN AND CO LTD
Little Essex Street London WC2
and also at Bombay Calcutta and Madras
Macmillan South Africa (*Publishers*) *Pty Ltd Johannesburg*
The Macmillan Company of Australia Pty Ltd Melbourne
The Macmillan Company of Canada Ltd Toronto
St Martin's Press Inc New York
Gill and Macmillan Ltd Dublin

Library of Congress catalog card no. 76-78814

Printed in Great Britain by
ROBERT MACLEHOSE AND CO LTD
The University Press, Glasgow

Contents

List of Plates	*page*	7
List of Maps		9
Preface		11

1	The Making of an Admiral (1859–1907)	13
2	The Coming Man (1907–14)	41
3	'Responsibility is the Devil' (1914–15)	59
4	The Long Haul (1915–16)	83
5	Jutland	99
6	After Jutland (June–November 1916)	132
7	First Sea Lord (December 1916–December 1917): The Submarine Peril	154
8	First Sea Lord: Dismissal	177
9	The Empire Mission	210
10	The Jutland Controversy and the Closing Years	230

Appendix	255
Notes	258
Bibliography	268
Index	271

Plates

Admiral Sir John Jellicoe when Commander-in-Chief of
the Grand Fleet *facing page* 48
    Lady Latham

Jellicoe's parents: Captain and Mrs Jellicoe 49
    Lord Jellicoe and Mr Richard Latham

Jellicoe in Captain's full-dress uniform shortly after the
Boxer Rebellion 64
    The Trustees of the National Maritime Museum

Two cartoons of Jellicoe 65
    *The Trustees of the National Maritime Museum and the
    Proprietors of Punch*

Admiral Jellicoe coming on to the bridge of his flagship the
Iron Duke while Commander-in-Chief 128
    Imperial War Museum

Admiral Sir David Beatty on the quarter-deck of his flagship the *Queen Elizabeth* 129
    Imperial War Museum

Jellicoe's flagship, H.M.S. *Iron Duke* 144
    Imperial War Museum

Sir David Beatty's flagship while he was in command of
the Battle-Cruiser Fleet, H.M.S. *Lion* 144
    Imperial War Museum

Vice-Admiral Sir Charles Madden 145
    Radio Times Hulton Picture Library

Admiral Sir Alexander Duff 145
    Trustees of the National Maritime Museum

Rear-Admiral Hugh Evan-Thomas 145
    Imperial War Museum

Commodore William E. Goodenough   145
  Imperial War Museum

Vice-Admiral Reinhard Scheer   176
  Imperial War Museum

Vice-Admiral Franz Hipper   176
  Imperial War Museum

Lady Jellicoe   177
  Lady Latham

Admiral Sir John Jellicoe at the time of his first sea
lordship, 1917   192
  Lord Jellicoe

Some of Lord Jellicoe's relaxations in later life   192
  Lord Jellicoe

Maps

1   The North Sea, 1914–18   108

2   Jutland from 2.15 to 6 p.m.   112

3   Jutland from 6.15 to 6.45 p.m.   117

4   Jutland. The second clash between the battle fleets   122

5   Jutland. The tracks of the two fleets during the night
      31 May–1 June   126

Preface

FOR a landsman to attempt to write the life of a great seaman requires some apology. Mine must be that after having spent some years, through a combination of circumstances too complex to be described here, in preparing for the Navy Records Society a two-volume edition of Lord Jellicoe's papers and of documents relating to his career, I have become very conscious that a new biography of him is needed. The two (one of them relatively brief) which appeared soon after his death were written by naval officers of distinction who, although they enjoyed the advantage of personal acquaintance with their subject, had been too close to him, and in the major case too warmly partisan and too deeply immersed in the controversies to which his wartime career gave rise, for an objective presentation to be possible. Nor did either have access to or liberty to use all the material that is now available. That even with this greater wealth of material I have achieved such a presentation I would not venture to claim, notwithstanding the technical and specialist aid which has been generously given me and on which I have leant heavily; but at least I have tried hard to hold the balance even, while steering my way through matters some of which are still subjects of debate or even yet of partisan dispute. Perhaps I may be permitted to emphasise that I am not striving to present a case for or against anyone, but only to set down the truth as I see it, with however blurred or limited a vision. As Luther said of an infinitely greater issue: 'Here stand I. I can naught else.'

I have the greatest pleasure in expressing my warm gratitude to the present Earl Jellicoe for placing much material at my service and drawing for my benefit on his personal recollections of the later part of his father's life; and similarly to Earl Beatty for the like access to papers and readiness to supply information. To Captain S. W. Roskill, R.N., I am most deeply indebted for much invaluable help and advice; as also to Professor Arthur J. Marder for the generous loan of much material, for stimulating correspondence and (as Pepys would have said) 'much good talk'; to the Hon. David Erskine, the Secretary of the Navy Records Society, for indispensable aid and counsel; to Lieutenant-Commander P. K. Kemp and Mr A. W. H. Pearsall for leave to consult collections of manuscripts in the Naval Library of the Ministry of Defence and the National Maritime Museum respectively; to Admiral Sir Charles Madden and Vice-Admiral Sir Geoffrey Barnard for helpful interviews and in the latter case the loan of documents; to Mr A. J. L. Barnes of the London School of Economics for the loan of papers; to Commander P. C. H. Clissold of the Warsash School of Navigation for kindly supplying information about the Cayzer family and its shipping lines; to Lord Keyes and Mr David McKenna for permission to consult the Keyes and McKenna Papers in the custody of Churchill College, Cambridge, and to Dr Edwin Welch the College Archivist for help in this consultation; to Lieutenant-Commander R. F. Cope, R.N.R., for more than one valuable suggestion; to the staff of Southampton University Library and in particular Mr G. J. Broadis and Mr G. Hampson for patient, frequent and invaluable aid; and to Mrs D. Moore and Mrs K. Sharpe for kindly typing my manuscript.

For leave to reproduce illustrations I am indebted, again, to the Earls Jellicoe and Beatty, as well as to Sir Charles Madden, the Imperial War Museum, the National Maritime Museum and the proprietors of *Punch*. Individual acknowledgements have been made in the list of plates. To Captain Geoffrey Bennett, R.N., and Messrs B. T. Batsford Ltd (as publishers of his *Naval Battles of the First World War*) I owe grateful thanks for permission to make use of his plans of the battle.

A. T. P.

1 The Making of an Admiral
(1859–1907)

THOSE who have held high command at the beginning of Britain's
wars have rarely ended them in that position, though perhaps this
has been truer of our generals than our admirals. As far as the
former are concerned our habit of fighting at least the first part of
every war with the weapons and methods of the previous one has
been largely responsible for this result. The spacing of our land
wars has been such, when taken in conjunction with the progress
of land warfare, as often to make our opening commanders and
matériel sadly out of date. At sea the pattern has been rather
different. Long generations of supremacy under sail were separated
from the naval warfare of the twentieth century by a hundred
years which saw on the one hand virtually no major sea battles
and yet on the other a complete naval revolution involving the
introduction of steam, steel, long-range guns, mines, torpedoes,
wireless, submarines and even the first aircraft. Here there could
be no question of using the weapons that had brought victory in
the past, nor in many cases the methods; but the traditions and
popular mythology of the triumphant age of sail lingered on into
this newer time, to which they were not always as relevant as the
courage and confidence that also survived unchanged.

The problems that confronted the first great British seaman who
held command in modern war were therefore enormous. A nation
and a navy bred to believe themselves invincible at sea looked to
him to repeat the glories of the past and produce a new Trafalgar.
Yet he himself understood better than most, or perhaps all, others
some of the great difficulties which stood in the way of so resounding an achievement. Nelson, genius though he was, had after all
worked with factors known and familiar. Those with which an
admiral of the early twentieth century had to cope were still
largely imponderables, menacing uncertainties on which the
recent Russo-Japanese war could throw little light. Nor was this
all that confronted Sir John Jellicoe when he assumed command

of the Grand Fleet in 1914, for he knew the rapid progress and technical efficiency of the German Navy, unhampered as it was by ancient habits and traditions. A sober and clear-headed realist, he was aware of or at least suspected its superiority to our own in several important respects. Even so, his difficulties were in actual fact still greater than he himself realised, for with all his talents he was the prisoner of his time and training, freer than many others from inherited fetishes and obsessions, but still not wholly free. Nevertheless he grasped the realities of the situation well enough for his sense of the vastness of his responsibilities to impose on him a ceaseless strain. Add to this that circumstances and the time required for even an able man marked out for advancement to climb the ladder of promotion brought these responsibilities upon him at a time when his powers were perhaps beginning to pass their peak, and the result becomes a burden that might well bend the shoulders of an Atlas. But if it was his fate to hold command at the moment when the anxieties of a commander-in-chief at sea were probably at their very highest, and if he won no dazzling victory, the service which he rendered his country was that of seeing her through the worst naval crises of that time.

John Rushworth Jellicoe, on whom this high destiny and heavy burden fell, was born at Southampton on 5 December 1859, of Hampshire stock on both sides that had many connections with the sea.[1] In the case of his paternal great-great-grandfather Adam Jellicoe, indeed, the connection was not one of the most creditable. As Pay Clerk to the Navy at Portsmouth he converted to his own use part of the funds which passed through his hands, by investing them in a partnership with the celebrated ironmaster Henry Cort of Fontley near Fareham, to whom the invention of the all-important process of puddling iron is chiefly credited. It was not uncommon in the eighteenth century for officials and even ministers to make profitable private use of public money while it was resting in their hands, but Adam's practices went far enough towards permanent embezzlement to earn him a term of imprisonment. This nevertheless did not prevent his son Samuel from becoming Cort's partner in his turn, and afterwards the owner or perhaps the tenant of the Fontley works.[2] He also came to possess lands which marched with the estates of Sir James Gardiner of Roche Court near Fareham, who was descended through females from the ancient and eminent Hampshire family of Brocas of Beaurepaire; and his son, another Samuel, married Sir James's eldest daughter Elizabeth.* This second Samuel became an actuary at Southampton, where he was a well-known and respected figure.[3] His second son John Henry entered the service of the Royal Mail Steam Packet Company, which was based on the town, and after commanding one of its vessels became its marine superintendent there and eventually Commodore of its fleet and a director of the Company. Captain Jellicoe's wife was Lucy Henrietta Keele, a lady of much strength of will and personal charm, whose family had played a prominent part in the administration and life of the town. Her father, John Rushworth Keele (from whom her second son inherited his Christian names) was a surgeon who had been thrice mayor and was distinguished as a magistrate for his vigorous enforcement of law and order. His three brothers, Henry, Charles and Edward, had all entered the Navy, Henry becoming a naval surgeon, Charles rising to the rank of admiral and Edward being killed in action in 1812, at the age of thirteen. Two of his maternal cousins, the Rushworths, were also naval officers, while his wife was a daughter of Admiral Philip Patton, who had fought with distinction under Boscawen, Hawke and Rodney, and had been Second Sea Lord at the time of Trafalgar.[4]

Born in a seaport and with such a heritage, young John Jellicoe and his brothers Frederick (two years older) and Herbert (two years younger)† naturally spent much of their spare time in the docks and on the waterfront. They soon acquired some experience of sailing, both in small craft and large yachts, and John set his heart on a naval career from the very first. After attending two private schools at Southampton between the ages of six and eleven, he was sent for a year to a boarding school called Field House in the seaside village of Rottingdean near Brighton. Here he showed an early bent for mathematics, though it seems to have been rather later that he developed his skill at games. Though never a

* It was on account of this descent that Jellicoe on his elevation to an earldom chose as his second title Viscount Brocas.

† Frederick, who entered the Church, eventually returned to his birthplace for a time as a much-respected Rector of Fremantle, was later Rector of Alresford, and died in 1927. Herbert and another brother, Edmond (born in 1875), both died young, in 1885 and 1904 respectively.

first-class performer at any (unlike his brother Frederick who won a cricket Blue at Oxford) he clearly had what is sometimes called 'ball sense' and played all the more common English games well, throwing himself into them with a zest that caused his sometime flag-captain William Goodenough to write in later years that his powers of enjoyment of a game 'made one marvel how . . . one who had borne such immense responsibility could still remain so young in heart.'[5] He continued to play cricket until late in life, whenever he could find an opportunity;* and although his days as a rugby footballer were long behind him when he became Commander-in-Chief of the Grand Fleet, he had on one occasion to be dissuaded with some difficulty from turning out at Scapa for a game against the gunroom of the *Iron Duke*.

In 1872, when he was twelve, Jellicoe was given a nomination for the Navy by a friend of his father's, Captain Robert Hall, who was then Naval Secretary to the Admiralty, and passed into the training-ship *Britannia* second in his term of thirty-nine boys. In this wooden three-decker of the old type, moored in the River Dart, cadets were given a two-year course in seamanship, navigation and a few miscellaneous subjects such as drawing and elementary French, before they were sent to sea. The course was a comparative innovation, dating only from 1857,† previously to which all youths aspiring to become naval officers had been sent to receiving ships moored in the naval ports until they were drafted to seagoing vessels in order to pick up seamanship and the other necessities of their profession. Although the *Britannia* represented some advance on this, her curriculum was still behind the times, being entirely geared to the sailing-ship era that was fast passing away, and ignoring the ungentlemanly and unwelcome intrusion of steam. 'Masts, yards, standing and running rigging, and how to work a ship under sail were the essentials of the practical instruction.' Jellicoe's chief recollections in later years were of spending

---

* Lord Hankey has recorded (*Supreme Command* i, 12) that it was thanks to his own cricketing activities at Eastney Barracks in his youth that when he left in 1898 for his first ship as a subaltern of Marines, Jellicoe knew him well enough to offer him a posting in the *Centurion*, as flag-captain of which he had just gone out to the China Station. Hankey, however, preferred to go to the Mediterranean.

† In 1857 naval cadets began to be sent to the two-decker *Illustrious*, specially commissioned as a harbour training ship, which was replaced in 1859 by the larger *Britannia*, berthed originally in Portsmouth Harbour.

much of his spare time aloft, like his fellow-cadets, and in boating (in which he revelled); and also of the fagging system which in retrospect he considered was 'perhaps overdone', and of the early morning drill imposed on those who had misbehaved themselves. Although he was very small for his age until some time after he left, he played cricket and football with zest and success, and grew tough and hardy. He also passed first of his term in each examination during his four terms and finished by passing out in 1874 with a first-class certificate in each subject, being immediately promoted to midshipman. He was in fact an 'all-rounder', good at work and games alike, and was described by the captain of the *Britannia* to a chance-met friend of his mother's as 'one of the cleverest cadets we have ever had'.

In September 1874 Jellicoe joined H.M.S. *Newcastle*, a 17-gun wooden sailing frigate with auxiliary steam-power, for what he afterwards recorded as a most interesting two and a half years' cruise. The ship was one of six, all wooden frigates except one composite vessel built partly of steel, forming a flying squadron such as was then periodically commissioned to visit off-stations and thus incidentally give the younger officers more continuous sea-training than they could get by service with the larger fleets. Under these circumstances much depended, for a midshipman in his first seagoing ship, on the character of his seniors and particularly of the officer of his watch. The latter was usually a lieutenant, from whom if he were a good officer a great deal could be learnt in the way of deportment and the handling of men. Here Jellicoe was fortunate in that all three of the lieutenants under whom he successively kept watch were of high quality.* He also had an excellent naval instructor, although in those days all that that officer could do for even an able and willing youngster while at sea was to help him to keep alive the elementary mathematics he had learned in the *Britannia*. The main body of the squadron was then lying at Gibraltar, and the *Newcastle* made the passage thither under sail in ten days, which was reckoned a reasonable average. In later life the only recollection which Jellicoe retained of his first visit to 'the Rock' was the excellence of the delicacies to be bought at Esmeralda's confectioner's shop. Similarly his

---

* They were Edmund Poe (afterwards C-in-C of the Mediterranean Fleet), J. Field (a future Hydrographer of the Navy) and H. J. May (the first President of the Naval War College).

recollections of Madeira, which the squadron touched after leaving
Gibraltar, were again of food – to wit, the delight of eating
custard apples. This apparent greediness when in harbour he was
afterwards inclined to ascribe a little apologetically to the marked
plainness of gunroom fare in those days, but for a growing boy (he
put on five inches during the cruise, while still remaining rather
small) an apology seems hardly needed.

From Madeira the squadron crossed the Atlantic to the West
Indies, negotiating the doldrums by having three ships raise steam
and tow the other three. The *Newcastle* then parted company to
visit Rio de Janeiro, afterwards rejoining the rest of the squadron
at Montevideo, where one of the periodical revolutions was in
progress, considerably reducing the opportunities of shore leave.
Hitherto the midshipmen had been drilled aloft regularly, and
frequently exercised at making, furling and reefing sails, but when
one of them fell during these exercises and injured himself
seriously they were henceforth curtailed. The next port of call
was the Falkland Islands, in waters which one of Jellicoe's fellow-
midshipmen, Doveton Sturdee, was to see again forty years later
in the very different capacity of commander of the British force
which destroyed von Spee's ships in them. At the Falklands,
although there were only seven British ladies in the scanty population, warm hospitality was shown and there was good shooting of
wild geese, duck, teal and snipe. Thence a passage was made to the
Cape of Good Hope, where a fortnight was spent at Simon's
Bay before returning to Gibraltar. Next the squadron received
orders to proceed to Bombay to meet and escort the yacht of the
Prince of Wales, who was making a visit to India. Afterwards it
went on to Singapore and then cruised in Chinese waters for some
time, remaining for two months at Woosung at the mouth of the
Yangtze River, where it was anticipated that a railway which had
just been built and opened might be regarded as a Western
abomination and thus lead to trouble. Nothing very serious
developed, however, and after a visit to Nagasaki in Japan the
squadron returned to England.

After a short spell of leave, Jellicoe joined H.M.S. *Agincourt* in
July 1877, his two fellow-midshipmen being his cousin Charles
Rushworth, who had also been one of his term-mates in the
Britannia, and Cecil Burney, who was afterwards to be his second-
in-command in the Grand Fleet and his lifelong friend. The

Agincourt was the flagship of the Channel Squadron, which was presently sent out to reinforce Vice-Admiral Sir Geoffrey Phipps Hornby's Mediterranean Fleet on account of the outbreak of war between Russia and Turkey, in which it seemed likely for a time that Britain would be involved in defence of her Near Eastern interests and therefore of Turkey. The two fleets concentrated at Besika Bay near the mouth of the Dardanelles, where the midshipmen's shore recreations consisted of cricket, the new game of lawn tennis and occasional picnics. In the *Agincourt*, however, an extra burden of work was soon cast on Jellicoe and Burney when Rushworth was drowned in a gallant but unsuccessful attempt to rescue one of the crew of his cutter who had fallen overboard in a heavy sea. The fleet then passed the Dardanelles and anchored in the Sea of Marmara, where Jellicoe found himself in charge of two steamboats and four cutters, as well as acting as one of his ship's three signal officers and also as aide-de-camp to the Admiral. In this last capacity he was occasionally called upon to ride across the Gallipoli Peninsula with letters to the senior officers of other British ships which were anchored in the Gulf of Xeros. For this purpose he was lent the Admiral's horse, and quickly became a very fair horseman.* Next he was detached to the *Cruiser*, a sailing sloop attached to the Mediterranean Fleet for the instruction of ordinary seamen and midshipmen in practical seamanship. This meant that he had to take charge of a watch, and his competent handling of the ship while Admiral Hornby was aboard on a visit of inspection brought him to the latter's favourable notice. Moreover, though these activities left no time for study, he managed when the crisis had eased to pass his mathematical examination for the rank of sub-lieutenant third out of 106 candidates in the two fleets. He then took his examination in seamanship at Malta, gaining a first-class certificate, and returned to England for a course of study at the Royal Naval College at Greenwich, followed by gunnery and torpedo courses at Portsmouth. In all of these he once more obtained his invariable first classes.

Next came eight months' service in the *Alexandra*, the flagship of the Mediterranean Fleet, during which he found Malta pleasant, improved his game of rackets, enjoyed dances and fell briefly in love with a young lady whose identity has not survived. Promoted

* In later life hunting became one of his pastimes.

lieutenant, he returned overland to England, contracting dysentery *en route* at Florence and being compelled to spend the next three months on half-pay as unfit for service. These months were the only period of his career during which he was on half-pay, though he made one or two attempts later on to get six months of it in order to study foreign languages abroad. His failure to achieve this he ascribed to the shortage of lieutenants in the eighties and nineties, a time when the Navy was being built up again after having been allowed to fall to a relatively low level of strength.

His real passion, however, was for gunnery, then a sadly neglected and backward branch of the service. Having made up his mind to specialise in it and applied for leave to do so, he was appointed again to the *Agincourt* as soon as he was fit, in February 1881, in order to complete the year of watch-keeping at sea which was obligatory on all lieutenants before they were allowed to qualify in any specialist branch. This brought him his first brief and peripheral experience of war service, since the Channel Fleet was again ordered to the Mediterranean as a reinforcement, this time because of the trouble which had arisen in Egypt through Arabi Pasha's revolt against increasing Western influence over the country. The *Agincourt* was detailed to convey troops from Malta to Port Said, but was temporarily diverted to Alexandria because of Admiral Sir Beauchamp Seymour's bombardment of the forts of that town, after which the troops were urgently needed to help to hold fortified lines outside it against Arabi's army. When the ship eventually reached Port Said, Jellicoe was sent with a party of seamen to the *Orion*, which was anchored off Ismailia on the west bank of the Suez Canal. Here Sir Garnet Wolseley intended to land the forces which had been prepared under his command for the suppression of the revolt, but since it was generally believed in Egypt that he would operate from Alexandria as a base this intention had to be kept as secret as possible.* Hence when three weeks later the captain of the *Orion* entrusted Jellicoe with a despatch for Admiral Seymour he ordered him to travel by night

---

* The distance to Cairo from Ismailia was much shorter than from Alexandria, and the route lay almost entirely over 'hard desert' of firm, smooth gravel; whereas an advance from Alexandria would have to be made through the difficult Delta country cut up by a vast network of artificial canals and lacking roads suitable for wheeled vehicles. B. Bond (ed.), *Victorian Military Campaigns*, pp. 251–2.

in one of the canal boats conveying refugees from Ismailia to Port Said and to disguise himself as one of them, since it was feared that an officer sent in a service boat by daylight might be intercepted by Arabi's troops holding the west bank of the Canal. After successfully completing this rather melodramatic and decidedly odorous journey Jellicoe remained at Port Said with his detachment, which returned from Ismailia a few days later, as part of the naval contingent which was helping to hold the town.

On finishing his year (actually a year and a half) in the *Agincourt* he went back to England for further courses at Greenwich and Portsmouth in order to qualify as a gunnery lieutenant. At Greenwich he passed out head of his class, while managing to find time for a good deal of rackets, tennis and rugby football, at which he played wing forward in a strong College side that met several first-class teams, such as Richmond, Blackheath and Oxford University. At Portsmouth he played in the United Services XV and emerged from his examination with flying colours to become a gunnery lieutenant first class. In so doing he caught the keen eye of 'Jacky' Fisher, the captain of the *Excellent* gunnery school, with whom his long and increasingly close connection now began. One result of this and of his gunnery specialisation was that while the first decade of his naval service had naturally been spent mainly at sea the greater part of the second was passed in shore service and much of it in the *Excellent*, to the junior staff of which he was now appointed in May 1884. The school had hitherto consisted of two old three-deckers joined together, but was now being transferred to Whale Island in Portsmouth Harbour, which was then being developed out of the mud excavated in making extensions to the dockyard. At the time of Jellicoe's appointment the new establishment was very much in its infancy. Field exercise was carried out on the parade ground, and the only buildings on the island were the house of the gunner in charge and a few small workshops.

In the following year the Russo-Afghan boundary dispute known as the Penjdeh incident led to a short scare of war with Russia and a fleet was hastily assembled at Berehaven in south-west Ireland under Admiral Hornby, to whom Fisher went as chief of staff, taking Jellicoe with him as his staff-officer. Since the latter was still only the junior lieutenant of the junior staff of the *Excellent* and Fisher had known him for only a year, this meant that he was already safely established in 'the Fishpond' – the collective nickname afterwards given to those officers of whom Fisher thought highly, by those of whom he did not think so highly. Against these last his countenance was set like flint, for he believed outrageously in favouritism, defending it with the argument that favouritism of merit was the surest road to efficiency. Merit, however, was for him synonymous with the sharing of his own views, without which there could be no salvation, nor any promotion so far as that depended on himself. At the same time it cannot be too strongly emphasised that while Fisher played a great part in moulding Jellicoe's career, the younger man was never regarded in the Navy as having owed his advancement to favouritism. His ability, industry and the powers of leadership which he presently developed and displayed were widely recognised, and Fisher was by no means the only senior officer who recognised early that he had the highest potentialities.

When the war scare had passed Jellicoe returned to the *Excellent* as assistant to the Experimental Officer whom Fisher had now appointed. In September 1885 he went to sea again as gunnery lieutenant of the *Monarch*, in which he experienced an adventure that might have cost him his life. One day when the ship was preparing to carry out target practice off Gibraltar a vessel was sighted aground on a lee shore to the northward with a stiff south-easter blowing, which meant that she was in danger of breaking up, with grave peril to her crew. All the *Monarch's* boats had been left behind because of their liability to be damaged by the blast of her guns when they were fired, except the captain's galley which was rather lightly built and thus unsuitable for work in a rough sea. Jellicoe, however, asked for and received permission to take volunteers in it and try to get the crew of the wrecked vessel ashore. By the time his boat had got under the lee of the wreck a rocket apparatus had come into operation from the shore and a rope had been sent aboard, but the crew of the ship seemed to be ignorant of how to use it to work the breeches buoy. What followed is best described in Jellicoe's own words:

> The bowman got hold of the rope and we started hauling the boat close to the ship. I hailed those on board to take the opportunity of jumping into the boat as we got close. . . . There was however . . . a very strong current running along the shore

which began to turn the boat broadside to the sea. Seeing this I ordered the bowman to let go of the rope, and the crew to turn the boat head to sea again (with the oars). At that moment, however, a huge wave broke on the ship and caught us partially broadside on, capsizing the boat and throwing the crew clear of her into the water. They all started to strike out for the shore. I feared that they would not be able to reach it in the heavy surf, and hailed them to hang on to the boat. They were however all too far off to get back to her, and only the coxswain and I stuck to the boat which was bottom up. The strain of holding on was considerable, but we gradually drifted towards the shore and when close in were rescued by the rocket apparatus party throwing us lines with sandbags attached. The whole crew got on shore safely, but we were all pretty well done up, and the coxswain, who had swallowed a good deal of sand by getting under the boat, never fully recovered his health. . . . The sea went down in the evening and boats from the shore rescued all the ship's company except one man who was drowned in jumping for the boats. We were awarded the Board of Trade Lifesaving Medal for our attempt at rescue.

In April 1886 he was transferred as gunnery lieutenant to the *Colossus*, a so-called 'mastless' vessel* which was then considered the most modern ship afloat. She was commanded by Captain Cyprian Bridge and her torpedo lieutenant was Lewis Bayly, between whom and Jellicoe a lifelong friendship now began. While she was lying at Spithead with a heavy gale blowing and a very strong tide running a seaman fell overboard from one of the ship's boats and was being swept away when Jellicoe jumped into the sea and swam vigorously to his aid, succeeding in reaching him before he sank and keeping him afloat until another boat which had been launched picked them both up. It was soon after this that in seeking for methods of stimulating interest in gunnery, at a time when through the continued influence of the sailing era the art of handling a ship was considered the only really important accomplishment, he hit upon an expedient which was to obtain some prominence and have a long history. While the *Colossus* was

---

* Her two masts, that is, were mainly for signalling purposes and carried no sails, and she thus marked the final break with the old sailing navy.

on duty as guard ship at Cowes during regatta week it occurred to him to land two field guns from her and hold a competition between their crews in assembling and serving them. This aroused so much interest that the practice caught on and spread to all the depots and fleets, and in a much developed form eventually became the main naval event of the annual Royal Tournament.

In December 1886 he returned to the *Excellent* as Experimental Officer, an appointment which carried with it the command of the gunboat *Handy*, in which all seagoing experiments with new ideas for naval mountings and guns were carried out. He also had to attend the gunnery trials of all ships commissioning. The first important trials with which he was associated were those of the Elswick breech-loading 30- and 70-pounders. These were so successful that it became possible to increase the weight of the projectiles to 45 lb. and 90 lb. respectively, the guns becoming known afterwards as 4·7-inch and 6-inch. The chief improvement, however, was that whereas the rate of fire of the old 5-inch gun was two rounds a minute at the most, the new 4·7 could fire ten; and whereas the old 6-inch could barely manage a round a minute the new one could easily achieve seven or eight.

It was at this time that his throat was temporarily damaged during a rugby match in which he was playing scrum-half, by an opposition forward coming out of the scrum who dug his elbow into his Adam's apple. The result was that he lost his voice completely for six weeks, had to take a curative course of Turkish baths, and was compelled to conduct the gunnery trials of two ships at Chatham in a whisper, with another officer repeating his orders.

After eighteen months as Experimental Officer Jellicoe was promoted to the senior staff of the *Excellent*, and sixteen months later again was asked in September 1889 by Fisher, who had become Director of Naval Ordnance, to go to the Admiralty as one of his three assistants. The Navy was then passing through a period of great changes. An agitation for its increase, dating from the Russian war-scare of 1885, had led to the Naval Defence Act of 1889. This provided for an unprecedented building programme and so brought more work to Fisher and his diminutive department. His two senior assistants, who were of commander's rank, were mostly employed in routine matters such as examining the returns of firing exercises and supervising in general the work done by ships in commission and the gunnery schools. To Jellicoe therefore fell the task of dealing with all questions concerning new ideas and improvements in guns, ammunition and mountings, and their installation on board the new ships; and according to his recollection in later days it was only by often working until 11 p.m. that he was able to keep pace with the resultant pressure.

Early in 1892, after his promotion to commander in June 1891 at the comparatively early age of thirty-one, another period of sea-service began when Captain A. K. Wilson (later the famous Admiral of the Fleet 'Tug' Wilson) invited him to become his executive officer in H.M.S. *Sans Pareil*. Since he had been ashore for well over three years and most captains preferred to take as their second-in-command someone fresh from seagoing experience as a first lieutenant, this was a compliment which implied that he already had a reputation for sea-efficiency and goes far to answer the criticism made long afterwards by an unfriendly pen that he 'spent only 16 months in a seagoing ship between the ages of 23 and 33 [*sic*]'.[6] A mercantile marine officer who did twelve months' R.N.R. voluntary training service in the *Sans Pareil* at this time subsequently recorded his lifelong recollection of the young commander's kindness, naturalness and lack of 'side', in a letter written after Jellicoe's death to his biographer Admiral Sir Reginald Bacon:

> . . . There was a certain amount of prejudice about R.N.R. men. . . . But . . . though in a few of H.M. ships R.N.R. officers had not a very pleasant time, it was all the other way in most ships, and I was lucky! . . . [Commander Jellicoe's] attitude towards R.N.R. soon became evident. It is one of my most pleasant sea memories. His treatment of the one R.N.R. officer on board was exactly the same as if I had originally come from H.M.S. *Britannia*. He honoured me too in 1895 by accepting an invitation to lunch on board R.M.S. *Ophir* at Naples, when I was but Third Officer. My invitation was made in fear and trembling, but to accept was just like him.[7]

By the time this little reunion took place Jellicoe had served as commander in two more ships and had almost lost his life in one of them. He had spent little more than a year in the *Sans Pareil* when he received another compliment in the shape of a request to Captain Wilson from the commander-in-chief of the Mediterranean

Fleet, Sir George Tryon, to let him be transferred to the flag-ship, the *Victoria*. This, however, was nearly his undoing for good and all, since it involved him in the disaster wherein she was sunk with a loss of 358 lives through collision with the *Camperdown*. On 22 June 1893, while the fleet was steaming between Beirut and Tripoli in two lines six cables apart, Sir George, wishing to reverse its course, made a signal for the leading ship of each column to turn in a half-circle, the others following round. By a tragic blunder the reason for which can only be guessed at, since he was one of the drowned, he signalled for both to turn inwards towards each other. For this there was insufficient room, and the result was that the *Camperdown*, the flagship of Rear-Admiral Markham, which was at the head of the other line, sliced into the *Victoria* and sank her. What is perhaps even more extraordinary than Tryon's action is that although Markham and both the flag-captains involved testified at the subsequent court-martial that they knew that the manoeuvre was impossible, none of them took any steps to avert the collision. All thought that the Commander-in-Chief, who was looked on as the finest tactician of the day, must have some method of carrying out this apparently impossible evolution, and waited for him to put it into operation. It was a supreme manifestation of the tradition of unquestioning obedience and subordination to the one directing brain which permeated the Navy then and was still evident at the time of Jutland.

When the collision occurred Jellicoe was in his berth, suffering from Malta fever and having in fact been in bed for a week. On feeling the shock and learning from his servant what had happened he put on a coat and a pair of trousers and went on deck to his station on the after-bridge. Since the ship seemed to him to be sinking fast, though his impression was that the Admiral and the Captain did not realise this, he began (as he recorded in a letter written next day to his mother)[8] 'to give orders about getting the boats out'. Leveson, the gunnery lieutenant, however informed him that the lifting power had failed and the boat-hoist was out of action. Immediately afterwards the ship heeled over and began to capsize. As she did so Jellicoe walked or clambered some distance down the port side and had just reached the jackstay of the torpedo nets in line with the upper deck when she turned bottom up. He held on to the jackstay as the hull turned over, letting go when he found himself under water and starting to swim away from the ship as soon as he came to the surface, in order to avoid being sucked down as she sank. He then managed to get rid of his hampering clothes in the water, but although he was normally a strong swimmer his illness had weakened him and he was beginning to feel very tired when a midshipman named Roberts-West swam up to him and asked if he needed help. Jellicoe told him that he would be glad if he might put a hand on his shoulder, which he did, and shortly afterwards he was picked up by a boat from the *Nile* and taken aboard that ship. One of the most horrified spectators of the disaster was his young brother Edmond, who was then serving in the *Sans Pareil* and, knowing that he was ill and probably in his bunk at the time, could hardly hope that he would survive.*

Despite Jellicoe's illness his immersion seemed at first to have done him no harm, and indeed his temperature, which was 103° before the collision, was down to normal next day. The mental resilience and recuperative power which he had in those days are shown by the fact that (according to an army officer who travelled home in the same ship as the surviving officers of the *Victoria*) whereas several of these were distinctly downcast Jellicoe was 'all over the place' doing physical exercises with a party of midshipmen who happened also to be taking passages to England.[9] It would be contrary to everything we know of his character to suppose that he could have been insensitive to the loss of so many shipmates; but even in his later years of vast responsibility he worried less over things that had happened and were past remedy than over what might happen in the future. Moreover it is likely that his outward cheerfulness was due more than a casual observer might realise to deliberate policy arising from a sense of his duty as a senior surviving officer to set a good example of 'carrying on'.

Sir George Tryon was succeeded as commander-in-chief in the Mediterranean by Sir Michael Culme-Seymour, who hoisted his flag in the *Ramillies* with Francis Bridgeman as his flag-captain and Jellicoe as commander. The two latter were already well acquainted, since Bridgeman had been a commander in the *Excellent*

---

* In Jellicoe's opinion Roberts-West never fully recovered from the effects of his immersion and efforts, and during the First World War he intervened to save him from a very severe penalty on account of a failure of nerve.

when Jellicoe was on the junior staff. The *Ramillies* was a new ship, of a class which represented a great improvement on anything hitherto built for the Navy, and he was detailed to supervise her fitting out at Portsmouth. This gave him the opportunity of ironing out many of the difficulties normally attendant on a newly commissioned ship by having some of her fittings adapted and improved in the light of his recent seagoing experience. The commission lasted three years, until the end of 1896, during which time considerable anxiety was caused in British naval and other circles by the *rapprochement* between France and Russia that led to their alliance and to the appearance of a Russian squadron in the Mediterranean. An increased programme of battleship construction was at once embarked on, but in view of the frequent friction between Britain and France over Egyptian or colonial questions it was felt that great circumspection and watchfulness were necessary at least until these ships were completed. The Mediterranean Fleet was therefore kept very concentrated during its cruises, and repeatedly carried out tactical exercises while at sea, mostly in the Levant, though also off the Italian and French coasts. This did not, however, prevent the Admiral and Jellicoe from spending many hours in playing rackets at Malta, and partnering each other in the competition for the Fleet Challenge Cup.

Of these years in the *Ramillies* Jellicoe wrote long afterwards:

We had indeed . . . a complement of officers second to none in the Service – all most delightful companions and most excellent officers. The warrant officers also were of the highest class. I am sure that any old *Ramillies* will agree that Mr Trice the Boatswain (who retired later on as Lieutenant Trice) was a splendid warrant officer and a delightful personality. In my later years (on the retired list) whenever I visited Portsmouth, where Lieutenant Trice was living, whether on British Legion or other work, he was always present at any meeting I attended and his presence ever afforded me the greatest possible pleasure. . . . With so fine a set of officers it was an easy matter to get the ship's company to attain a very high standard, and I have no hesitation in saying that the ship was most efficient in every way. . . . A great feeling of loyalty was apparent, and after three years of a most happy commission I found it a real pleasure to meet men who had served in the *Ramillies*, as we all shared the pride with which we remembered our time on board. In all sports the ship took a high place, whether rowing, sailing in regattas, shooting at the rifle range at Malta, competing in athletic sports, etc., etc. The field guns' crews . . . did particularly well in competitions, which were frequent. The officers shone at polo and other games and sports; at drill or in coaling ship the *Ramillies* always did well.

Her efficiency and happiness were undoubtedly due in large measure to the commander, as those of any ship must be; and one of the secrets of Jellicoe's success in this rank was his meticulous attention to detail, a propensity which he later found it impossible to shed in a more exalted sphere where its value had become dubious. As far as gunnery was concerned, however, his eulogy of the *Ramillies* must be taken as merely relative and perhaps owed something to a retrospect through the arches of the years, for it was of this period that he also wrote: 'Gunnery efficiency in the modern sense was I fear non-existent. An annual competition prize-firing was carried out off Malta at a range of some 1600 yards and fire control was unheard of, as was long-range practice. . . . Gunnery work took rather a back seat in considering the smartness and efficiency of a ship's company.'

During 1896 the Anglo-Egyptian expedition for the reconquest of the Sudan was being mounted, and naval officers were needed to command the gunboats that were to be used for the ascent of the Nile – a service in which Lieutenant David Beatty presently distinguished himself. Jellicoe, however, lost his chance of taking part through his liability to Malta fever. Sir Herbert Kitchener, then the Sirdar of the Egyptian army and the commander of the expedition, telegraphed a request to Admiral Seymour to allow Jellicoe to go in command of a gunboat. The telegram arrived while he was at sea in the *Ramillies* carrying out target practice, and the Admiral without consulting him replied that he could not be spared, meeting his subsequent protests by declaring his firm conviction that if he had been allowed to go he would have gone down with fever, of which indeed he had recently had a particularly bad attack. As a result Commander the Honourable Cecil Colville of the *Trafalgar*, which was second flagship, went in his place, did splendid service, and was severely wounded and promoted captain, thus leap-frogging Jellicoe in seniority. This, however, Colville generously waived during the First World War in order to serve under his old friend.*

Jellicoe's own promotion to captain came on 1 January 1897 after his return to England at the end of the *Ramillies* commission. In the same month he was appointed a member of the Ordnance Committee, to which all questions relating to the experimental trial of guns and ammunition for both the Navy and Army were referred. The Committee had been established for the purpose of keeping armaments in both services of uniform standard and design, but with the increasing divergence of their requirements this was no longer desirable nor even possible, though there were some things that still remained common to both. His year in this appointment, however, meant that whereas his recent service as commander in a succession of battleships had temporarily taken him away from direct association with gunnery, he now returned to his element at a higher level, and acquired knowledge and experience which he found valuable later when he became Director of Naval Ordnance. It was during this tour of service also that he became friendly with the eminent shipping magnate Sir Charles Cayzer and his family, with whom he stayed during a holiday in Scotland. This was a friendship which was to have important consequences.

Towards the end of 1897 he was invited by Vice-Admiral Sir Edward Seymour, who was taking command of the China Station, to go with him as his flag-captain in the *Centurion*. Such an invitation implied that he was considered among the most promising of the junior captains, by one of whom a flag-captaincy was normally held. A senior captain usually preferred the command of an independent ship, but for a junior a flag-captaincy meant the command of a much larger vessel than he would otherwise have had, together with the gratification of acting as his Admiral's deputy, while shielded by his authority, in all routine matters affecting the squadron. The chief requisites for the post were ability, popularity and tact, all of which Jellicoe possessed in large measure. It was during this commission that a midshipman recorded in his diary: 'Captain Jellicoe seems to please everybody because he is so polite, even to a humble midshipman.[10]

China at that moment was being opened up by the Western

* See below, p. 65.

Powers, and even seemed likely to be broken up by them. In 1898 Russia took Port Arthur, nominally on a 25-year lease. Germany took Tsing-tao; France 'leased' Kwang-chow-wan; and Britain, in order not to be behindhand, did likewise with Weihai-wei. All these powers, besides the United States, Italy and Austria, were now maintaining squadrons or ships in Chinese waters. The taking-over of Weihaiwei involved Jellicoe in much administrative work; but he also busied himself in organising boat-sailing, with weekly races, as a diversion for the large parties of seamen who had been landed. He found time, too, for cricket, which was played on the parade-ground on a coconut-matting pitch that encouraged fast and heavy scoring and on which he scored his first and only century – 120 in an hour. At Hong Kong he won the squadron tennis tournament and saw a good deal of the German Emperor's naval brother Prince Henry of Prussia, who was there in his flagship the *Deutschland* and who challenged him to a shooting-match on a rifle range, in which Jellicoe came off best. The squadron also paid visits to Japan, during the first of which he and several fellow-officers of the flagship had a short but pleasant holiday in a somewhat primitive Japanese hotel, where (he recorded) he was 'greatly struck by the politeness and delicacy of manner of the Japanese fair sex'. On a second visit he and his friend Colville (who had come out as flag-captain of the *Barfleur*, the rear-admiral's flagship) were received by the Mikado in a very formal audience, the effect of which was a little spoilt by the fact that the imperial trousers were much too long.* The squadron also visited Manila early in 1899, soon after the end of the Spanish-American War, where it met Admiral Dewey's American squadron which had won the battle of Manila Bay six months before, and the want of discipline in which (by British standards) struck Jellicoe very much.

Resentment against the foreigners was naturally now running high among the Chinese, and rumours were being set afoot that all misfortunes such as droughts, floods, epidemics and so forth were due to the anger of the gods at their being admitted to the country. Secret societies arose and flourished, especially one whose violent xenophobia was at first rather thinly disguised under the pretext

---

* Ill-fitting clothes were an affliction from which modern emperors of Japan frequently suffered, since nobody was allowed to profane their august persons by measuring them.

of the promotion of gymnastics and boxing and whose members were therefore known as the Boxers. Neither the Dowager Empress, who had seized control of the government, nor her ministers and regular troops made any serious attempt to conceal their sympathy with this society, and by June 1900 the foreign embassy staffs and residents in Peking were besieged in the Legations. Sir Claude Macdonald, the British Minister, had telegraphed to Admiral Seymour on 28 May, asking for a guard to be provided, and a body of marines had been sent up; while on the 31st the Admiral had taken his squadron to Taku at the mouth of the Pei-ho river, which was eighty miles in a direct line from Peking and was the coastal terminus of the railway leading to it, in order to be prepared for eventualities. The senior naval officers of the other foreign powers, including Japan, followed suit, so that in effect an international squadron was assembled in which Admiral Seymour took the lead by virtue of seniority, though he had of course no direct authority over the personnel of other nationalities. At a conference on board his flagship it was decided that if the situation made it necessary a joint naval force would be landed and pushed up to Peking.

On 5 June Seymour sent Captain Jellicoe to Tientsin, some twenty-five miles up-river, to find the best route for such a force to take if required. Since the road from there to Peking was impossible and the river was shallow and winding he decided that only the railway was feasible, and returned on the 9th to Tongku near Taku, where a somewhat panicky message reached him from Sir Claude that the Legations were besieged and unless help was sent at once it would be too late. A naval brigade of 2129 officers and men with seven field guns and ten machine-guns was promptly put together and despatched in five trains under Seymour's command, with Jellicoe as chief of staff and commander of the British contingent of 915. There were also 512 Germans under Captain von Usedom and smaller contingents from each of the other nations. A press correspondent who accompanied the column wrote long afterwards:

It was to Captain Jellicoe that I was referred for permission . . . and I can see him now as he put a few terse direct questions to me before granting the required permit. A man below the middle height, alert, with that in the calm brown eyes which spoke of decision and a serene confidence in himself, not the confidence of the oversure, but that of the real leader of men. A man whose features would have been unpleasantly hard but for the lurking humour of the eyes and for certain humorous lines about the mouth that on occasion could take the likeness of a steel trap. A man to trust instinctively and one to like from the beginning. . . . Later, when I came to know him, he inspired me with the same feeling of affection with which he was regarded by everyone with whom he had occasion to come into close contact. There was, and is, a magnetism about the man which stamps the personality of one who is indeed a commander . . .[11]

The enterprise was a gamble, undertaken because of the seeming urgency of the need, and dependent for success on the railway line being more or less intact and the Chinese regular troops not joining the Boxers, neither of which conditions was fulfilled. The force reached Yangtsun, fifteen miles beyond Tientsin, without much difficulty, but after that the line was found to have been damaged in several places, so that repeated stoppages had to be made to repair it. Eventually the expedition came to an enforced halt at Lang Fang, another fifteen miles or so forward, which it reached on 12 June. Here the station had been wrecked, the sleepers burnt, the rails twisted or carried off and the water-tanks destroyed so that the engines had to be watered by chains of men passing buckets from hand to hand. The temperature was torrid, the soil was mostly sand, and the wind, blowing from the Gobi Desert, parched the skins and throats of the men. A large force of the enemy lay ahead, and it was becoming increasingly obvious that the line of communication with Tientsin could not be kept open with the small numbers available. On 14 June a fierce surprise attack on the halting-place of the trains at Lang Fang was beaten off with heavy loss to the Boxers; but on the 16th a German officer who had been sent back to Tientsin with a train for supplies returned to report that he had been unable to get there, since a stretch of the permanent way had been completely destroyed. The column, that is, was cut off from its base; ammunition and provisions were running short; Chinese Imperial troops had begun to help the Boxers; and since there was now no possibility of rushing a relief force to Peking in quick time a council of war held on the 19th resolved to retreat.

c

Even this was a difficult and dangerous undertaking, which had to be carried out along the banks of the shallow and winding river, since the railway was now impossible and the column had no land transport in which to carry its growing number of wounded. These were placed in junks towed from the bank, and the force set off to fight its way from one river village to another, each of which was held by the enemy and had to be stormed with the bayonet. It was while Jellicoe was leading one such attack on 21 June that, as he recorded later in his diary:

> I was hit on the left side of the chest, the shock turning me half round. I thought my left arm had gone. Sat down on a stone, and Cross, Gunnery Instructor, came and cut away the sleeve of tunic and shirt and helped me behind a house where I lay down. After a bit Dr Sibbald came up and bandaged wound and told me that he thought I was finished. I made my will on a bit of paper and gave it to my coxswain. I was spitting up a lot of blood and thought the wound probably mortal, so asked Pickthorn [another naval surgeon] who came after a short time to rebandage me, if this was so. He said it was very dangerous and injected morphia. This stopped the internal bleeding. Harrison Smith, our chaplain, came along afterwards. . . .

Captain von Usedom now replaced Jellicoe as chief of staff, and the fighting retreat continued. On the following day the column had an immense stroke of luck, which was perhaps its salvation, in the capture of Hsiku Arsenal. This was found to contain Krupp guns (on which the Germans fell with delight), Maxims (which the British appropriated), thousands of modern rifles and millions of rounds of ammunition, as well as large supplies of rice and medical and other stores. These made it possible for the force to hold out with ease until another international column under a Russian colonel arrived from Tientsin to relieve it. The wounded were then safely evacuated, including Jellicoe, who had already taken a turn for the better in spite of the surgeons' gloomy prognostications. Nevertheless it was some months before he recovered the full use of his left arm, and for the rest of his life he suffered occasionally from cramp and rheumatism in the part of his body where he had been wounded. The bullet, too, had remained in his lung, as was revealed by an X-ray in 1934. Another legacy, of a different kind but equally lasting, which he carried away from the Boxer campaign was a keen admiration of the efficiency of the Germans and the smartness of their ships and men. With Captain von Usedom, who had himself been wounded in the knee at Lang Fang, and several of his officers he had formed friendships which were kept alive during the years before the First World War by occasional meetings and in Usedom's case by an intermittent correspondence[12] and a visit to Kiel in 1910.*

Jellicoe remained on the China Station for another year after his recovery, during which period the relief of the Legations was eventually accomplished by a much larger international force under a German general, Count von Waldersee. In this operation he had no part, nor did he see any more fighting, but while hostilities lasted he gained further experience of co-operation with senior naval officers of other countries and learnt some of its trials and tribulations. These years of service in the Far East, indeed, represented an important stage in his development. Brought into contact with a wide variety of personalities of diverse races, he had shown firmness and tact in dealing with them; his outlook had been broadened; and he had displayed conspicuous courage in action, resource in facing unforeseen difficulties, and in general all the gifts of leadership.

In August 1901 the *Centurion* returned to England, steaming past the shores of the Isle of Wight (where Jellicoe's parents were now living and to which he was always particularly attached) on a lovely Sunday morning whose sights and sounds – the church bells pealing from the land – were still clear in his recollection thirty years later.

After a period of leave he then went to the Admiralty again as assistant to the Third Sea Lord and Controller, Sir William May. His post was a new one; the Controller was responsible for superintending the departments which built, fitted out and repaired ships, and the chief duties of his assistant were to visit and inspect those under construction at private yards and make suggestions for their improvement in the light of his practical seafaring experience. This work involved a great deal of travelling, including

* Among the other German naval officers who served in this campaign were von Holtzendorff, who was Chief of the Naval Staff in Berlin during the intensive submarine campaign, and von Pohl, who commanded the High Seas Fleet for twelve months in 1915–16.

for part of the time an average of three overnight train journeys a week. While visiting the great shipbuilding yards on the Clyde, however, Jellicoe was able to renew contact with the family of Sir Charles Cayzer, and in February 1902 he became engaged to Sir Charles's second daughter, Gwendoline. In the following July they were married, and established themselves in a flat in London. This marriage was of great consequence to the fortunate bridegroom. First and foremost it gave him that possession of immense value, domestic happiness throughout life. As he wrote towards the end of it: 'My dear wife was ever a most helpful companion in whatever appointment I found myself. Our love grew if possible stronger and stronger as the years passed by and she was besides a most loving mother to our dear children. I do not think many men could have been so fortunate in their married life as I was.' In addition, although Jellicoe was already a marked man whose professional advancement was assured (barring misadventure), a marriage into the wealthy and important Cayzer dynasty* meant for a career officer a widening of contacts and an enlargement of horizons that were bound to be of much value. Moreover Lady Jellicoe (as she became) was one of the most powerful and dynamic personalities of a family which contained several such. Tireless, fearless in every way, forthrightly outspoken and full of vitality, she created for her husband a rich social and domestic life through which he steered quietly, competently and happily.

In August 1903 he went to sea again in command of the armoured cruiser *Drake*, as senior captain of a cruiser squadron under Rear-Admiral Fawkes. The first part of this commission was spent in the West Indies, where target practice was carried out. A much-needed gunnery renaissance was now under way, thanks largely to Captain Percy Scott, whose assistant Jellicoe had been when Scott was Experimental Officer in the *Excellent* and who had

* Charles William Cayzer, born in 1843, had settled in Liverpool in 1877 after working as a clerk in Bombay with the British India Steam Navigation Company. He became a partner in a firm of ships' store merchants and then developed as a shipowner, establishing in partnership with a friend who died soon afterwards the house of Cayzer, Irvine and Co., and launching the Clan line of steamers in 1878. Under the successive direction of three generations of his family the enterprises of the Company expanded until on the outbreak of the Second World War it could claim that its fleet was the largest devoted exclusively to cargo that had ever operated under one house-flag.

afterwards become the captain and director of that establishment in April of this same year. Firing at much longer ranges had been realised to be not only practicable but essential in view of the increasing range of torpedoes, and Scott had devised methods of faster loading and more accurate sighting that were beginning to produce a marked improvement in the previously poor shooting of the Navy. These methods Jellicoe was quick to absorb and put into practice.

A very pleasant feature of the cruise to the West Indies for him was that his wife came out to Bermuda while the squadron was staying there for some weeks, accompanied by her sister Miss Constance Cayzer. An eventual outcome of this, which must have added to his pleasure, was Miss Cayzer's engagement to the flag-captain of the squadron, Charles Madden, who was afterwards his chief of staff in the Grand Fleet.

During the *Drake*'s passage across the Atlantic it was found that neither she nor any of the other cruisers could keep their lower-deck 6-inch gun-ports open in a sea-way without flooding the decks. Jellicoe reported this to Admiral Fawkes, who referred the matter to the Admiralty. On the squadron's return they were both summoned, together with Captain Madden, to a conference there with the First Sea Lord, the Controller and the Director of Naval Construction. From this emerged a recommendation, which was duly carried into effect, that in designing future armoured cruisers all armament should be put on the upper deck.

During the later part of the commission the squadron carried out manoeuvres in the Mediterranean, and afterwards with the Channel and Reserve Fleets under Sir A. K. Wilson. The latter of these fleets was a new creation and an outcome of the reforms made by Admiral Sir John Fisher as First Sea Lord from 1904 to 1910. The main features of these were the scrapping of obsolete warships, the creation of this Reserve Fleet on the basis of a nucleus crew system, the redistribution and concentration of our fleets, and the introduction of the dreadnought battleships and battle-cruisers. More than 150 gunboats and second- and third-class cruisers which were scattered round the waters of the world showing the flag and performing police duties – survivals of the days before steam, telegraphy and wireless had made centralisation possible – were struck off. Their crews provided the personnel needed for the new Reserve Fleet, which in 1906 was reorganised and became a new Home Fleet. Along with the former Home Fleet (now renamed Channel Fleet) and the former Channel Fleet (renamed Atlantic Fleet), this enabled a greater concentration of force in home waters to be effected. Fisher's critics, however, accused him of depriving the Navy of the large number of small ships which would be needed for trade protection in time of war. To this his answer was that if attacks on trade were undertaken on any large scale they would be made by strong cruiser squadrons, to cope with which the Admiralty was maintaining and developing a sufficiency of powerful armoured cruisers that could also be used for scouting, reconnaissance and cruiser work in general. Small ships, he asserted, would be useless for commerce protection. The First World War, however, was to prove the critics right in their contention that Britain would be left without sufficient of the smaller craft, through for a reason neither they nor at this stage Fisher had foreseen – the development of the submarine.

The most revolutionary of Fisher's changes, however, was the introduction of the 'all-big-gun' battleship of which H.M.S. *Dreadnought* was the prototype. This was the logical outcome of the new long-range firing, since in order to find the range salvo-firing was necessary, and this required 8 or 10 guns of one uniform size, at first 12-inch, later 13·5-inch, 15-inch and sometimes even 16- and 18-inch. Since the dreadnoughts made all their predecessors obsolete the critics also fell on this new building policy as throwing away Britain's advantage and enabling her rivals to start again level with her. Fisher's contention here ('defence' is not a word appropriate to his personality) was that the change was inevitable in view of the developments in gunnery and that it was vitally necessary to get away to a flying start with it and so gain a lead that could then be maintained. Jellicoe, when he was Controller later, put the point thus:

In peace strategy the initiative is probably as important as in war. So long as we retain the initiative we keep our rivals in a chronic state of unreadiness, confuse their building policy, and by maintaining a perpetual superiority in each individual unit, tend to preserve peace by postponing the moment when they could make war at an advantage.[13]

These reforms inaugurated a new era in the history of the Navy, especially since they coincided with the diplomatic revolution represented by the Entente Cordiale, which ended our differences with France at the same time as the growth of the German Navy and other causes of friction were substituting Germany for her as our potential enemy. Of that new era Fisher was the presiding genius, and Jellicoe now began to move forward towards the position of his right-hand man.

In November 1904 he was recalled from sea by Fisher, who already regarded him as one of 'the five best brains in the Navy under the rank of Admiral',* in order to serve on a committee which had been set up to consider the designs of the new dreadnoughts. After this he was appointed Director of Naval Ordnance in February 1905, and had then to provide the heavy gun-mountings for them. During his term of office he was successful with Fisher's aid in wresting the control of the supply and to some extent the design of naval guns from the War Office, in whose hands it had been since the Ordnance Department came to an end in 1858; and he also inaugurated a small department of trained inspectors of the manufacture of these guns. The question of fire-control at the new long ranges was another matter to which he gave much attention, encouraging the work of several gunnery officers who were studying the problem, and in particular of Lieutenant F. C. Dreyer of the *Exmouth*, who had brought that ship to the top of the Navy list in gunnery practice. Meanwhile Rear-Admiral Percy Scott, as he now was, had been appointed in March 1905 Inspector of Target Practice, a new post created with the idea that its holder should attend the gunnery practices of the various fleets and squadrons and suggest improvements designed to promote efficiency. There was still considerable opposition to Scott's ideas in many quarters, but Jellicoe as D.N.O. did everything he could to support his efforts. It was at this time also that he entered into correspondence with Captain W. S. Sims of the United States Navy, who was an old friend of China

* Fisher to Lord Selborne (First Lord of the Admiralty), 19 October 1904, quoted in A. J. Marder, *Fear God and Dread Nought*, I, 330. The other four, Captains Henry B. Jackson (First Sea Lord, 1915–16), Reginald Bacon (afterwards Jellicoe's biographer) and Charles Madden (his brother-in-law and afterwards his chief of staff in the Grand Fleet), and Mr W. H. Good, then Chief Constructor of Portsmouth Dockyard, were also members of this committee.

Station days and another keen follower of Scott's methods of improving the shooting of heavy guns. In 1906 Sims was Adviser in Gunnery to the United States government and Director of Target Practise (in effect Scott's American 'opposite number') and Jellicoe learnt from him that the American results compared quite favourably with the British. Their friendship afterwards proved of the greatest advantage to both countries when Sims came to Britain in 1917 to command the United States Naval Forces in Europe and act as the American Navy's liaison officer with the Admiralty.*

* See below, p. 169.

2 The Coming Man
(1907–14)

JELLICOE's naval career was now assuming a pattern of service alternately at sea and in the Admiralty, under the patronage of Fisher, whose favourite protégé he was fast becoming. In February 1907 he was promoted rear-admiral and sent to sea again for a year as second-in-command of the Atlantic Fleet, hoisting his flag in the *Albemarle* with William Goodenough, who was afterwards to serve him so devotedly at Jutland, as his flag-captain. According to Goodenough, he was still 'in the full tide of physical strength and health, enjoying with equal zest cricket, golf, a day with the Calpe hounds* or a walk over the hills from Berehaven'.[1] In October he was made a Knight Commander of the Victorian Order on the occasion of a royal review of the fleet at Cowes, and in 1908 he came back to the Admiralty as Controller.

By this time the growing naval rivalry with Germany and the danger, or supposed danger, of being overtaken by that power in the number and size of capital ships had become the major preoccupations of the Board, which had formed the impression that the completion of German capital ships was being pushed on in advance of the dates previously announced. Germany, it was thought (wrongly as the event proved), would probably have 17 dreadnoughts by 1912 and might even have 21, while Britain at her current rate of construction would have only 18. The Sea Lords therefore urged as forcibly as possible that the building programme of capital ships for 1909–10 should be increased from four, or even six, to eight.[2] Reginald McKenna, the new First Lord, accepted their view and made himself their able spokesman, backed by much vociferous support in the country to the tune of the slogan 'We want eight and we won't wait!' As a result the Cabinet was persuaded to sanction this addition. In this battle Jellicoe played a full part, pointing out in his capacity of Controller

* The Calpe hunted the country just over the Spanish border from Gibraltar.

something not generally realised, namely that the governing factor in our rate of production was the time required to construct the necessary turret gun mountings. From private sources of information he had learnt that in this matter the productive capacity of the Krupp works in Germany considerably exceeded that of the British gun-mounting firms, and he issued a warning that whereas the latter were prepared to increase their plant in order to improve their rate of output provided they were assured of sufficient orders, they could only be expected to take this step if our building programme was big enough to give them this guarantee.[3] Winston Churchill (at that time) and Lloyd George headed the 'economists' who opposed the bigger programme, and it was over this question of German superiority in the manufacture of gun mountings that the latter delivered himself of an ill-tempered and ill-founded remark that evidently rankled sufficiently with Jellicoe to make him send a memorandum about it to the sympathetic McKenna. At the close of a meeting in Sir Edward Grey's room in the Foreign Office to discuss the question, Lloyd George, who was walking excitedly up and down the room, burst out with: 'I think it shows extraordinary neglect on the part of the Admiralty that all this should not have been found out before. I don't think much of any of you admirals and I should like to see Lord Charles Beresford [the head of the anti-Fisher party among naval officers] at the Admiralty, the sooner the better.' To this McKenna made the crushing reply: 'You know perfectly well that these facts were communicated to the Cabinet at the time we knew of them, and your remark was "It's all contractors' gossip", or words to that effect.'[4]

The Controller's work was regarded by many of those qualified to judge as heavy at the best of times, and the post was believed to have worn out more than one of its holders. Jellicoe, who occupied it at a critical and controversial time, found it decidedly trying. He realised, and sought to make others realise, that the German dreadnoughts now being built were probably superior to their British rivals. It was true that they were less heavily gunned, carrying 11-inch and 12-inch guns as against 12-inch and 13·5-inch, and this led some people (including Winston Churchill when he was First Lord later) to think them less powerful. But, as Jellicoe repeatedly emphasised, the only true criterion of power in a capital ship was size or displacement; and if in ships of equal displacement British guns were heavier than German guns and more weight was thus expended in gun armament, it was obvious that in some other direction the German ships must have advantages. In fact, as Jellicoe had deduced, these advantages were their greater armour-protection both above and below water and their more complete watertight subdivision below water as a defence against torpedo and mine attack. This subdivision and under-water protection were facilitated by the greater beam of the German ships, for while our vessels were limited in this respect by the width of our existing docks the Germans were building their docks to take their ships and not their ships to fit their docks. Jellicoe, of course, could not hope to persuade the British Government to build new and wider ones, but for purposes of repairing vessels he managed to secure approval for the construction of two floating docks capable of taking the largest battleships. These were moored in the Medway and at Portsmouth respectively, and after the outbreak of war in 1914 one of them was towed to Invergordon and used for docking the ships of the Grand Fleet, thus saving the longer absences from service that passages to and from Plymouth would otherwise have involved both for them and their escorting destroyers so long as the dock at Rosyth remained uncompleted. The possibilities of such floating docks had incidentally been brought to Jellicoe's notice by his observations during his visit to Kiel Regatta in 1910 at the warm invitation of his old comrade-in-arms of Boxer days, von Usedom, who was now also an admiral.

He was likewise uneasy about the relative ineffectiveness at long range (and hence oblique impact) of the shells fired by our heavy guns, and arranged firing trials in 1910 against an old battleship which had been specially strengthened for the occasion by the addition of modern armour plates. These trials showed that in many cases the shells burst on impact without penetrating the armour, instead of going on to explode in the target ship's vitals. In other words, the advantage which British capital ships did possess in the greater calibre of their guns was being nullified by the inferiority of their shells. Jellicoe therefore asked the Ordnance Board to produce an armour-piercing shell that would be more adequate to the long ranges at which future sea-battles would be fought, but when his term as Controller came to an end a few weeks later this matter was afterwards allowed to drop until the battle of Jutland belatedly and tragically underlined its importance. Nor was he successful in his efforts to get the development of Rosyth pushed on. The previous government had approved the establishment of a major naval base here, since our main existing bases faced our former enemy France, which had now become our friend, and it was felt that a new one confronting Germany was needed. Their Liberal successors, however, had decided to slow down the work from motives of economy and a desire not to increase causes of friction with Germany, and Jellicoe could not get this decision altered. On the other hand he met with rather more success in his efforts to give the new battleships better armour-protection; and attempts were also made to strengthen their resistance to attack in other ways, as for example by the fitting of three engine-rooms abreast of each other in the *Hercules* and later types, so that as long as the central one remained intact they would still be able to steam at considerable speed. When he left the Admiralty again in December 1910 the professional journal of the engineering industry, with which he had naturally had much contact, commented:

> Sir John Jellicoe has been a strong Controller, and his departure from the Admiralty is a matter of personal regret which is not by any means confined to members of the Board. . . . No Controller has been more popular, none has commanded greater respect as an administrator. Sir John had the reputation of being a very hard worker, working for 15 or 16 hours a day when necessary. He never worried, fussed or drove his subordinates. His words were few but to the point. And he had never been known to make a request or give an order twice.[5]

The strain which, despite this encomium, these labours may already have begun to impose on Jellicoe* was now lightened by two more years of sea-service, the first of which he spent as Acting Vice-Admiral in command of the Atlantic Fleet. By now Fisher had made up his mind that Jellicoe and no other must lead the British battle fleet in the war with Germany which he was convinced must come. He later forecast its outbreak for 1914, but at this time he wanted to cover the possibility that it might happen before the man of his choice had reached the top of the ladder, and to ensure that even in that case he should play the

---

* I am indebted for this suggestion to Mr Bernard Pool.

decisive part. Although his term as First Sea Lord had now ended and he had been succeeded by Sir Arthur Wilson, he therefore held a colloquy with Admiral Sir Francis Bridgeman, Jellicoe's former captain in the *Ramillies*, who was then commanding the Home Fleet. The results of this conference he announced to his protégé in a letter of 10 January 1911:[6]

> I wanted much to see you, as so difficult to put in a letter what transpired between myself and dear Bridgeman. . . . What I wish to convey to you is that he is prepared and wishes to lean wholly on you as regards war operations and gave me to understand that he would be prepared so to manipulate matters as to put you in the forefront of the battle. . . . It is both obvious and certain that when the actual conflict becomes imminent . . . the Atlantic Fleet will then be joined up with the Home Fleet . . . and the gravity of the case lies in the fact that hardly anyone but yourself – and this I pointed out to Bridgeman – clearly realises the immense alteration in both tactics and strategy which the development of the submarine now causes. . . . Of course I can't write down all that passed between Bridgeman and myself, but I assured him that . . . it would be perfectly easy for him so to manipulate the Home Fleet as to place you in command of the van and . . . come in and pick up the pieces. That was my advice to him and which he appeared to swallow. . . .

The combined Home, Atlantic and Mediterranean Fleets carried out tactical exercises early in 1911, including a night action of which Jellicoe wrote: 'The difficulty of distinguishing friend from foe, and the exceeding uncertainty of the result, confirmed the opinion I had long held that a night action was a pure lottery, more particularly if destroyers took part in it.'* After the exercises a friendly meeting had been arranged between the Atlantic Fleet and the German High Seas Fleet in Norwegian waters where the latter had recently been in the habit of making an annual summer cruise. Jellicoe was anxious for this meeting to take place, both because he hoped that since he knew many of the German senior officers personally it would have a good effect on relations between the two countries, and because he felt that he ought to know as

---

* To this judgement on night-fighting may no doubt be traced Jellicoe's omission, when Commander-in-Chief, to train the Grand Fleet in night action, for which he has been criticised. See below, p. 128.

much as possible about the German Navy in case war should come. Unfortunately the Agadir crisis developed just at that juncture and Sir Arthur (A. K.) Wilson who had succeeded Fisher as First Sea Lord instructed Jellicoe that nothing but official courtesies were to pass between the two fleets and that he was under no circumstances to offer or receive any private hospitality. To this Jellicoe replied that he felt it would be a great mistake for the meeting to take place under such restrictions and that it would be far better to cancel it, which was done. When the crisis had passed and he was spending a few days' leave with his wife and her parents at their Isle of Wight residence, St Lawrence Hall, he visited Cowes Regatta and there encountered Prince Henry of Prussia, who took him to task about the cancellation, saying that his brother the Emperor Wilhelm had worked very hard to bring about the meeting in order to improve relations and was very angry and disappointed. Since all mention of the crisis which had just been surmounted was strictly taboo, Jellicoe could only say that the Admiralty had ordered the fleet to its home ports for some reason of which he was unaware, though he much regretted it. Prince Henry, however, was not much mollified.

The next step in Jellicoe's progress was that in December 1911 he was offered the command of the Second Division of the Home Fleet under Sir George Callaghan, who by now had replaced Sir Francis Bridgeman on the latter's becoming First Sea Lord. The significance of Jellicoe's appointment was twofold. In the first place he had not yet served in a dreadnought battleship or battle-cruiser, and it was essential that he should have experience of a fleet of these in order to be fully qualified for the destiny Fisher had marked out for him. Bridgeman in fact put his finger more acutely on the spot than Fisher probably realised in writing to him:

> [Jellicoe] has had no experience of fleet work on a big scale, and is so extremely anxious about the work in it that he really does too much. He must learn to work his captains and staff more and himself less! At present he puts himself in the position of, say, a glorified gunnery lieutenant. This will not do when he gets with a big fleet. He must trust his staff and captains and if they don't fit, he must kick them out![7]

Unhappily this was a lesson that Jellicoe never fully learnt.

By this time Fisher with his characteristic extravagance was describing Jellicoe in his correspondence as the future Nelson, and in his mind the paramount importance of this new appointment was that it would almost automatically make him the successor to Callaghan as commander-in-chief of the Home Fleet at the end of the latter's term. Thus he would be where he was most needed in time for the clash with Germany and the great sea-battle which Fisher expected and to which he was now alluding apocalyptically as Armageddon. McKenna was no longer First Lord, since his complete identification of himself with the opposition of Fisher and Wilson to the creation of a Naval Staff analogous to the Army's General Staff (which Haldane the brilliant Secretary for War was pressing in the hope of securing the harmony between the war plans of the two services that at present was lacking) had led the Prime Minister to transfer him to the Home Office. His successor was Churchill, now a convert to a strong naval armament programme and to the probability of war with Germany, who was throwing himself into the work of his new office with all a convert's zeal and all the gusto with which he did everything. Between him and Fisher a strong mutual liking had developed, and the veteran, acting as his unofficial adviser and so still pulling the strings of the Navy, had persuaded him to promote Jellicoe (who at the moment was 21st on the list of 22 vice-admirals) over the heads of all those senior to him to the command in question. To Lord Esher he wrote exultantly afterwards: 'I owe . . . much to Winston for scrapping a dozen admirals . . . so as to get Jellicoe Second in Command of the Home Fleet. If war comes before 1914 then Jellicoe will be Nelson at the Battle of St Vincent.* If it comes in 1915 he will be Nelson at Trafalgar.'[8]

Meanwhile Jellicoe himself, not fully aware of the point of the move and preferring sea service away from England to home waters, had at first replied to Churchill's telegram offering him the new appointment that he would rather retain his command of the Atlantic Fleet. In return he received a second and characteristically peremptory wire telling him that this command would be terminated in any case† and that no other post but the one offered

---

* Fisher evidently meant that though in the former case Jellicoe would not yet have succeeded to the command-in-chief he would nevertheless play the decisive role.

† By a fresh reorganisation in 1912 the Atlantic Fleet was merged into a new First Fleet.

was open to him. He therefore bowed to the will of the ill-assorted pair of demi-gods who were directing his destiny almost in his own despite, and hoisted his flag in the *Hercules* at Portsmouth on 19 December 1911, his old friend Burney taking over the Atlantic Fleet.

A few days later and before the Home Fleet left for exercises he had a short talk with Churchill during a visit to the Admiralty, in which the First Lord asked for his views on relieving the Controller of some of the burden of his work, of the weight of which Jellicoe had had such recent experience. His uncompromising reply, however, was that it was unnecessary to take any of the Controller's work from him so long as his Naval Assistant was given more power, since it would be most unwise to let it go out of naval hands; a pronouncement that reflected his own readiness to work himself to the limit rather than delegate responsibility to any but a very few trusted subordinates. Churchill, he recorded, 'did not seem to agree'. In the following March, according to the autobiographical fragment which he wrote many years later, he had another conversation with the First Lord, this time about the design of the proposed *Queen Elizabeth* class of fast battleships, which were to carry eight 15-inch guns and to be capable of 25 knots. Of these he states that he expressed disapproval because he saw no advantage in reducing armament by two guns per ship in order to gain a mere 3 or 4 knots and would have preferred 10-gun battleships of 21 knots' speed. It seems likely, however, that this is one of the occasional cases in which this autobiographical matter, written up long afterwards, can be seen by comparison with more contemporary sources to have suffered from a lapse of his memory. The value which was claimed for these *Queen Elizabeths*, both then and later, was that in battle a squadron of such ships could be used to operate separately in order to head off the enemy's movements or perhaps enable a concentration to be made on a part of his line in the old Nelsonian way; and it is clear that at this time Jellicoe was opposed neither to independent action nor to special fast squadrons. On one occasion during the spring manoeuvres of this year, carried out by the combined Home and Atlantic Fleets under the command of Sir George Callaghan, he departed without orders from the single line-ahead formation which was then the Navy's basic principle of battle and took successful independent action with his squadron **against**

Admiral Sir John Jellicoe when Commander-in-Chief
of the Grand Fleet

Jellicoe's parents: Captain and Mrs Jellicoe

the rear of the 'enemy', Sir George subsequently approving.[9]
This, it must be remembered, was the kind of operation which
Fisher in his letter of 10 January 1911* had envisaged for him,
and which may conceivably have been discussed between them,
though Jellicoe does not seem to have left anything on record to
that effect. Moreover in the secret 'War Orders and Dispositions'
which he drew up at this time in order that flag officers and
captains under his command might be fully aware of the principles
that would guide him in fighting an enemy's fleet should he be the
senior officer, he emphasised that his subordinate commanders
would have a wide discretion in the conduct of their divisions in
action so long as they observed the general principles which he laid
down. In these Orders he definitely envisaged the employment of
fast divisions, placed if possible on either wing during his approach
to battle, to make separate attacks if circumstances were favourable. He also stated that the object of his destroyers would be to
attack the enemy's battle-line, as well as to protect his own from
torpedo craft.[10]

In the autumn of 1912 Jellicoe took his squadron to Berehaven,
where he superintended a trial of the system of director firing
which Sir Percy Scott had devised. This system centralised and
synchronised the aiming and firing of all the heavy guns of a ship
under the control of a single officer stationed aloft in a position
where, being above any low-lying smoke and shell-splashes, he had
the best view obtainable. Operating a master-sight electrically
connected to the sights of each gun, he then aimed the whole of his
ship's broadside and fired it by pressing a single key. Since the
chief objection to the director system was the chance of the aloft
position or the electrical communication being damaged by shell-
fire, in armoured ships an alternative director sight was fitted in an
armoured tower on deck to cover this possibility. This director
system had been fitted to the *Thunderer*, and competitive firing
now took place between her and a sister ship employing the
previous methods. The trial proved conclusively the superiority
of the new system, and Jellicoe proceeded to advocate its general
adoption most strenuously. There was nevertheless very strong
opposition to this in the fleet and at the Admiralty, and in spite
of all that he could do only eight British battleships had been

* See above, p. 45.

fitted with the system before the outbreak of war in 1914. After that, however, he was able to press the Admiralty hard enough to ensure that by the time of the Battle of Jutland all except two of our capital ships had been so fitted for their main armament.

In December 1912 he returned once more to the Admiralty, this time as Second Sea Lord, though without prejudice, in the minds of Fisher and Churchill, to his ultimate succession to the chief command at sea. It did not take him long to realise that Churchill as First Lord was interpreting his position and duties in a way which, although within his constitutional rights, differed considerably from the practice of his predecessors and especially of McKenna. They had been content to supervise and co-ordinate the work of the Board of Admiralty and to act as its spokesmen. But Churchill held emphatic views on technical matters which, although they were sometimes sound or even brilliant, often took little or no account of realities or practical difficulties. Moreover he was inclined, with all his tremendous powers of exposition and argument, to seek to impose these views upon the Board and have them put into execution. Since on several matters Jellicoe was far from seeing eye to eye with him, and since the First Sea Lord, Prince Louis of Battenberg, in spite of his talents was not the strongest of men, it fell chiefly to the former to stand up to Churchill. Always impatient of opposition, the First Lord took exception to this, and relations between the two occasionally became strained.* One of the first matters over which this occurred was, at least in Jellicoe's eyes, a question of naval discipline, a subject which lay largely within the province of the Second Sea Lord. Churchill, like Lloyd George and other civilian ministers after him, was in the habit of seeking information or inviting suggestions from all and sundry, irrespective of rank, and acting or ordering action on what seemed to him the merits thereof, which for him were the supreme consideration. It sometimes happened that by doing this he outraged the principle that on service matters communication with junior officers must be held only through

---

* It must be borne in mind, however, that a main source of evidence about their relationship during this period is Jellicoe's autobiographical fragment, which was written after the publication of Churchill's book *The World Crisis*, to many statements in which he took strong exception and which would hardly lead him to view the author retrospectively in the most favourable light.

their seniors, in order to guard against their coming to look disrespectfully on the latter. He was particularly prone to this practice in matters affecting the Royal Naval Air Service, which was then in its infancy and in which on the one hand he took a keen interest (his energy and encouragement being indeed largely responsible for its progress in the pre-war years) while on the other hand he had asked Jellicoe, also much interested in aviation, to be its Superintending Sea Lord. The issue in question was the use to be made by that Service of some ground on the bank of the Medway near Sheerness. Captain Vivian, commanding the *Hermes*, which was the parent ship of the R.N.A.S. and was at anchor off Sheerness at the time, had given a decision on the subject. One of his lieutenants held other views, which he expressed to Churchill while the latter was visiting Sheerness. The First Lord then sent for Captain Vivian and told him that he agreed with the lieutenant, whose proposals were to be carried out. The captain reported the matter to his commander-in-chief at the Nore, Admiral Sir Richard Poore, who wrote a letter on the subject to the Secretary of the Admiralty which he sent first of all under private cover to Jellicoe, asking the latter's opinion as to whether his remarks were too strong. Jellicoe in returning the letter replied that in his view they were. Churchill, however, had not only learnt of this exchange of correspondence but had managed to become aware of its contents, and declared his intention of dismissing Poore. Jellicoe thereupon informed him that in that event he himself would not only resign but make public his reasons for doing so. Eventually an arrangement was arrived at which saved face all round and the matter was dropped; but a little later Jellicoe felt constrained to tell Churchill that as he could not agree with his methods of handling the R.N.A.S. he wished to resign his own control of it as its Superintending Lord, and the Fourth Sea Lord accordingly took over this function.

Another cause of dispute arose out of a temporary shortage of officers of the rank of lieutenant and below. To meet the difficulty Churchill suggested that officers of the Accountants' Branch should undertake lieutenants' duties, including that of watch-keeping; whereupon Jellicoe pointed out that no officer could properly take charge of one of the King's ships at sea unless he had been certified as fit to do so, which accountant officers in virtue of their training could not possibly be. 'The First Lord', he records, 'took great exception to my opposition and said that I was always trying to thwart him. I replied that I only did so when his proposals were of an impossible nature.'

There was more agreement between them, however, on matters of major importance; though when the shipbuilding programme for 1914 came up for consideration Churchill at first alarmed Jellicoe by showing signs of a desire to reduce the number of battleships to be built from four to three. He produced papers purporting to give the comparative strengths of British and German ships, in which he quoted only the number and calibre of guns in each, and proceeded to argue from that basis alone. As Jellicoe pointed out in the course of debating the question with him at considerable length on paper, not only was the striking energy of the projectiles from the German 11- and 12-inch guns not far short of that from British 12- and 13·5-inch guns respectively, owing to their much higher muzzle velocity, but this method of comparing the power of ships was quite misleading. The only true standard of comparison, he reiterated, was displacement, and if this were examined it became apparent that the German ships must have advantages in other respects. He succeeded in converting Churchill to his programme, if not entirely to his contention, with the result that the First Lord stood out for the four battleships against the opposition of Lloyd George and others in the Cabinet, and gained his point. As late as July 1914, however, it was still necessary for Jellicoe to counter an over-optimistic minute of Churchill's on the probable relative dreadnought strength of Britain and Germany in 1917 by a detailed memorandum[11] proving, as he put it, that 'far from the British ships showing a superiority the exact opposite is usually the case, and . . . it is highly dangerous to consider that our ships as a whole are superior or even equal fighting machines.'

Difficulties also arose in 1913 on the subject of the Admiralty reserve of oil fuel. The authorised reserve at that time was three months' war consumption, which was distributed in oil tanks at the dockyard ports and elsewhere. In view of the fleet's increasing dependence on this fuel and the fact that most of Britain's supply came from the United States and was therefore open to attack on the sea while being transported to this country, Jellicoe felt that this reserve should be increased and proposed to the Board that it should be gradually augmented to six months' war consumption.

On raising the question in the Cabinet, Churchill encountered strong opposition to any increase, while not all the Sea Lords were agreed on its necessity. Jellicoe, however, felt that the matter was so important that he was prepared to resign unless some action was taken, and a compromise was effected by which a gradual increase to $4\frac{1}{2}$ months' war consumption was approved. 'These conclusions', wrote Churchill in *The World Crisis*, 'stood the test of war';[12] a statement from which Jellicoe forcibly dissented in his autobiography, on the ground that for a considerable period in 1917, at the height of the German submarine blockade, our shortage of oil fuel became in his opinion very serious.

The sun of the First Lord's favour, however, came out again and shone upon him with full force after his brilliant showing in the naval manoeuvres of 1913. For these he was granted leave of absence from the Admiralty in order to take command of the Red Fleet, representing a hostile force convoying and clearing the way for an invading army. Outmanoeuvring Sir George Callaghan who commanded the defending Blue Fleet, he succeeded in landing the troops he was escorting in the Humber and on the north-east coast, with the result that the manoeuvres were hurriedly ended lest they should give information and encouragement to Germany. It seems probable, indeed, that he was then at the peak of his powers, not yet worn down by long-continued strain and ceaseless and manifold anxieties. Even so, Churchill (who wrote to congratulate him on 'the brilliant and daring manner' in which he had executed the difficult task entrusted to him and to express his conviction that the future would furnish him with 'new opportunities of showing those qualities of enterprise and audacity which play so decisive a part in the art of making war')[13] seems to have been swept by the warmth of his enthusiasm into attributing to him more dash and daring than he actually possessed and believing him a commander more after his own heart than he really was, with consequent greater scope for disappointment in the long-drawn-out sequel.

In actual fact, Jellicoe's inclination to caution and in particular his strong sense of the dangers to be feared from submarines in modern naval warfare must have been intensified shortly afterwards by a memorandum 'On the Oil Engine and the Submarine' which Fisher sent to Churchill at the beginning of 1914 and of which he received a copy.[14] Among the more emphatic passages in this were the following:

> The use of submarines in the last two annual manoeuvres has convinced most of us that in war time nothing can stand against them, and broadly speaking it may be stated with confidence that – THE SUBMARINE IS THE COMING TYPE OF WAR VESSEL FOR SEA FIGHTING . . .*
>
> And what is it that the coming of the submarine really means? It means that the whole foundation of our traditional naval strategy . . . has broken down! The foundation of that strategy was blockade. . . . But with the advent of the long-range ocean-going submarine that has all gone. Surface ships can no longer either maintain or prevent blockade, and with the conception of blockade are broken up all the consequences, direct and indirect, that used to flow from it. . . .
>
> Even three years ago the distance at which it was found to be *dangerous* for a vessel to stay off an enemy's submarine base was demonstrated *as a result of trial* to be no less than 300 miles. . . . On the other hand in case of war an English blockade of the German ports is just as essential as ever. . . . In this new form, however, blockade can never be really 'close'. . . .
>
> *It has to be freely acknowledged that at the present time no means exist of preventing hostile submarines emerging from their own ports and cruising more or less at will. . . .*
>
> The question being what is to prevent German submarines from infesting the approaches to British ports, the answer must certainly be:
>
> (a) *In the North Sea* – Nothing is so far known that can prevent them doing so, but a very large number indeed . . . would be required to do so effectively.
>
> (b) *In the English Channel and on the Western Coasts* – Nothing but the distance from the nearest German base and the difficulties of passing the cordon we . . . ought to have established in the Straits of Dover, but even then *it is . . . not impossible.*
>
> In both cases, in fact, the risk will have to be reckoned with. IT WILL BECOME INCREASINGLY DIFFICULT FOR ANY . . . POWER TO OBTAIN THE COMMAND OF NARROW SEAS. . . .
>
> Again the question arises as to what a submarine can do against

---

* The capitals and italics in these extracts are Fisher's.

a merchant ship. She cannot capture [it], she has no spare hands to put a prize crew on board, little or nothing would be gained by disabling [its] engines or propeller, and in fact it is impossible for the submarine to deal with commerce in the light and provisions of accepted international law. Under these circumstances, is it presumed that the hostile submarine will disregard such law and sink any vessel heading for a British commercial port? . . .

There is nothing else the submarine can do . . . and it must therefore be admitted that . . . this submarine menace is a truly terrible one for British commerce . . . for no means can be suggested at present of meeting it except by reprisals. . . . It is not invasion we have to fear but starvation . . .

Although Jellicoe's mind was very far from being a mere *tabula rasa* for the reception of Fisher's ideas, it is difficult to avoid the assumption that his own anxieties and eventual pessimism on this subject owed something to the views of his mentor.

The concept of close blockade, however, died hard. Although it had been replaced in the War Orders of 1912 by a plan for an 'observational blockade' of the Heligoland Bight by a line of cruisers and destroyers at a considerable distance, with the battle fleet still further to the westward,[15] it was brought forward again as late as the latter part of July 1914, on the very eve of war, in a memorandum which was submitted to Jellicoe for criticism. Churchill also passed to him for his opinion a report which had been drawn up* on the possibility of seizing the German island of Borkum as a forward base in the event of war. Against both ideas he pronounced strongly and decisively,[16] though Churchill long continued to hanker obstinately after the Borkum project.†

Meanwhile a test mobilisation of the Navy which by a fortunate coincidence had been arranged months beforehand began on 15 July and was followed by a review after which, on Churchill's responsibility, the First (or, as it was soon renamed, the Grand) Fleet did not disperse but steamed to its war station at Scapa Flow.

---

* By Rear-Admiral Lewis Bayly (who was always inclined to favour bold and sometimes rash courses), Major-General Aston of the Royal Marine Artillery and another officer.

† See below, p. 81.

The whole of our mobilisation arrangements [he wrote later] were thus subjected for the first time in naval history to a practical test and thorough overhaul. Officers specially detached from the Admiralty watched the process of mobilisation at every port in order that every defect, shortage or hitch in the system might be reported and remedied. Prince Louis and I personally inspected the process at Chatham. All the reservists drew their kit and proceeded to their assigned ships. All the . . . ships coaled and raised steam and sailed for the general concentration at Spithead. Here on the 17th and 18th of July was held the grand review of the Navy. It constituted incomparably the greatest assemblage of naval power ever witnessed in the history of the world. . . . It took more than six hours for this armada, every ship decked with flags and crowded with blue-jackets and marines, to pass, with bands playing and at 15 knots, before the Royal Yacht, while overhead the naval seaplanes and aeroplanes circled continuously. . . . [Then] one after another the ships melted out of sight beyond the Nab. They were going on a longer voyage than any of us could know.[17]

A few weeks previously Jellicoe, writing to his friend Vice-Admiral Sir Frederick Hamilton (who had commanded the cruiser squadron of the Atlantic Fleet under him and was soon to succeed him as Second Sea Lord), had voiced doubts whether the succession to the command of the Home Fleet was going to come his way after all:

When I came to the Admiralty [he wrote] the First Lord indicated to me pretty clearly that he intended to offer me the command . . . in succession to Callaghan. He has spoken frequently since I have been Second Sea Lord as if this was settled. . . . But up to date he has not offered it, and as we so constantly disagree, it is quite possible that he may think I am not the right person for it.[18]

At the end of July, however, when the war-clouds were darkening and what was to become known as the Grand Fleet was already concentrating at Scapa Flow in the Orkneys, he was appointed second-in-command to Sir George Callaghan; and on 30 July he was told by Churchill and Prince Louis of Battenberg that in view of Callaghan's age (he was verging on sixty-two) and the

fact that his command was due to end in any case in the following
October he himself was to take over at once if war broke out.
When he left London by train on his way to Scapa an officer
from the Admiralty handed him a sealed envelope to be opened in
Sir George's presence in that event, which contained his appointment as commander-in-chief. Although he appreciated the force
of the argument that Sir George's health was unlikely to stand the
strain of command in war, Jellicoe was very strongly conscious of
the invidiousness of superseding him in such circumstances and
the difficulty of establishing relations with officers who might well
feel resentment at what they would consider the injustice done to
him (though it may perhaps be conjectured that after the 1913
manoeuvres there would be many who preferred to go to war under
Jellicoe's command). There were also the practical problems of
taking over at such short notice, while the fact that Callaghan was
an old friend would make it a horribly painful task. From Wick,
where he was detained by fog, he therefore sent the following
telegram to Churchill:

> Am firmly convinced after consideration that the step you
> mentioned to me is fraught with gravest danger at this juncture
> and might easily be disastrous owing to extreme difficulty of
> getting into touch with everything at short notice. The transfer
> even if carried out cannot be accomplished for some time. I beg
> earnestly that you will give matter further consideration before
> you take this step.

From Scapa on 2 August he wired:

> Am more than ever convinced of vital importance of making no
> change. Personal feelings are entirely ignored in reaching this
> conclusion.

At 8.30 that evening he received a reply from the First Lord:

> I can give you till 48 hours after joining Fleet. You must be ready
> then.

At 11.30 p.m. he telegraphed to both Churchill and Prince Louis:

> Can only reply am certain step contemplated is most dangerous
> beg that it may not be carried out. Am perfectly willing to act
> on board Fleet Flagship as assistant if desired to be in direct

communication. Hard to believe it is realised what grave difficulties change Commander-in-Chief involves at this moment. Do not forget also long experience of command of Commander-in-Chief.

And on the following morning:

Quite impossible to be ready such short notice. Feel it my duty to warn you emphatically you court disaster if you carry out intention of changing before I have thorough grasp of Fleet and situation.

Two hours later he sent another message to both:

Fleet is imbued with feelings of extreme admiration and loyalty for Commander-in-Chief. This is very strong factor.

In answer to these he received a final ukase at 12.45 p.m.:

. . . I am telegraphing to the Commander-in-Chief directing him to transfer command to you at earliest moment suitable to the interests of the Services. I rely on him and you to effect this change quickly and smoothly, personal feeling cannot count now only what is best for us all, you should consult with him frankly. FIRST LORD.[19]

Jellicoe was therefore compelled to carry out this heartrendingly distressing duty, though it was made easier by the gallant and gentlemanly behaviour of Sir George. To Hamilton he wrote later: 'I hope never to live again through such a time . . . My position was horrible.'[20]

Meanwhile on 1 August Churchill had written to Lady Jellicoe: '. . . We have absolute confidence in his services and devotion. We shall back him through thick and thin. Thank God we have him at hand.'[21]

3 'Responsibility is the Devil'*
(1914–15)

THE man into whose hands the most powerful fleet that had ever yet sailed the seas had been entrusted was then in his fifty-fifth year, small, spare, wiry, alert and quick of movement, a vigorous walker and a devotee of outdoor games and sports who sought from now on, when he was largely deprived of them, to keep himself fit by physical exercises and deck-hockey with the officers of his flagship. He was also neat and methodical, quiet (some called him 'Silent Jack'), polite and outwardly always calm and self-controlled, though it may perhaps be wondered whether his tightly pressed lips meant that it was already beginning to cost him some effort to maintain this imperturbability against a tendency to worry which grew with his responsibilities. A tireless worker with great technical knowledge and expertise, he was a first-class administrator and might have been a superlative one but for his excessive preoccupation with detail and the difficulty which he found in delegating responsibility. It is perhaps hardly true that he could not delegate, but he delegated too little and to too few. Throughout his busy career he had been more concerned with the *matériel* and administrative sides of his profession than with strategy and tactics, and though he was gifted in these too his approach to them was somewhat empirical, since unlike several of his near-contemporaries he was not well read in naval history. Though he was capable of bold actions, his inclinations in Service matters (as in others) were to orthodoxy, tradition and convention. Fundamentally cautious, 'his precise brain made such a cold analysis of each problem that he tended to reach the more cautious solution',[1] and this tendency was powerfully reinforced henceforward by a strong and even oppressive sense of the vital importance of his task.

The sudden supersession of Sir George Callaghan at the very moment of the outbreak of war on 4 August took the Grand Fleet

* Roger Keyes, in another connection.

by surprise and dismayed at least the officers and ship's company of the flagship, the *Iron Duke*. However after the first hectic month of sorties, coalings, firings, exercises, alarms and excursions, it was generally realised that the command under these conditions would indeed have been too much for a man of Sir George's age; and meanwhile Jellicoe had rapidly gained the confidence of the Fleet. He inspired affection and trust in officers and men alike, endearing himself to the lower deck by his care to provide every possible facility for recreation and his interest in their welfare, and inspiring in his senior officers reliance on his leadership and often personal devotion. Some of them indeed, such as Vice-Admiral Sir George Warrender commanding the Second Battle Squadron and Commodore Goodenough who led the First Light Cruiser Squadron,* were old friends and shipmates, and his brother-in-law Rear-Admiral Charles Madden had been sent post-haste after him at his request to be his chief of staff.

The Grand Fleet at the outset of the war comprised four battle squadrons, one of which (the Third) consisted of pre-dreadnought battleships, the First Battle-Cruiser Squadron under Vice-Admiral Sir David Beatty (which was moved to Cromarty late in October and to the Firth of Forth in December), the Second and Third Cruiser Squadrons, First Light Cruiser Squadron, Second and Fourth Flotillas of twenty destroyers each, six mine-sweeping gunboats and some other miscellaneous craft. Two other flotillas under Commodore R. Y. Tyrwhitt, based on Harwich, were in theory part of the Grand Fleet and were intended to join it at sea if possible, should a fleet action appear imminent. In actual fact, however, the Harwich Force never succeeded in doing so. The Channel Fleet under Vice-Admiral Sir Cecil Burney, a still older friend of Jellicoe's and his one-time fellow-midshipman in the *Agincourt,* included most of the older pre-dreadnought battleships; and patrol flotillas under the overall command of an Admiral of Patrols were based on Dover, the Humber, the Tyne and the Forth. In October the Dover Patrol was detached and given to Rear-Admiral the Hon. Horace Hood, who was succeeded by Vice-Admiral Sir Reginald Bacon in April 1915 on being transferred to the command of the newly-formed Third Battle-Cruiser Squadron with the Grand Fleet.[2]

* In a reorganisation during February 1915 Goodenough was transferred to command the Second Light Cruiser Squadron.

Public opinion in Britain, and on the whole naval opinion as well, expected a major sea-battle to be fought early in the war, which it was assumed would be a great British victory. The Germans preferred, however, to keep their High Seas Fleet as a 'fleet in being', remaining in harbour ready to sally forth at any favourable moment. Restrained by the Emperor under the influence of the Army's general staff, it did not even try to interfere with the transport of the British Expeditionary Force to France, since the generals preferred to let that 'contemptible little army' come across the Channel in the expectation that it would then be destroyed or captured. Among the advantages of this strategy of a 'fleet in being' was that the British commander-in-chief would always have to keep as many as possible of his ships in a state of readiness in case the enemy left harbour, while for his German opponent this was necessary only when he intended to come out. Since the Grand Fleet was liable at any given time to have at least two battleships, three or four cruisers, six destroyers and perhaps a battle-cruiser under refit, while other vessels might be temporarily disabled or detached, and since its numerical superiority was not at the outset so great as it afterwards became, the possibility that the Germans might have equality or even superiority at their 'selected moment' was a cause of constant anxiety to Jellicoe. Moreover, while the High Seas Fleet waited in harbour for its 'day', the Germans could hope in any case to whittle down the British preponderance in capital ships by mining and submarine attacks and perhaps by contriving means of catching some part of the Grand Fleet at a disadvantage, so that their chances of bringing on that favourable moment when battle could be ventured with a prospect of success would be increased.

On the other hand, even though the Germans refused battle under any but the most favourable conditions (and provided that they could be prevented from achieving and exploiting such conditions), Britain's geographical advantages and overall numerical superiority seemed to be sufficient to gain without battle her main strategic aims at sea – the economic blockade of Germany and the sufficient security of her own seaborne supplies, together with safety from invasion on any scale large enough to be dangerous. It would not even be necessary to bottle up the High Seas Fleet in its harbours (which in any case would not have been possible under conditions which had rendered close blockade no longer practicable), provided that its surface ships at least could be confined to the North Sea and kept from doing any considerable damage there. What in fact had to be achieved was a blockade, not of the German harbours, but of the North Sea. The means employed to this end were the holding of its two exits, the Straits of Dover by a mine barrage and patrol with the Channel Fleet to back them, and the wider passage between the Shetland Islands and the Norwegian coast by a patrolling squadron of cruisers (the Tenth, which eventually reached a maximum strength of 24) with the Grand Fleet available in case of a major German venture. This state of affairs meant on the one hand that the Germans had a considerable but precarious freedom of movement within the North Sea, and on the other that in at least its northern waters the Grand Fleet could make sweeps in the hope of catching the High Seas Fleet or some part of it in the act of availing itself of that freedom and could also in due course carry out training exercises. Only after the potentialities of the submarine had been fully realised and exploited by the Germans did a different and almost reversed situation emerge, with a new and highly dangerous form of counter-blockade operating against Britain.

Within the framework of the first phase of the naval war, as set out above, four major considerations governed the operations of the Grand Fleet during the opening months: the need to ensure the safe passage of the Expeditionary Force to France, which it was not known that the Germans had no intention of preventing; the possibility of an attempted invasion; the partial realisation, soon after the commencement of hostilities, of the impact of the submarine on naval strategy and tactics; and, arising chiefly out of this last, the lack as yet of a secure base.

During the period while the Expeditionary Force was crossing the Channel the Grand Fleet spent 19 days out of 26 at sea, and on 15 and 16 August carried out a sweeping movement which brought it to a point ten miles south of the line from Horns Reef to Flamborough Head, in the hope of being able to pounce on any German attempt to attack the Force in its passage.[3] Whether it could in fact have interfered with any such attempt is questionable, however; and Jellicoe seems to have had his doubts on the matter, and certainly to have regarded the enemy's omission to make one as evidence of a lack of enterprise. A few days later he planned a sweep in strength at dawn to within thirty miles of Heligoland with the flotillas leading, the cruisers covering them and the battle fleet supporting. This, however, the Admiralty countermanded, since the bulk of the Expeditionary Force was already across;[4] but it almost immediately afterwards approved a raid into the Heligoland Bight by the Harwich destroyers with the two light cruisers which were their flotilla leaders, supported by two battle-cruisers from the Grand Fleet. On being informed of this proposal Jellicoe got leave to increase the support to the whole of the battle-cruiser squadron under Beatty's personal command. This was a fortunate move, for in the Battle of the Bight which resulted on 26 August the British light forces were being roughly handled before Beatty, ignoring the risk of mines, stood in at full speed through the mist and turned the tables. Nevertheless the reaction of Jellicoe and his staff seems to have been that although Beatty's boldness had paid dividends on that occasion, the first phase of the action had been a narrow escape from disaster, owing to the over-confidence and under-estimation of the enemy which permeated the Navy and must in future be prudently guarded against.[5]

By this time or soon afterwards a brief experience of war had shown that the ideas previously held about the capabilities of submarines needed revision. It quickly became apparent that the radius of action and sea-keeping qualities of the German U-boats were appreciably greater than those of our own underwater craft. The occasional sightings of enemy submarines as far north as the Orkneys and Shetlands early in the war, the torpedoing of the light cruiser *Pathfinder* off St Abb's head on 5 September, the sinking of the cruisers *Aboukir*, *Cressy* and *Hogue* by a single submarine in the 'Broad Fourteens' off the Dutch coast on 22 September, and of the cruiser *Hawke* to the east of Aberdeen on 15 October,[6] made it evident that the U-boats could constitute a very serious menace. It was realised that vessels moving at slow to moderate speeds, and above all a number of capital ships in company, would run very considerable risks in waters where German submarines were operating, unless they were screened by a strong force of destroyers. This realisation affected the operations of the battle fleet, since its total of forty destroyers was quite inadequate to form screens for both it and the Battle-Cruiser Squadron. Moreover the fuel capacity of destroyers was only sufficient for them to remain at sea in company with a fleet for three days and nights, whereas the Fleet itself could remain out for three or four times that period. Again, destroyers could not be kept nearly so frequently at sea as larger ships owing to their requirements in the way of boiler-cleaning and the refit and adjustment of their more delicate machinery, as well as the necessity of giving their crews periods of rest. There were thus two alternatives for the capital ships of the Grand Fleet, either to return to harbour with the destroyers or to remain at sea without a destroyer screen. For the time being Jellicoe adopted the latter alternative, accepting the risk, but minimising it as far as possible by keeping henceforward to the northern part of the North Sea.[7] The German High Seas Fleet, it should be pointed out, reacted in a somewhat similar way to the sinking of the old cruiser *Hela* by a British submarine six miles south of Heligoland on 13 September. Hitherto it had occasionally exercised in the Bight, but its commander-in-chief Admiral von Ingenohl now decided that future exercises must be carried out in the comparative safety of the Baltic, at the cost of a double passage of the Kiel Canal for the purpose.

A further danger which soon made itself apparent was that from mines, which the enemy could easily lay in the central and southern waters of the North Sea, especially under cover of darkness, with little risk of his activities being witnessed. The only safeguard for our battle fleet, if it operated in these waters, would be to keep minesweepers constantly working ahead of it. Not only would this have meant reducing the Fleet's speed to the minesweepers' maximum of ten knots, but the number of minesweepers we then possessed was in any case wholly inadequate for such a task. The combined effect, therefore, of the submarine and mine threats was to cause the Grand Fleet to confine its movements, at any rate under ordinary conditions, to the more northern parts of the North Sea, where the risk of cruising without a destroyer screen might be taken, and where it was unlikely that the Germans would be able to lay mines without discovery, owing to the distance from their bases. For a little longer cruiser patrols without destroyers were maintained in the central waters, but after the loss of the *Hawke* these also were withdrawn to the northward.[8]

An additional complication and anxiety was that some months elapsed before Scapa Flow could be made secure against submarines. At the outbreak of war, having previously been intended only as a war anchorage for light forces, it was wholly undefended

Jellicoe in Captain's full-dress uniform shortly after the Boxer rebellion

Two cartoons of Jellicoe: that by Spy was done just before his promotion to Rear-Admiral

HIS BARK IS ON THE SEA.

Mr. Punch. "AND WHAT DID YOU THINK OF COLONEL CHURCHILL'S SPEECH, SIR?"
Admiral Jellicoe. "I'M AFRAID I DON'T UNDERSTAND THESE THINGS. I'M NOT A POLITICIAN."
Mr. Punch. "THANK GOD FOR THAT, SIR!"

by nets and booms. Jellicoe therefore set to work at once to give it such protection as he could by sinking merchant vessels to block some of the entrances of the vast natural harbour and placing batteries on either side of the main channel, Hoxa Sound; but until more adequate defences could be provided he preferred to keep the Fleet at sea as much as possible, engaged in gunnery practice, exercises, and sweeps between the 58th and 54th parallels of latitude. Indeed, after it had been discovered in the opening days of the war that German U-boats could reach the Orkneys* he was twice driven by subsequent alarms to withdraw altogether from Scapa for short periods; to Loch Ewe on the west coast of Scotland for three weeks after a false report that a submarine had penetrated the Flow on 1 September, and to Lough Swilly on the north coast of Ireland after a similar scare on 16 October. At one point so much of his time was occupied in planning the defences of Scapa, pressing forward the work on them, dealing with various questions relating to the patrolling of the coast by watchers, arranging for the guarding and disposal of merchant ships sent in for examination, requisitioning trawlers and drifters, and other matters which should have been delegated at the outset, that he began to find it difficult to deal with the Fleet work proper. However the appointment of his old friend Sir Stanley Colville, who waived his seniority in order to serve under him, as Vice-Admiral Commanding the Orkneys and Shetlands relieved this part of the pressure upon him. In the middle of November the Admiralty made a rather tentative suggestion, with which he complied, that he should return to Scapa; but it was not until the middle of 1915 that the base could be considered reasonably safe.[9]

Another related problem was that of obtaining sufficient gunnery practice. No facilities for this originally existed at Scapa, which had not been used as a base for such work in peacetime, except for destroyers; and although Cromarty had been so used it was at first not much better protected against submarines. At the beginning of the war, therefore, not only was it necessary to depend on the Fleet's own resources for the provision of targets, but the practices were carried out under conditions which laid the

---

* On 8 August a torpedo was fired at the battleship *Monarch* while she was engaged in firing practice to the south of Fair Isle. The enemy was probably U15, which was seen, rammed and sunk by the cruiser *Birmingham* next day.

E

ships open to submarine attack. This was most unsatisfactory, and the work suffered considerably as a result. Not until the latter part of 1915 did it become possible, owing to the increase in the number of destroyers attached to the Fleet and the provision of anti-submarine obstructions at Cromarty, to carry out practices at long ranges in the Moray Firth, and real improvement dated only from that period. Later still, battle-practice targets were brought to Scapa Flow and the long-range firing was carried out in the Pentland Firth, a more convenient place except for its very strong tides. By 1916, however, a marked advance had been made in the Grand Fleet's gunnery efficiency.[10]

Jellicoe's early realisation of the dangers to be expected from submarines and mines also contributed to the anxiety which from the outset he felt about the Grand Fleet's relative shortage of destroyers and light cruisers, although at first the main consideration which weighed with him was not so much the consequent lack of anti-submarine screening as the superiority in the destroyer arm which he ascribed to the Germans and the use which he feared they might make of it in a fleet action, especially since he believed wrongly that all German destroyers carried mines.* As early as 18 August he expressed his misgivings on this point in a letter to Prince Louis of Battenberg:[11]

> I am strongly of opinion that as soon as the Expeditionary Force is across, it is most desirable and essential that one, if not both, of the Harwich Flotillas should be attached to the Grand Fleet. You have always expressed the opinion that when the High Sea† Fleet comes out intending to fight, it will be accompanied by practically the whole German T.B.D. force. Such reports as we have received at present confirm this view entirely. . . . Some of the German T.B.D.'s will undoubtedly have as their task the laying of mines. The rest will attack with torpedoes. My few light cruisers and 40 T.B.D.'s will be no match for them so far as *torpedo* armament goes, and the superiority on the German side may well make up for our superiority in battleships or indeed turn the scale in their favour considerably. . . .

* In the whole war only 25 German destroyers or torpedo-boats carried mines.

† This, which Jellicoe consistently employed, is a correct literal translation of the German *Hochseeflotte*, though 'High Seas Fleet' is the more common English usage.

The problem of the mines laid in action is a difficult one. I fully expect the Germans to deploy in the opposite direction to ourselves. . . . If they do this I must immediately start to circle their rear. . . . Their T.B.D.'s in *rear* of their line will lay mines across my van as soon as my circling movement begins and unless I am very strong in light cruisers and T.B.D.'s I can't stop the mine-laying. . . .

He went on to add, however:

The weather is fine, the spirit in the Fleet excellent . . . and when we do meet the High Sea Fleet I believe we shall give a very good account of ourselves. Only I want to fight them fairly, not with a great superiority in T.B.D.'s and mines in their favour together with what they may well scheme for, viz. a locality adjacent to some of their submarines.

To this appeal he received an official reply (which time proved to be unduly optimistic) that he could rely on having the Harwich flotillas with him in the event of a fleet action.[12] On 31 August he wrote formally to the Admiralty asking for more light cruisers, which were needed to support destroyer raids, act with the battle-cruisers in offensive sweeps, patrol the areas covering the approaches to Scapa, cover the front of the battle fleet at sea and protect its van and flanks in action.[13] This time, however, there was no response, for the demands on our relatively limited number of light craft were multifarious.

The same concern about submarines and mines, especially the latter, emerges in the Grand Fleet Battle Orders which Jellicoe drew up in August and amplified in September.[14] These orders were much more elaborate and detailed than his pre-war ones, and indeed verged upon an attempt to foresee and provide for all contingencies. It was still laid down that vice-admirals commanding squadrons would have discretionary powers to act independently in certain circumstances, but the use of separate fast divisions which he had formerly proposed was ruled out for the time being by the dictum that 'in all cases the ruling principle is that the fleet keeps together, attempted attacks on a portion of the enemy's line being avoided as liable to lead to the isolation of that division which attempts the movement.' Subsequently, however, the notion of a detachable division reappeared before Jutland with

the creation of the fast Fifth Battle Squadron of *Queen Elizabeths*.*
'Generally speaking', another paragraph pronounced, 'so long as
the action is being fought on approximately parallel courses, the
whole fleet should form one line of battle.' A slight shift of
emphasis can perhaps also be detected in the orders for destroyers,
a little more space being given to their defensive duties, though the
necessity for attack was still stressed.

The possibility of an attempt at invasion or a raid was not considered very great in the earliest days of the war, when the nights
were comparatively short and it was probable that the enemy had
not many troops to spare for the purpose. In October and November 1914, however, by which time conditions on the Western
Front were approaching a deadlock and Britain had been virtually
denuded of trained men, more earnest consideration was given to
the matter, and a secret memorandum drawn up by Churchill
on the subject was conveyed personally to Jellicoe by the First
Lord's Naval Secretary.[15] In this it was laid down that the Grand
Fleet's primary task if such an attempt were made would be to
deal with the High Seas Fleet should it come out to cover the
operation, while Admiral Burney with the Channel Fleet and the
flotillas attacked the enemy's transports and their escort. In reply
Jellicoe pointed out that owing to the activity of the German submarines and the consequent withdrawal of the cruiser patrols
from the central part of the North Sea no warning of the departure
from German ports of a raiding or invading force could be
expected.[16] It must therefore be realised that the fleet could not
undertake to prevent the landing of a large force, though it might
make the maintenance of that force when on shore difficult or
impossible. On the other hand, he went on to comment, it was
highly improbable that such a landing would be attempted on open
beaches, especially during the winter months, and the danger
points were therefore the rivers, harbours and estuaries on the
east coast. These could be guarded, he suggested, by placing
merchant ships fitted with explosive charges in position ready to be
sunk across the channels at a moment's notice.

All these anxieties were augmented by the fact that Jellicoe knew
or in some cases suspected that there were many matters in which
the German Navy was the equal of or superior to our own. In
addition to the better armour protection and more complete

* See above, p. 48.

watertight subdivision of its capital ships and the superiority of its shells, which have been referred to in the previous chapter, and the greater range of operation which its submarines had now revealed themselves to possess, its torpedoes* and mines proved to be better than ours. Its Zeppelins too could serve, at least in clear weather, as far-ranging and invaluable scouts. Even in gunnery, on which together with numerical superiority Jellicoe relied for victory in battle, the German director pointer gave an advantage when the visibility was poor. Other superiorities, in night-fighting practice and in signalling, were to be made manifest at Jutland. In part, at least, the British inferiority in technical matters arose from the inferior status and consideration still accorded (in spite of Fisher) to engineers and technicians in the Royal Navy. Although their German opponents were much more alive to the effects and implications of the technological revolution of the late nineteenth and early twentieth centuries – indeed the material superiority of the German Navy may be said to have been a reflection of Germany's general lead over Britain in this 'Second Industrial Revolution' – the British Sea Lords and higher command continued to be drawn exclusively from the executive or seaman branch of the Service until after the Second World War.

In Britain's favour, on the other hand, were the splendid seamanship produced by longer and greater experience, the confidence born of centuries of success, and the longer service and on the whole more maritime instincts of our men. Nevertheless it was incumbent on Jellicoe, while straining every nerve to train the gunnery of his crews, to shun or guard against any danger that threatened to reduce or destroy the superiority in numbers that was his chief though unromantic asset. He therefore took care to make plain the cautious strategy and tactics which he intended to follow, first in a letter to Churchill and then more explicitly still in a memorandum to the Board of Admiralty. In the letter, written on 30 September, he emphasised that it would be suicidal to throw away our advantage in capital ships by risking them in

* British torpedoes had a hitherto unsuspected defect, which caused them to take much longer to pick up their set depth than was realised (since peace-time practices had been carried out with practice heads 40 lb. lighter than the warheads). Hence even when otherwise dead on the target they sometimes passed under it.

waters infested by submarines, since the result 'might easily be such a weakening of our battle fleet and battle-cruiser strength as seriously to jeopardise the future of the country by giving over to the Germans the command of the open seas.' Until the submarine menace could be minimised, he urged, 'we must give up the idea . . . of southerly battle fleet movements. The battle and light cruisers could still do it occasionally when I get a few more of the latter.' To this Churchill replied that he was in full agreement.[17] The memorandum sent on 30 October was a trenchant statement of the principles by which Jellicoe proposed to be guided in a fleet action, and in view of its importance calls for quotation at some length:

The Germans have shown that they rely to a very great extent on submarines, mines and torpedoes, and there can be no doubt whatever that they will endeavour to make the fullest use of these weapons in a fleet action, especially since they possess an actual superiority over us in these particular directions. It therefore becomes necessary to consider our own tactical methods in relation to these forms of attack. In the first place it is evident that the Germans cannot rely with certainty upon having their full complement of submarines and minelayers present unless the battle is fought in waters selected by them and in the southern area of the North Sea. . . . My object will therefore be to fight the fleet action in the northern portion of the North Sea, which position is incidentally nearer our own bases, giving our wounded ships a chance of reaching them, whilst it ensures the final destruction or capture of enemy wounded vessels, and greatly handicaps a night destroyer attack. . . . Owing to the necessity that exists for keeping our cruisers at sea, it is probable that many will be short of coal when the opportunity for a fleet action arises, and they might be unable to move far to the southward for this reason. . . .

Secondly, it is necessary to consider what may be termed the tactics of the actual battlefield. . . . *If, for instance, the enemy battle fleet were to turn away from an advancing fleet, I should assume that the intention was to lead us over mines and submarines, and should decline to be so drawn. I desire particularly to draw the attention of Their Lordships to this point, since it may be deemed a refusal of battle, and indeed might possibly result in failure to bring the enemy to action as soon as is expected and hoped.** Such a result would be absolutely repugnant to the feelings of all British Naval Officers and men, *but with new and untried methods of warfare new tactics must be devised to meet them. I feel that such tactics, if not understood, may bring odium upon me*, but so long as I have the confidence of Their Lordships I intend to pursue what is, in my considered opinion, the proper course to defeat and annihilate the enemy's battle fleet, without regard to uninstructed opinion or criticism.

The situation is a difficult one. It is quite within the bounds of possibility that half our battlefleet might be disabled by underwater attack before the guns opened fire at all, if a false move is made, and I feel that I must constantly bear in mind the great probability of such attack and be prepared tactically to prevent its success.

To this uncompromising declaration from the man who, as Churchill wrote long afterwards, 'could lose the war in an afternoon' by an error of judgement, the Board replied that they approved his views, as stated therein, and assured him of their full confidence in his contemplated conduct of the Fleet in action.[18]

Soon afterwards, however, a situation developed which opened a rift between Jellicoe and the Admiralty and began to sap the confidence that Churchill had hitherto felt in him despite their temperamental incompatibility and earlier disputes. The Grand Fleet's original numerical advantage had soon begun to dwindle dangerously, owing to the loss of the battleship *Audacious* by a mine and the frequent need for ships to go into dock because of engine trouble or for other reasons. This was a necessity which Churchill could never fully grasp; and another difficulty of which he showed little understanding, apt as he was in both World Wars to count heads without weighing other considerations,† was that when new ships joined the Fleet it was some time before they were fully fit for battle. The most critical period came towards the end of October, when for these various reasons the Grand Fleet was eight capital ships short and the Germans could have given battle

---

* The italics are the present writer's.

† Cf. his repeated attempts to prod General Wavell and then General Auchinleck into premature offensives in the Western Desert by assessments of their forces based on ration strengths only.

with 15 dreadnoughts and 5 battle-cruisers (counting the *Blücher*, which was really only a large armoured cruiser) against Jellicoe's 17 and 5. A few days later Lord Fisher, who had just been recalled to the post of First Sea Lord,* took the calculated and successful risk of detaching three of the battle-cruisers to deal with the situation produced by von Spee's destruction of Cradock's squadron off Coronel on the west coast of South America. Again only inadequate information combined perhaps with lack of enterprise caused the High Seas Fleet to miss its opportunity. Jellicoe's estimate of the probable forces on either side at this point was embodied in a memorandum of 12 November to the Admiralty[19] and showed 19 British dreadnoughts available as against 16 Germans supported by 10 pre-dreadnought battleships, 3 battle-cruisers against 4, 7 cruisers against 6, 10 light cruisers against 15 and 40 destroyers against a conjectural 66. He also credited the Germans with a possible 16 submarines present on the day of action. Certainly this, especially the last item, was an *ex parte* calculation which even Fisher, though he was more sympathetic to Jellicoe's predicament than Churchill, declined to swallow wholesale. Nevertheless when Jellicoe's justifiable doubts of the supposed superiority of British capital ships are also taken into account, the position goes far to explain the vehement protests he now made, both informally in letters to Fisher[20] and more formally to the Board. In particular he pleaded to be allowed to keep the third battle-cruiser, the *Princess Royal*,† pointing out that he had recently raised no objection when the Third Battle Squadron (of eight old pre-dreadnoughts of the *King Edward VII* class) had been taken away from him to reinforce the Channel Fleet, whereas he would have objected most strongly if he had known that he was soon to lose three battle-cruisers as well. The immediate result, however, was a telegram which he described to

* Fisher had been raised to the peerage when he left the Admiralty in 1910. Prince Louis of Battenberg, who was First Sea Lord at the outbreak of the war, had almost immediately been driven into retirement by ignorant clamour against his German birth.

† Fisher had despatched the *Invincible* and *Inflexible* to the Falkland Islands, where under the command of Vice-Admiral Sir Doveton Sturdee they avenged the Coronel disaster by destroying von Spee's squadron in its turn. He had also sent the *Princess Royal* to guard against the possibility that von Spee might go north and come through the Panama Canal into the North Atlantic.

his sympathetic subordinate Beatty as a direct snub[21] and about which Fisher wrote apologetically a few days later:

I'm distressed above measure that you should have been harried in any way by Admiralty action. . . . There was never the very faintest idea of finding fault with you. I did not make out the telegram, but I see it is faulty and open to the construction you were justified in putting upon it. It won't happen again! Just then I was sore pressed. . . .[22]

By the time Fisher wrote this, however, fresh fuel for argument and protest had been provided. On 3 November the German battle-cruisers carried out the first of what came later to be called their 'tip-and-run' raids, making a dash across the North Sea and bombarding Yarmouth. This provoked the fears, or at any rate uneasiness, about invasion already referred to, and Jellicoe was informed that in order to strengthen the east coast deferces the Third Battle Squadron would be brought round again from the Channel to Rosyth.[23] He was also told that after Admiral Burney's Channel Fleet had disposed of the enemy's transports and their escort it would come under his command for the main battle with the High Seas Fleet if it had not yet been fought. A brisk exchange of memoranda followed. Jellicoe pointed out that since Burney would have to negotiate minefields with no destroyers and only two cruisers he was unlikely to arrive in time, which meant that if he himself was to have the superiority needed to cope with everything he must have the Third Battle Squadron sent back to him at Scapa. The Board's rejoinder was that the squadron must go to Rosyth, since it was imperative to have a force nearer the probable points of attack than Scapa was, and because the east coast had been so stripped of destroyers for the benefit of the Grand Fleet (which the Board claimed had now 71) that there were only a few patrol vessels available on it. Jellicoe, moreover, was now instructed to send a half-flotilla of his 71 to Rosyth to act with the squadron. 'We are sending you', the telegram continued, 'a carefully compiled table of the comparative strength of your fleet and the German High Seas Fleet which makes it clear that without the Third Battle Squadron you have such a preponderance of gun power that with equal gunnery efficiency a successful result is ensured' – a conclusion which smacks of the First Lord's old and fallacious argument based on guns alone. Jellicoe, shifting his ground, returned to the charge on the destroyer questions which had now been raised:

> With reference to your telegram 293 [he wired] the 71 destroyers mentioned include 10 . . . [which] are absent refitting . . . I regret to appear importunate but must beg for reconsideration of order detaching a half-flotilla with the Third Battle Squadron. . . . Without [these] additional 12 T.B. destroyers the safety of the dreadnought battlefleet is seriously endangered. A submarine attack here is quite feasible and as I am directed to use this base I trust that I shall not be held responsible for any disaster that may occur. The question of the relative strength of the High Seas Fleet and the fleet now with me cannot of course be decided without reference to the cruiser and destroyer strength of the two fleets. It is my comparative weakness in these two essentials that counterbalances any battleship superiority I may possess. . . .

The Board, however, made only a slight concession in the number of destroyers to be transferred, closing the argument with:

> We have carefully reviewed the position and given the fullest consideration to your wishes. We are confident that your fleet with its destroyers and flotillas is strong enough for the defensive work entrusted to it. In view of the grave needs we have to meet elsewhere we cannot reinforce you at present nor alter the dispositions communicated. The Third Battle Squadron . . . and 8 destroyers should proceed to Rosyth as ordered.[24]

Again Fisher sought to gild the pill by writing on the same day a placatory letter in which he promised more cruisers presently and jocularly declared that the Board thought Jellicoe's battle-line already so long that one end would barely see the other, ending with what was perhaps a hint – 'Let everyone be optimistic, and shoot the pessimists!'[25]

If Jellicoe had carried out this injunction, however, the first victim might have been the commander of the Battle-Cruiser Squadron. Sir David Beatty was fully as disquieted as his chief by the absence of the three battle-cruisers and had sent him a memorandum which Jellicoe forwarded to the Admiralty and which should suffice by itself to dispose of the ancient legend that he was a mere reckless thruster. In this Beatty pointed out that he was faced by the possibility of an unexpected and difficult situation, since whereas he had always assumed it to be his duty to engage the German battle-cruiser squadron when and where it could be found, he was now (he declared) markedly inferior to it in numbers, especially as the new battle-cruiser *Tiger* was not yet fit to take her place in the line He therefore asked for a ruling as to how he should act if he encountered the German squadron. In Jellicoe's covering letter to this memorandum he endorsed what it said of the squadron's inferiority in numbers and the unreadiness of the *Tiger*, and went on:

> We cannot rely on much if any superiority in gunnery in my opinion. The German Fleet has shown itself to be highly efficient and their gunnery in any action in which they have not been hopelessly inferior* has been markedly excellent. I can only repeat once more my request for the *Princess Royal*. . . . I can only inform Sir David Beatty as I have done, that he must do the best he can with the force at his disposal . . . but I hold a very strong opinion that we are running the greatest risk of losing an opportunity of inflicting a severe defeat on the enemy, if nothing worse, by not adhering to the principle of concentration in the decisive theatre.[26]

The Board replied with an instruction based almost word for word on a minute that had been made on Jellicoe's and Beatty's representations by Sir Arthur Wilson (who had been brought back to the Admiralty at the same time as Fisher returned, though in an undefined capacity, to work on high-level strategic problems). Stripped of formalities, it ran:

> The inferiority of the 1st Battle Cruiser Squadron to the German Cruiser Squadron . . . is so slight that it should not make any difference in the Vice-Admiral's duty to engage the latter if opportunity offers.
>
> The *Derfflinger* [the latest German battle-cruiser] has not had much more time than the *Tiger* to get into gunnery order, and it is on gunnery efficiency more than numbers that the result of an action depends.[27]

This last rather sententious pronouncement was soon afterwards

* Jellicoe was probably referring on the one hand to Coronel and on the other to the Battle of Heligoland Bight.

stripped of such point as it had by the transfer of the Battle-Cruiser Squadron from Cromarty to the Forth in December, which made it difficult to arrange gunnery exercises for it with anything like the frequency with which Jellicoe was exercising the Grand Fleet. They were only possible if it came north, which it could rarely leave its station to do; and the result of its lack of firing practice was that far from its shooting being or becoming better than that of its rival, as Wilson implied, the reverse was the case, as became all too evident later in the opening phase of the Battle of Jutland.

Meanwhile on 4 December Jellicoe had sent another memorandum to the Admiralty on the subject of what he considered the inadequacy of his destroyer force. Estimating the probable destroyer strength of the High Seas Fleet as 88, he claimed that since he could not be certain of having the Harwich flotillas with him in a fleet action he could reckon on only 33 destroyers to counter the attack of these 88. The only course left to him would be the objectionable and difficult one of turning the battle fleet away if such an attack took place. Nor had he the superiority in light cruisers which would have enabled him to use some of them to take the place of destroyers. 'I cannot but feel', he summed up, 'that with my present weakness in destroyers I am greatly handicapped in obtaining the crushing victory over the High Seas Fleet that is expected of me.' This time the Admiralty's response was to attach the First Destroyer Flotilla of three light cruisers and twenty destroyers formally to the Grand Fleet, but station it at Rosyth under the immediate orders of Vice-Admiral Bradford commanding the Third Battle Squadron. Here, it pointed out, the flotilla, like the squadron, was both available for use in the event of a raid or invasion in the north of England or south of Scotland and also in a position to join Jellicoe at sea if required. In return, he was instructed to detach eight of the oldest of the destroyers which he had at Scapa and send them south as a partial replacement for the First Flotilla.[28]

The private correspondence which Jellicoe maintained with Fisher and of which Churchill was understandably rather jealous* increased in frequency towards the close of the year and may have served as a slight safety-valve for some of his worries and

* Fisher urged Jellicoe on 11 January to write occasionally to the First Lord to prevent this.

annoyances – besides performing the same service for Fisher himself. The latter was rarely able to meet Jellicoe's requests, but he was sympathetic in his attitude and usually soothing in his language. On the other hand Churchill, unable to appreciate all Jellicoe's difficulties, became exasperated by his memoranda of dissent and what he regarded as his loud and prolonged complaints. It was these which caused him to refer in his *World Crisis* long afterwards to Jellicoe's 'continuous protests' and the Admiralty's 'efforts to reassure and placate him'. In this book he also wrote that:

> If at any time from any cause two or three ships were absent from the Grand Fleet for a week or two* he drew severe comparisons between the German Fleet and his own. . . . From his own side he deducted any ship which had any defect, however temporary, however small. . . . He sometimes also deducted two or three of the most powerful battleships in the world because they were not trained up to the full level of efficiency of the others. . . . He always credited [the enemy] with several ships more than we now know they had, or were then thought likely to have.[29]

There was some weight in this last criticism, though a tendency to over-estimate the enemy's force is not uncommon in commanders, as Beatty indeed had shown in his memorandum about the battle-cruiser situation; but the others were exaggerated and unfair. One recognises in Churchill's irritation with Jellicoe's caution and careful consideration of possibilities and details something of the same clash of temperaments which British naval and military commanders and Chiefs of the Imperial General Staff – Cunningham, Tovey, Dill, Wavell, Auchinleck and Alanbrooke – were to experience in the Second World War. Yet it has to be borne in mind that these strictures were set down in after years, and it would be a distortion of the facts to imagine that the relationship of the two had now become one of continuous bickering. Churchill could still write, for instance: 'I admire the patience you have shown and the wonderful success which has attended and rewarded your efforts to guard the Grand Fleet from loss hitherto'; and again a few days later: 'I am so

---

* The three battle-cruisers about which Jellicoe chiefly protested were absent from home waters for about seven weeks.

glad you will rest for a few days. . . . Your health and poise are vital to us.'[30]

A notable stroke of good fortune had now befallen the British Navy. On 26 August the German light cruiser *Magdeburg* had run aground in the Gulf of Finland and the Russians had salvaged from the body of a drowned signalman copies of the German Navy's cipher signal books and squared charts of the North Sea and Heligoland Bight, by which the position of their own and enemy forces were indicated. These had been sent by our allies to the Admiralty and had in due course been decoded. As a result, when Admiral von Ingenohl, the German commander-in-chief, sent Vice-Admiral Hipper's battle-cruisers out again on another tip-and-run raid on Scarborough, Whitby and Hartlepool on 16 December, with the High Seas Fleet in support, the British had sufficient warning of at any rate the battle-cruiser sortie for the Admiralty to order out the Second Battle Squadron under Warrender and Beatty's force from Cromarty.* Jellicoe, for his part, gave them a well-judged rendezvous that should have enabled them to catch Hipper on his return, and submitted to the Admiralty that the Harwich destroyer flotillas should also be directed to this rendezvous. Both sides, however, missed their opportunities. First Ingenohl threw away his chance of destroying Warrender's squadron and so reducing the Grand Fleet to something like parity at one blow, by turning the High Seas Fleet back to its base as soon as his destroyer screen encountered Warrender's, in the mistaken belief that he had the whole of the Grand Fleet in front of him. 'Ingenohl', groaned Grand Admiral von Tirpitz, the virtual creator of the German Navy, when he heard of this, 'held Germany's fate in the hollow of his hand.' Then a combination of mischances, bad weather, poor visibility, errors of judgement and a badly worded signal from Beatty's flagship enabled Hipper in his turn to escape. Jellicoe, writing to Fisher that he was 'intensely unhappy' about this failure to seize 'the opportunity of our lives', ascribed it in part also to the lack of sufficient destroyers, since his suggestion that the Harwich Force should be ordered out had not been taken up.[31] When the Admiralty made a mild

* It was not until after this unsuccessful operation that Beatty's battle-cruisers, with Commodore Goodenough's light cruiser squadron, were moved down from Cromarty to Rosyth to give them a better chance of intercepting future raids. See above, p. 60.

criticism of Beatty for not spreading his battle-cruisers sufficiently, however, he leapt so sharply to his subordinate's defence
that he obtained a partial retraction.[32] Beatty himself had written
to him:

> It was terrible to have had opportunities apparently within our
> grasp and nothing to have come of it. Would to God that you
> had been there and I feel we should have had a grand day! . . .
> Truly the past has been the blackest week in my life and I trust
> earnestly to have the opportunity in the *very near* future to
> obliterate it. But next time come in command yourself or let
> me do it.[33]

A month later Beatty had the opportunity he wanted. When on
24 January the German battle-cruisers sallied out again, this time
not to bombard our coast but to investigate some reported
activities of British forces in the Dogger Bank area, his squadron
succeeded in catching them there. But even though the Battle
of the Dogger Bank was a British success, it was made less con-
clusive than it should have been by errors on the part of two of
Beatty's subordinates – Rear-Admiral Moore on whom devolved
the pursuit of the fleeing Germans after the flagship *Lion* had been
disabled and who (partly because of an ambiguous signal from the
Lion) gave up the pursuit too soon, and Captain Pelly of the
Tiger who reduced the effect of his ship's already poor shooting by
firing at the wrong opponent. The only German ship which was
sunk, the *Blücher*, was not a true battle-cruiser but a heavy
cruiser which was deputising for a temporary absentee, the *Von
der Tann*. Almost all the hits scored by the British were on her,
very few shells hitting any of the German battle-cruisers in their
retreat, so that the misgivings which Jellicoe was beginning to
have about the gunnery of his own battle-cruiser squadron were
confirmed. Moreover, one of these comparatively few hits scored
on the German battle-cruisers had consequences which ultimately
worked out to the serious disadvantage of the British later, at
Jutland. A shell from the *Lion* partly penetrated the armour of
the after turret of the *Seydlitz*, igniting waiting charges in the
working chamber, the spreading flames from which would have
exploded the after magazines and probably destroyed the ship,
but for the prompt action of the executive officer in flooding both
magazines. After the battle the German Naval Command introduced

into their capital ships the anti-flash arrangements which enabled them (and the *Seydlitz* in particular) to take such heavy punishment at Jutland and yet survive. The British, on the other hand, still had to learn this lesson there, and at a heavy cost.

Despite these adverse features the moral effect produced on the German fleet by the Battle of the Dogger Bank was sufficient for more than a year to elapse, under the cautious command of Ingenohl's successor Von Pohl, before any capital ships of the High Seas Fleet ventured far into the North Sea again. In expectation of further sorties, however, Churchill and Fisher now wished to move the Grand Fleet to Rosyth and the battle-cruisers to the Humber, in order to give each a better intercepting position; but they met with the united and uncompromising opposition of both Jellicoe and Beatty.

> I have looked at the Humber as a base [Jellicoe wrote to Fisher].[34] It is quite impossible. A few reasons are –
>   1. You could only get in about 12 or 14 large ships.
>   2. No submarine obstruction could remain efficient in the strong tides there.
>   3. A destroyer boom would be essential, as it is so well within range of German destroyers.
>   4. It is so easily mined off the approaches.
>   5. When there is a fog *anywhere*, it is sure to be there. I am sure Scapa can't be beaten as a base for the Grand Fleet.

To Beatty he wrote on February 7:[35]

> The difficulty in both cases [i.e., Rosyth and the Humber], in addition to the fogs, seems to me to be that neither anchorage is defended against torpedoes fired through the obstruction. I know you hate Rosyth from the point of view of mining and submarines. I think the Humber is possibly even worse. The one redeeming feature [of the double change] would be that . . . of course one is very much nearer to support you and the strategic advantages are considerable. But [Rosyth] is really only from 60–90 miles nearer the required position and the lack of facilities for practice is serious . . . and I'll be hanged if I can see where you, 3rd Battle Squadron, 3rd Cruiser Squadron, light cruisers and possibly Channel Fleet are going to find room in the Humber.

To this Beatty replied:

> On the subject of the change of bases I talked to 1st Lord about
> it and I certainly thought I had made it plain that I did not
> agree with putting battle-cruisers at the Humber. First of all
> and lastly it is impossible, as there is insufficient water. . . . I
> also think it would be a mistake to move the battlefleet to
> Rosyth. It no doubt could be made safe with extra craft and
> extra vigilance, but it seems to me it would be playing into the
> enemy hands to bring within nearer reach our capital ships, and
> in a position where going in and out (no matter what precautions
> we take) they would be far more vulnerable to submarine attack
> than at Scapa, also destroyer attack if they ever develop it, and
> most certainly mine-laying, and take them away from a place
> where they can enjoy some measure of opportunity for gunnery
> practices . . . I cannot see that you are any more likely to catch
> the enemy battlefleet from Rosyth than you are from Scapa. In
> fact unless he makes up his mind to fight you, I do not see how
> you are going to make him, any more than I could make their
> BC's turn round and fight the other day.[36]

In face of this opposition Churchill and Fisher dropped their
idea; though by the following May, Beatty was beginning to
change his attitude, writing to Jellicoe on the 26th:

> If the Battle Cruiser Force were at the Humber then the whole
> of the rest of the Grand Fleet could be based here [Rosyth];
> that would be worth a great deal. But can they make the
> Humber capable of taking us all? . . . A good deal of dredging
> would be required so that we can get out at any state of tide.
> That is not insurmountable.[37]

At the beginning of 1915 Churchill's volatile mind had also
returned to the Borkum project of pre-war days. Perhaps not fully
appreciating (though he claimed to do so) the decisive influence
which the Navy could exercise by blockade even if not given the
opportunity of fighting a fleet action, he had from early in the war
been considering and proposing a variety of offensive and mainly
amphibious operations, whose difficulties he was inclined to ignore
or gloss over. Fisher's return to the Admiralty had given him an
ally in advocating projects for penetrating the Baltic and landing
troops on the coast of Pomerania, but the general opinion was

F

unfavourable to these. His attention had then swung back to schemes for seizing some island off the German coast in order to facilitate intensive mining of its channels and river-mouths, enable submarines and destroyers to be maintained in German waters, and serve as a base for an invasion of Schleswig-Holstein. In letters of 4 and 11 January he urged on Jellicoe the possibilities and advantages of Borkum for these purposes, but found him as resolutely opposed as he had been in the previous July. As late as March, however, he was still hoping for an attack on Borkum in May,[38] but in the meantime his main attention had been diverted to the Dardanelles.

It was in January also that Jellicoe's health began to show the first open signs of deterioration. Behind the outward calm which he maintained in front of his subordinates the strain imposed on him by his unique position was beginning to wear him down. His awareness of the weak points of the British Navy and the strong points of the enemy and his sense of the vastness of his responsibilities worked upon his naturally cautious temperament to increase his tendency to worry, even over minor matters. Inevitably, this nervous strain began to have its physical repercussions. He still took exercise, sometimes in the form of golf on the course which had been laid out at Scapa, but he played in such haste ('almost sprinting between the strokes') that he can hardly have derived much benefit from it. By the beginning of 1915 he was suffering from the painful and weakening though undignified complaint of piles, and had already decided to take a short rest when on 25 January a particularly bad attack caused something like a breakdown. 'I am not at all well', he wrote to Beatty on the following day: 'Crocked up yesterday. Very bad attack of piles and general run down.' 'You must take the greatest care of yourself', replied Beatty: 'What we should do without you the Lord knows.' To Hamilton Jellicoe wrote: 'I am laid up for a bit. It is of course due to the worry of trying to get things done which ought to be done without my having to step in' – a sentence eloquent of that difficulty in delegating responsibility which was his most serious weakness. A minor operation cleared up this particular physical trouble, but even so it was a month before he returned to duty, 'feeling really fit for work though going a little slow at first',[39] and the nervous strain of which it had probably been a manifestation soon reappeared as the long months of constant watchfulness wore on.

4 The Long Haul

(1915–16)

THE main features of the twelve months after the Battle of the Dogger Bank, so far as operations in home waters were concerned, were the dangers from submarines and mines and the efforts to cope with them. During this period, and despite the enemy's adherence to his strategy of attrition, the Grand Fleet's margin of numerical superiority grew again through the building of new ships; while the unenterprising Von Pohl peeped out only five times, never going more than 120 miles beyond Heligoland, and the British public continued to be disappointed of its hoped-for new Trafalgar.

During the first six months of the war the Germans had made no attempt to use the potentialities of their submarines to the full against Britain's trade, and indeed had not realised them. No general policy of attacks on merchant shipping without warning had been adopted, and when such attacks occurred they were due to the actions of a few individual submarine commanders. On 4 February 1915, however, after all the German surface commerce-raiders that were at large in the oceans at the beginning of the war had been accounted for, the first such 'unrestricted' campaign began, though still with a comparatively small force of U-boats. On 29 March the separate Flanders Flotilla, based on Ostend and Zeebrugge, was created to campaign against our shipping off the east coast and in the Channel. On our part numerous counter-measures were devised and explored, but none with any great success. Before the war it had been believed that high speed and zig-zagging would offer the best protection, and little progress had been made in the development of anti-submarine weapons. Depth charges, sweeps, indicator nets, auxiliary patrols of small craft and the arming of merchant vessels so far as our resources and their great numbers allowed were now resorted to; but the results were not impressive.

Jellicoe at this stage continued to be more concerned about the submarine menace to the Grand Fleet than the threat to commerce. On 18 March, while the Fleet was returning from tactical exercises to the eastward of Scapa, a submarine* fired a torpedo at the *Neptune*, but was rammed and sunk by the *Dreadnought*. Less than a fortnight later, after a sweep in the North Sea on 29 and 30 March, he complained strongly to the Admiralty that its instructions for this sweep had involved both Beatty and himself in needlessly grave risks of submarine attack. These instructions had been sent to him so late that in order to reach the rendezvous with the Battle-Cruiser Fleet,† which they assigned to him, he had been compelled to take the fleet to sea in daylight and insufficiently screened, since he had only sixteen destroyers available at Scapa at that moment. His return in bright moonlight, he considered, had perhaps been even more risky, while the dangers for Beatty had possibly been still greater, except that he had had more patrol vessels at his disposal.[1] Jellicoe's own proposed solution to the submarine problem, which he urged upon the Admiralty both before and after the departure of Fisher and Churchill,[2] was that a single energetic officer, preferably Vice-Admiral Sir Lewis Bayly, should be appointed to co-ordinate and direct the activities of the patrols. In this the Admiralty concurred only to the limited extent of making Bayly in July Admiral Commanding the Western Approaches with his headquarters at Queenstown in Ireland and the duty of protecting traffic in this important area through which, in particular, American supplies to Britain passed. Bayly, however, was not very successful, since the submarines could on the whole work effectively outside the limited range of his patrols. The vehement protests of the United States after the sinking of the *Arabic* on 19 August with the loss of three American lives nevertheless obliged Germany to bring this first unrestricted campaign to an end; and the subsequent difficulties and dangers of operating in accordance with international law by surfacing and stopping vessels that might prove to be armed or might bring British warships quickly to the spot led to a marked decline of submarine warfare in the waters around the British Isles after the end of September.

* This was the U29, commanded by Commander Weddingen, which on 22 September had sunk the cruisers *Aboukir*, *Cressy* and *Hogue*.

† The Battle-Cruiser Squadron had been thus renamed in February, while remaining an organic part of the Grand Fleet.

Fisher and Jellicoe had to some extent been drifting apart since the former's return to the Admiralty and perhaps especially since the beginning of the year. The old warrior was becoming increasingly cranky and unpredictable, and some of his strategic notions, notably his hankering after operations in the Baltic, were unrealistic to the extent of flying in the face of common sense. On the other hand, he was even more nervous of submarines than Jellicoe was, and for that reason fiercely critical in their private correspondence of the Grand Fleet's sweeps in the North Sea. His letters were peppered with such comments as: 'In my decided opinion . . . no big ship of your Fleet should EVER be in the North Sea', while his grumbles about Jellicoe's opposition to the proposed change of bases alternated with apologetic recantations and assurances that these complaints need not be taken too seriously.[3] Jellicoe for his part was growing more and more critical of the Admiralty and no doubt tended to include Fisher in that criticism, even if only mentally. Nor does he seem to have been completely mollified when Fisher's Naval Assistant, Captain T. E. Crease, wrote to him after his chief's exasperated and almost runaway resignation of the First Sea Lordship:

> I can only say that he has fought continuously for the Grand Fleet and for its proper strength and maintenance. Not always as successfully as he wished, but sometimes taking what he could get rather than nothing. I don't think you can possibly have realised the obstruction and difficulties here which he has had to face during the last six months in his efforts to meet all your wishes as much as possible.[4]

Within a few days of this letter Churchill had also departed from the Admiralty, removed as a condition of the Conservatives' entry into a coalition with Asquith's government. His successor was Arthur Balfour, and for a moment there was perhaps a possibility that Jellicoe might be Fisher's. There was no one clearly marked out for the post. Sir Arthur Wilson was seventy-three, had made an unfavourable impression on the War Council, and was given to favouring plans that were generally thought reckless. Hankey, the secretary of the War Council and almost the *éminence grise* of the British war effort, wrote in his diary on 20 May: 'Jellicoe is the only alternative to Wilson and Jackson, but everyone agrees that Jellicoe is indispensable in the Grand Fleet.'[5] Balfour, therefore, after a visit to Jellicoe at Edinburgh on 27 May, finally decided on Admiral Sir Henry Jackson, a seaman of scientific bent who had been another of Fisher's 'five best brains in the Navy . . .' ten years earlier but had latterly had little seagoing experience. Moreover, like Jellicoe, he was prone to worry, and his health was not of the most robust. The Balfour–Jackson regime could hardly have been more unlike that of Churchill and Fisher. Placidity replaced pyrotechnics; but if there was less friction there was also a good deal less drive. The correspondence between Jellicoe and Fisher now fell off for a while, and in November Jellicoe was writing to his friend Hamilton, who at the outset of the war had become his successor as Second Sea Lord:

> I don't believe J. F. [Fisher] will get on the War Council, but if you really think there is danger I will take steps which may *help to stop it*. Please let me know about it. I think I can do something *very much 'entre nous.'**** It would be a fatal step. I don't agree with you as to all his sins, as I think without his energy *re* new construction we should now be in a shocking state, but I am fully aware of his totally wrong strategical notions and so are others to whom I should write.[6]

It was not Hamilton, however, to whom Jellicoe chiefly unburdened himself on paper for the greater part of 1915, so much as Beatty. The squadron commanders of the Grand Fleet were of course much more available for oral discussion, but although several of them were old comrades and personal friends they were mostly rather colourless men. The chief exception was Vice-Admiral Sir Doveton Sturdee, the victor of the Falkland Islands, who had replaced Sir Douglas Gamble (whom Jellicoe considered 'not up to the mark nor his health good')[7] in command of the Fourth Battle Squadron in February; but Sturdee besides being personally difficult in some ways was in Jellicoe's eyes a tactical heretic who could not be trusted. Sir Cecil Burney, who had been transferred from the command of the Channel Fleet to that of the First Battle Squadron at the end of 1914, was a cautious man after his own heart, whose caution degenerated into pessimism when he was in poor health, which was often the case. Sir George Warrender, who commanded the Second Battle Squadron, had not

***** The italics are Jellicoe's.

distinguished himself in independent command on 16 December 1914.* Of him Jellicoe wrote to Jackson in June that he became 'awfully deaf at times' and was inclined to be absent-minded, but had had unique experience in command and was excellent as a squadron admiral in peace – the last a rather curious and left-handed tribute under the circumstances. Not surprisingly, he added that he was not always quite happy about him; and in December he was replaced by Sir Thomas Jerram, another rather unenterprising man who for his part lacked recent fleet experience at sea. In the letter to Jackson just quoted, which reveals something of Jellicoe's lack of ruthlessness in making changes, especially where old friends were concerned, he had confessed that his vice-admirals as a whole were 'always a little shaky' and had gone on to add: 'Any replacements should I think be . . . young men. The strain is too much for older people unless wonderfully fit physically.' 'Beatty is splendid', he concluded.[8]

Although this last comment presumably referred at least partly to the younger man's physical vigour, their correspondence at this time shows much mutual confidence and even similarity of outlook. 'I know that on all the large questions we are of the same opinion', wrote Beatty in August, with only a little exaggeration. On his side at least an element of affection and even perhaps a tinge of admiration seem to have entered into the earlier phases of their relationship, and it may have been a pity that Jellicoe's outwardly more restrained nature did not allow him to respond with equal warmth.† In addition to discussing the possibilities and problems of getting the Grand Fleet and the battle-cruisers together for exercises or of managing gunnery practice for the latter, they exchanged views on submarines, mines, Zeppelins, the tactics to be employed in a fleet action and the shortcomings of the Admiralty. 'I should dearly like to see you again', Beatty commented after one of their rare meetings, 'there is so much to talk about and it is so much easier than writing.' On the gravity of the threat from submarines and mines they were in agreement, except that Beatty did not fully share his commander-in-chief's cautious view of their effect on battle tactics. 'I have been most fully alive ever since the war began', Jellicoe wrote, 'to the extremely important part which mines and submarines are likely

* See p. 78 above.
† I owe this suggestion to the present Earl Jellicoe.

to play in the fleet action, if fought where the Germans want it.'
Beatty's opinion was that 'it would be extremely difficult for them
to lay mines unobserved once the fleets get into touch'; and he
queried in the margin Jellicoe's statements in the same letter that
'both in the case of submarines and of mines the only real cure is
not to fight on the enemy's prepared ground' and that in the early
stages of a battle he would be obliged, in order to avoid losing a
large number of ships, to seek to manoeuvre them off their ground.
Jellicoe on the other hand had already written a friendly word of
warning to Beatty in March about the risks of over-boldness:

> I should imagine that the Germans will sooner or later try to
> entrap you by using their battle-cruisers as a decoy . . . to bring
> you into the High Seas Fleet . . . They know that if they can
> get you in chase the odds are that you will be 100 miles away
> from me, and they can under such conditions draw you well
> down to the Heligoland Bight without my being in effective
> support. It is quite all right if you keep your speed, of course,
> but it is the reverse if you have some ships with their speed
> badly reduced in the fight with the battle-cruisers, or by sub-
> marines. . . . The Germans also probably know you and your
> qualities very well by report, and will try to take advantage of
> that quality of 'not letting go when you have once got hold'
> which you possess, thank God. I am therefore writing these few
> lines (not as a warning, as you have probably the matter fully
> in mind) but as a reminder of the possible difficulties of the
> situation.
>
> The Admiralty's and country's attitude would certainly be
> one of great praise . . . in case of success and one of exactly the
> opposite should you have ill luck over such a venture. One
> need not worry about the attitude of others, possibly, but one
> must concern oneself very seriously with the result to the country
> of a piece of real bad luck culminating in a serious decrease in
> *relative* strength. Of course the whole thing is a question of the
> game being worth the candle, and only the man on the spot can
> decide. If the game looks worth the candle the risks can well
> be taken. If not, then . . . I think one's duty is to be cautious. . . .
> One could discuss it all so much better if we could meet.[9]

In the light of Jutland and what followed, some passages of this
last paragraph are heavy with significance.

Jellicoe's anxieties about mines were by no means limited to the risk of his ships being drawn over them by a German manoeuvre during an action, or striking them while cruising. He was always aware of the danger that the enemy, before making an offensive move, might mine the exits from the Grand Fleet's bases or sow minefields across its probable path southwards to cope with such a move. 'I have constantly told the Admiralty', he wrote to Beatty on 4 June, 'that my view is that sooner or later we shall be lured out over a trap of mines or submarines.' He therefore sought to ensure the adequate patrolling of the waters to the south-east of the Pentland Firth, and when the Admiralty declined to countenance any longer the use of cruisers for these patrols he resorted to armed boarding steamers supplemented at night by destroyers. This system received something of a shock, however, when on 8 August one of these steamers was sunk by a seeming merchant ship, the *Meteor*, which was actually a German armed auxiliary vessel in disguise and which then proceeded to lay a large minefield in the entrance to the Moray Firth.* Nevertheless the minefield proved in the end a contribution to the safety of the Firth, since after his first dismay Jellicoe left it down and merely had side-channels cleared. He also sought constantly to persuade the Admiralty to use similar tactics on a larger scale against the enemy, by laying mines in the Heligoland Bight close to the shore and so hampering their operations. In this he was partly successful, inasmuch as by the end of the year a more or less complete line of mines had been laid across the Bight, and was occasionally reinforced in 1916. Even so, it fell short of what he wanted and its success was marred by the inadequacy of the mines both in numbers and efficiency.[10]

The loss of the pre-dreadnought battleship *King Edward VII* by a mine at the beginning of 1916 revived or increased Jellicoe's worries about the shortage of minesweepers with the Grand Fleet. He therefore asked the Admiralty to send him fifteen minesweeping sloops to reinforce the nine which he already had, and got in response thirteen Admiralty trawlers whose sweeping speed was much less than that of sloops, together with an explanation that the latter could not be supplied because our French and Italian allies were crying out for them in the Mediterranean. Since

* The *Meteor* did not escape, however, but was scuttled by her crew on the approach of British cruisers next day.

he was very much the naval equivalent of the military 'Westerners' who were insisting on the concentration of all our available troops in France and Flanders,* this provoked from him some strongly-worded comments to both Balfour and Jackson on the danger of weakening the Grand Fleet and perhaps losing the command of home waters for the sake of pleasing our allies:

> The danger is very real [he added in his letter to Balfour] and the disaster may occur in a few minutes without warning. It only requires the fleet to be inadvertently taken over one minefield for a reversal to take place in the relative strength of the British and German fleets. The existence of the Empire is at once in the most immediate and grave danger.[11]

Another source of anxiety and of impatience with the Admiralty, which Beatty fully shared, was the advantage which the use of Zeppelins as scouts gave or might give to the High Seas Fleet. Jellicoe had been interested in aircraft since his days as Second Sea Lord, when for a time he had been officially responsible for the infant Royal Naval Air Service and had made passenger flights in its aeroplanes and in the Army's airships. He had also, while visiting Berlin in 1913, got leave from Admiral von Tirpitz to make a flight in a Zeppelin. At that time the radius of action of aeroplanes was so small that he felt they had little value for naval scouting work, but he had been much impressed by the possibilities of airships in that way. Not fully appreciating the navigational and wireless weaknesses of the Zeppelins, nor how far their activities would be curtailed by the rough weather of the North Sea, he feared that when the day of the great battle came at last they would be able to give his opponent every detail of the British dispositions and movements, while he himself would be left half-blind. Nor could he see any means of coping with the problem as it appeared to him. A converted passenger liner, the *Campania*, had been attached to the Grand Fleet as a seaplane-carrier, but the early attempts to fly off planes from her deck had not proved very successful and had led him to the conclusion that

---

* He wrote to Hamilton, for instance, in November 1915: 'I am one of those who believe in concentrating on the main theatre of operations . . . I am afraid many people are losing sight of the first principle, that the main theatre of war is the place where we should be strong'. Hamilton MSS: Jellicoe to Hamilton, 9 Nov 1915.

they would be ineffective against Zeppelins. Since the latter could fly at a height above the range of ships' guns, the only remedy he envisaged was for the Admiralty to build airships against them, and this it was very slow to do.*[12]

Not least of Jellicoe's cares, perhaps, was the need to keep the 60,000 officers and men of the Grand Fleet happy and occupied during that considerable part of their time which they would otherwise have had to spend in semi-idleness. For this purpose the provision of facilities for games became a matter of great importance. The first steps in this direction were taken under the superintendence of Sir Lewis Bayly, who commanded the First Battle Squadron at the outset of the war and in pre-war days had been in the habit when ashore of playing tennis at 6.30 a.m. on fine mornings, going for a run round some convenient park at 5.30 p.m. and walking at least twenty miles on Sundays. Besides employing the men in building landing-piers and erecting batteries for the defence of the anti-submarine obstructions, he had football grounds constructed for them, together with a golf course for the officers and a rifle and pistol range for the small-arm practice of the ships' companies. Commodore Halsey, the Captain of the Fleet, whose primary responsibility was the organisation of all coaling, victualling, taking in stores, routine overhauls and repairs, also gave assistance in the arrangement of sports and games; and the Commander-in-Chief, himself a keen games-player all his life, threw himself wholeheartedly into these projects and found time amid so much else to take a lively interest in the inter-ship competitions, regattas and athletics meetings which gave the men fixtures to which to look forward and food for animated discussion both before and after. An invaluable contribution to the harbour life of the Grand Fleet was presently made by the appearance of the canteen-ship *Gourkho*, which not only carried stores and provisions of all sorts, available for use by all ships, but was soon fitted out by the Fleet's artificers with a theatre, lecture-hall and boxing ring. Thenceforward these were in constant demand. Programmes were arranged and the stage, hall and ring were booked weeks in advance. Officers gave popular

---

* In the event, Zeppelins took no part in the Battle of Jutland, while one R.N.A.S. pilot, Flight-Lieutenant Rutland, flew a successful reconnaissance, though the information which he brought back had no practical result.

lectures, both in the *Gourkho* and in their own ships, on famous naval battles, great explorations, visits to the Western Front and many other subjects. Education was also developed; the Admiralty, at Jellicoe's request, provided large numbers of naval schoolmasters, and classes for the boys and well-attended voluntary classes for the men were held in the evenings. 'Occupation and interest' he wrote later, 'are the surest antidotes to discontent and unrest';[13] and never in the two and a half years during which he held the command-in-chief did he see any signs of either.

Before the end of the summer his health had begun to deteriorate again. It seems probable that in spite of his efforts to take such exercise as he could aboard his flagship or occasionally ashore the prolonged semi-confinement to the *Iron Duke* in a remote and unattractive base so lacking in shore facilities was beginning to tell on him and make him less and less able to withstand his manifold anxieties. A strained and sometimes almost querulous note now crept into his correspondence, or at least into the criticisms of the Admiralty which it more and more often contained. It was probably this which moved Beatty (to whom he does not seem to have made any open admission of ill-health) to write: 'Please don't overdo yourself. You are our only hope and must take care of yourself.'[14] In September he thought it advisable to send for a civilian doctor of some repute, who diagnosed pyorrhea. The Admiralty thereupon suggested that he should take a period of rest ashore, which he spent at Kinpurnie Castle in Forfarshire,* paying several visits to a leading Edinburgh dentist for treatment. After about a fortnight he returned to Scapa Flow, still under medical supervision for some time but at least temporarily refreshed and declaring himself 'a totally different being'.[15]

The increasing dissatisfaction with the Admiralty which runs through his correspondence during these months was far, however, from being either a mere product of ill-health or peculiar to himself. From the first there had been much that was open to criticism in the Admiralty's conduct of the naval war – a reluctance to delegate proper authority and discretion to commanding officers, slowness in supplying or failure to supply all the information available about the enemy's movements, failure to co-ordinate the operations of different commands and to facilitate contacts and

---

* This house belonged to his father-in-law, Sir Charles Cayzer.

conferences between their commanders, and particular errors and omissions – faults most or all of which stemmed from the lack of a properly organised Naval Staff. 'There is no doubt whatever', Jellicoe had written shortly before Fisher's resignation, 'that the Fleet is rapidly losing confidence in the administration.'[16] The advent of the Balfour–Jackson regime had somewhat revived that confidence for a time (though not very markedly in Jellicoe's case), but it soon waned again. 'I hope you will not think because I criticise . . .', wrote Beatty who fully shared his chief's views in this as in much else,

> that I am in any way disloyal. If the criticism is unfair or conten-
> tious then I agree it is most undesirable and objectionable. But
> when on the other hand it is fair it is not only loyal to the
> Country whose servants we are but . . . loyal to the Admiralty
> itself whom we are endeavouring to assist. It cannot be patriotic
> to sit down and say nothing when we see ourselves walking
> into a morass and clogging ourselves so effectually that we
> cannot retaliate when somebody else endeavours to strike us. As
> you say the leopard can't change his spots; the only remedy is to
> change the leopard. Well, that must be done if necessary.[17]

Jellicoe's main discontent was now due to the delays in naval construction, especially of submarines, light cruisers, destroyers and minesweepers, on which he enlarged in a letter to Fisher on 18 January 1916:

> There is not a single ship that was laid down during your tenure
> of office that has not been delayed in completion for *months*, as
> far as I can see. Destroyers that should have been delivered in
> October have not yet arrived. Submarines due between June
> and November have not turned up yet. I should put the average
> delay at 3 to 9 months for all classes of ships. I don't know
> whether real efforts are being made to get the ships completed.
> All I know is that for several months I have not been allowed
> to send ships to home ports to refit, on the plea that I am
> delaying new construction by doing so. . . . I confess to feeling
> weary of protests.[18]

Notwithstanding this, he wrote privately to Balfour on the following day:

I think it right to let you know that I am much disturbed at the increasing delays that are taking place

(*a*) in the completion of repairs to ships;

(*b*) in the completion of new ships building . . .

I presume the cause of many of our difficulties comes under the head of 'Labour Troubles'. I submit that there should be no 'Labour Troubles' in war. If there is shortage of labour may it not be due to the fact that the Munitions Department [Ministry] is taking away men who should be engaged on naval work?[19]

To Beatty a few days later he was more succinct:

The shipbuilding delays are awful. No one seems strong enough to prevent Lloyd George [who was then Minister of Munitions] taking away all our men. . . . I am continually pressing for light cruisers and shall go on doing so although the Admiralty won't give them and get cross at being pressed.[20]

The Admiralty were indeed beginning to get cross. At this time there was a possibility of Fisher's return to the Board, which was favoured by some of those who felt that more drive, ingenuity and foresight were needed there. He himself in the early months of 1916 had taken on the role of a critic of the delays in Admiralty shipbuilding and consequent shortage of ships. Since this harmonised with Jellicoe's main anxiety, the latter had renewed the correspondence with him that had practically lapsed since his resignation. In this, as well as in his letters to Beatty and somewhat more guardedly in his private correspondence with Hamilton and even in that with Jackson the sorely overstrained commander-in-chief ventilated his dissatisfaction. 'The delays are terrible', he groaned to Fisher on 29 January:

In August last it was anticipated that I should have received by *now* an addition of *17* new destroyers. I have actually got 2 and the rate of delay is a progressive one. The case is almost worse in light cruisers, and is equally bad as regards submarines. Of course battleships are also delayed . . . but my most pressing need is and *always has been* destroyers and *minesweepers*. The latter don't come at all. I don't want to go behind the back of the Board, or I would write to the Prime Minister. . . .[21]

This, however, was precisely what Beatty did five days later. Loyal and attached to his commander-in-chief, equally convinced of the dangers of the situation, less perhaps of a respecter of persons and possibly (but only possibly) relying somewhat on the background and connections which had helped him to dare and dare again during his career, he wrote to Asquith a characteristically forceful letter which deserves quotation in part:

> I have just left the Commander-in-Chief, whom I have not seen for five months, and left him so perturbed and despondent about the delays in new construction that I feel impelled to write to you privately on matters which I feel to be of the greatest importance.
>
> The Admiralty I understand are powerless to prevent the depletion of the shipbuilding yards of labour which goes away daily to supplementing the making of munitions, with the result that the programme of completing destroyers and light cruisers and battle-cruisers has been thrown back four to eight months. No doubt you are aware of this . . . but what you cannot be aware of is the very serious view of the situation taken by the Commander-in-Chief, which I feel is of national importance and so take the liberty of calling your attention to it . . .

After detailing the shortages of destroyers and light cruisers and the possibility which he at least visualised of an inferiority in battle-cruisers, he went on:

> No remedy can avert the risks we are now accumulating unless immediate action is taken to avert delays in construction. Also, I am not presenting to you new or controversial opinions, but merely supporting the views of all sea officers. . . . No doubt the heads of the Admiralty will have made similar representations to you, but I feel that I must bring to your notice from personal knowledge how gravely this responsibility is weighing on the Commander-in-Chief and how deeply he feels about it. . . .
>
> The final responsibility for fighting and winning battles must rest with the sea officers alone. They desire, as the whole nation desires, that when we fight the result should be decisive and overwhelming. This can be done if the shipyards give us punctually the new construction promised, and it is for this

reason that I have felt it my duty to write to you. My letter is of course quite unofficial but I know that, as the leader of the nation, you would wish to have matters which must be vital brought to your notice no matter from what source . . . more especially as I recognise that the subject is one on which my Commander-in-Chief feels so strongly. I shall send him a copy of what I have written to you . . . I offer no apology for the length of this screed.[22]

Meanwhile the Board of Admiralty had become aware of the almost *frondeur* correspondence between Jellicoe and Fisher, and partly for this reason and partly because of Beatty's intervention he was invited to a meeting of the War Committee* on 17 February in order to air his grievances. Although agreement was reached on the urgent need to accelerate the building of light craft, the interview, which Jellicoe afterwards described to Jackson as degenerating into 'a mere rambling conversation',[23] gave him little satisfaction, and he renewed his complaints in a memorandum to the Prime Minister. For this he was rather gently reproved by Jackson in a private letter of 2 March:

Your papers to the Prime Minister were discussed yesterday. Your views are now known to all responsible, and you know the situation as far as new construction, etc., is concerned, and how anxious we are to hasten it. Don't you think it is time the matter was dropped, as if continued it may set an example to others, and we or you may have juniors setting forth the inadequacies of their ships and complaining of their tools, instead of trying to make the most of what they have got, in the spirit of the true seaman of old.[24]

To this Jellicoe, not minded to be altogether put down, retorted with a good deal of historical truth:

As regards 'doing the best with what we have', I take it we shall do that, but the seaman of old was never satisfied with what he had any more than we are, witness Nelson and the cruiser question.† It is merely history repeating itself, but for

* The War Committee had replaced the Dardanelles Committee, itself the successor of the War Council, in November 1915.

† This was presumably a reference to Nelson's complaints about his lack of frigates during his search for Bonaparte's Egyptian expedition in 1798.

'cruisers' read 'cruisers and destroyers'. Also we are faced now with entirely new methods of warfare and to meet these methods . . . we also must adopt new tools and if I don't ask for them I should be to blame.[25]

The general tone of this letter was conciliatory, however, and for some time afterwards he moderated or suppressed his criticisms. Nevertheless if the tired and worried commander of the Grand Fleet had stepped somewhat out of line in his behaviour at this juncture, it remained true that there was widespread discontent with the Admiralty's administration of the Navy, and it was not until the Board had been stung and stirred up by the realisation of this that it began to come properly to grips with the constructional delays and their basic causes, the shortage of and competition for labour and also competition for scarce materials such as steel.

On one matter, however, Jellicoe and the Admiralty achieved agreement. In January 1916 an inter-Service conference had reported that there was again a possibility of invasion. Its findings were forwarded to him by the Admiralty for comment and suggestions for possible counter-measures. Since they arrived at the moment of his maximum irritation with the Board, his first reaction was to describe them to Beatty as 'a wonderful screed . . . the most childish paper you ever saw'. Both he and the Admiralty agreed, however, that any large-scale attempt at invasion was most unlikely; and the Board approved the draft orders for the Grand Fleet in the event of an attempt being actually made which he prepared and submitted. It also conceded his claim that in that case it must be left entirely to him this time to decide whether he would attack the High Seas Fleet (if it came out) or the transports.*[26]

Another problem which faced both Jellicoe and Beatty during the winter of 1915–16 was the difficulty of managing gunnery practice for the battle-cruisers and combined exercises for them with the Grand Fleet. On the one hand the need to be ready for a possible German raid on the east coast made it undesirable for them to go too far north for either purpose; while on the other Jellicoe, who did not 'think it wise to have the whole fleet in the North Sea exercising south of 61°' was averse from coming too

---

* Contrast Churchill's instructions in November 1914 (see p. 68 above).

far to meet them for manoeuvres. Their gunnery had already suffered in any case from the fact that their annual pre-war battle-practices, carried out at a range of only 9000–10,000 yards and a speed of 12 knots, had been completely unrealistic. Even in the practice of 1914, which was the one partial exception with 16,000 yards range and 22 knots speed, the target had been towed slowly; and the war had prevented further progress.[27] It is true that at Jutland afterwards their shooting on the whole was not so bad as has sometimes been made out, and there were a number of extenuating circumstances during the period when it was at its poorest; but the bad effect of shortage of practice revealed itself in November, when both the *Lion* and the *Tiger* showed up poorly in one of their rare shoots. Beatty, confessing in a letter to Jellicoe that this had been 'a terrible disappointment', added that he was consoling himself with the thought that there was more to be learnt from a bad shoot than a good one, and went on optimistically: 'I do not think you will be let down by the gunnery of the battle-cruisers when our day comes'. However a hoped-for opportunity of joint manoeuvring exercises, to which Beatty looked forward since he confessed that his ships were 'all sadly in need of sea experience of that nature', failed to materialise soon afterwards, though the Battle-Cruiser Force was able to carry out exercises and gunnery practices on its own in the northern part of the North Sea towards the end of the month.[28] Meanwhile the Grand Fleet itself was able to keep up its target practice despite occasional postponements and to maintain the high standard of shooting which Jellicoe demanded of it, especially after the Pentland Firth had been substituted for the Moray Firth as a practice area, being more convenient to Scapa and requiring the use of fewer screening and protecting destroyers. The Germans, for their part, always had the opportunity open to them of slipping out through the Kiel Canal into the Baltic for practice, especially after the significant change of command which occurred early in 1916.

5 Jutland

In the spring of 1916 both the British and German main fleets became rather more venturesome, each seeking to take the other at a disadvantage. On the British side, although confidence in Jellicoe was still widespread in the Navy, discontent with his apparently unenterprising strategy was growing in certain quarters outside the service and could even be found within it. In the latter case it was partly an emotional reaction to the strain of uncertainty and boredom; but there was also more reasoned criticism based on study of the naval history of the sailing-ship era and on an interpretation of it which stressed the offensive spirit and saw his sober policy as a departure from the British way of making war at sea. In February Colonel Hankey, the secretary of the War Committee of the Cabinet, wrote to Captain Herbert Richmond of H.M.S. *Commonwealth* in the Third Battle Squadron (with a reference to Jellicoe's appearance before that Committee a few days earlier):[*] 'I have been hammering hard at the demoralising want of offensive, and even succeeded in bringing a distinguished person to London from a great distance. It is no good. The Navy has completely lost the spirit of the offensive.'[1] Richmond for his part was an uninhibited critic of the commander-in-chief in private, and one of the most notable members of the small minority of officers who justified their disquiet at the seeming passivity of the Grand Fleet by the lessons which they claimed were to be learnt from the writings on naval history of A. T. Mahan, Sir John Laughton, Admiral Philip Colomb, Julian Corbett and others. It is, however, at least arguable[†] that in this they were failing to realise that the

[*] See above, p. 96.

[†] And has been argued by Mr A. N. Ryan in an as yet unpublished paper, for private access to which the writer is greatly indebted to him, and from which the quotations in the concluding sentence of the above paragraph are drawn. It is not, of course, suggested that Jellicoe, who was no great student of naval history, was aware of the precedents on his side.

traditions of the great age of 'wooden walls' to which they appealed spoke with two voices and that there had been two schools of thought among its most distinguished figures on the question of how far risks should be taken and losses incurred in seeking out the enemy. As regards the strategy of remote blockade, indeed, 'there seems little doubt that some of the dissatisfaction with Jellicoe's policy (or rather the policy of the Admiralty) owed something to a misconception of the past [and that] . . . there was as much strategic precedent on his side as upon that of his bellicose critics.'

Even in the Admiralty there was what Jellicoe described in a letter to Beatty as 'a feeling to persuade me into a more active policy', which both men regarded with equal misgivings and Beatty indeed described as 'truly deplorable'.[2] Nevertheless the mounting pressure for more offensive moves led to two attempts to lure the High Seas Fleet out by seaplane raids on the Zeppelin base at Tondern in Schleswig, with covering forces supported by the battle-cruisers and more remotely by the Grand Fleet. No success was achieved, however, and after the first of these on 24–25 March Jellicoe wrote to Jackson: 'I have given much con-sideration to your suggestion that air raids or mining activities might be made the means of drawing out the High Seas Fleet for action. The matter is not so simple as it appears at first sight, and it is difficult to discuss it except at some length. . . .'[3] This he proceeded to do in a memorandum which contained the following passages:

> It is not, in my opinion, wise to risk unduly the heavy ships of the Grand Fleet in an attempt to hasten the end of the High Seas Fleet, particularly if the risks come not from the High Seas Fleet itself, but from . . . mines and submarines. There is no doubt that, provided there is a chance of destroying some of the enemy's heavy ships, it is right and proper to run risks with our own . . . but unless the chances are reasonably great, I do not think that such risks should be run, seeing that any real disaster to our heavy ships lays the country open to invasion. . . . Having started on these assumptions, I propose now to examine the chances of getting the High Seas Fleet into a position in which it can be attacked by means of an air raid or other threat on the German coast.

It is obvious that any such attack must take place at daylight [i.e., daybreak], because otherwise the approach of the raiding force . . . is certain to be reported by the enemy's air scouts and the attack therefore unquestionably would fail. Let us assume that it does take place at daylight, say 5 a.m. It is probable that the news would reach the High Seas Fleet at 6 a.m. and . . . the heavy ships might begin to move at about 10 a.m. . . . It is therefore very improbable that any action could possibly commence before 5 p.m. or later, and as the enemy [i.e., his advanced forces] would probably fall back on the battle fleet it is most probable that they would not be within range until much later than 5 p.m. My opinion is that this would be a most unsuitable time to commence an action. . . . It would be much too late for any decision to be arrived at, and probably . . . the enemy would have some wounded ships and so should we. The enemy would send an immense force of destroyers to screen their wounded ships during the dark hours, and to attack ours. Our destroyer force would be numerically very inferior, and the result in all probability would be the total loss of our wounded ships and the return to harbour of those belonging to the enemy, with a corresponding loss of prestige.

After thus forecasting several of the difficulties which he subsequently experienced at Jutland, though with some pessimism about the number of the German destroyers, he continued:

There is another consideration . . . of great importance. The main difficulty with which we are always faced is the depletion of fuel on the part of our destroyers during the movement south, the result being that we cannot afford to wait once we have got south, but must join action almost at once, otherwise the destroyers will not have sufficient fuel to fight the action and return to a refuelling base. . . .

Therefore any movement south which involves waiting about for any considerable time on the chance of getting the High Seas Fleet out raises great difficulties . . . The conclusion at which I arrive . . . is that air raids and mining activities cannot be used as a means of drawing the High Seas Fleet to sea but must be treated as a definite minor operation.[4]

Beatty expressed the same conclusion less grammatically but with characteristic force and succinctness in a letter to his chief:

. . . You ask me what I think. Well, I think the German Fleet will come out *only* on its own initiative when the right time arrives. Air raids on our part will not bring him out. It may, and probably will, bring out a portion which could be snapped at by the supporting force we choose to utilise to support the air raiding force. . . . It is on such occasions we might be able to inflict some damage, risking something to do it. But I am firmly convinced that under no circumstances could we ever by taking the initiative induce them to commit themselves to an action which in any way could be considered decisive.

I am not arguing against air raids. Anything we can do to harass and annoy has great advantages. . . . But it is certain that he will *not* come out in grand force when we set the time, i.e. to fight the great battle we are all waiting for. Your arguments *re* the fuel question are unanswerable and measure the situation absolutely. We cannot amble about the North Sea for two or three days and at the end be in a condition in which we can produce the whole force to fight to the finish the most decisive battle of the war: to think it possible is simply too foolish and tends towards losing the battle before we begin. As I said, my contention is that when the great day comes it will be when the enemy takes the initiative.[5]

That, indeed, was more or less what eventually happened. On the German side the new year had also brought a quickening of the tempo. Von Pohl, who was dying of cancer, had been replaced on 24 January by the more enterprising Vice-Admiral Reinhard Scheer, a torpedo specialist and a strong advocate of unrestricted submarine warfare. Failing to secure the resumption of this, he resorted instead to a series of cautious sorties in which he sought to trap and destroy a part of the British fleet and so achieve the long-desired parity of forces – on 5–6 March by a venture off the Texel, on 21 April by a sally in the mistaken belief that there was about to be another raid on Tondern, and on 24 April by a tip-and-run bombardment of Lowestoft by his battle-cruisers with the High Seas Fleet in support. Each time the Grand Fleet put to sea but could not make contact; indeed when Jellicoe struggled south on the last occasion against heavy seas that compelled him to leave his destroyers behind he could not come within 200 miles of his objective. It was partly by way of retaliation for the Lowestoft raid that the second air attack on Tondern with the Fleet in support was made on 3–4 May; but the High Seas Fleet did not learn of it and emerge until Jellicoe had been obliged to return to Scapa.

Scheer's appointment and activity had meanwhile led the Admiralty to reopen the question of concentrating the Fleet in the Forth, and in discussions with Jellicoe and Beatty the obvious strategical advantages of this were weighed against the physical limitations of Rosyth as a base for so many ships. Finally a rather indefinite decision was arrived at, to move the battle fleet there when sufficient outer defences had been built, but these were not finished until 1917.[6] Also under the stimulus of the Lowestoft raid the Third Battle Squadron of pre-dreadnought battleships and the Third Cruiser Squadron were transferred again from Rosyth to Sheerness and the Swin* to guard against any southerly move by Scheer.[7] In their place it was proposed that the new Fifth Battle Squadron should be brought down from Scapa to join Beatty's battle-cruisers, but to this Jellicoe offered an obstinate resistance for some time. 'My view is', he wrote to Jackson on 5 March, 'that the stronger I make Beatty the greater is the temptation for him to get involved in an independent action'.[8] Eventually he agreed to the squadron replacing temporarily the Third Battle Cruiser Squadron, which was due at Scapa for exercises with the main fleet. 'So', as Sir Julian Corbett wrote later, 'it came about that when the long-expected day was at hand, the distribution was not that on which his considered battle orders were based.... The free fast squadron was no longer under his hand.'[9]

These battle orders had been completely revised in December 1915 and reissued in the following month, some further changes being made between then and Jutland.† Covering seventy printed pages, they were now even more elaborate than before.[10] Three dominant conceptions stood out – 'a subordination of the offensive spirit to defensive precautions, especially against the torpedo; the single line, parallel course and long range of the plan of battle; and centralised command.'[11] In considering the first, it has to be borne

---

* Between Harwich and the mouth of the Thames.

† I must here acknowledge my indebtedness to Professor Arthur J. Marder's masterly analysis of these battle orders in the opening chapter of his *From the Dreadnought to Scapa Flow*, vol. iii, 'Jutland and After'.

in mind that Jellicoe's wariness about torpedoes, mines and submarines was still common to practically the whole Navy. As regards the submarine, though the war was to reveal that its inherent limitations prevented it from being used effectively with a battle fleet, this was not yet evident in 1916. Moreover since Jellicoe's own submarine tactics were essentially offensive he inclined naturally to expect the enemy's to be the same, and was unaware that they had never practised using them in co-operation with the High Seas Fleet in action. He still considered the situation which he had envisaged in his letter of 30 October 1914 to Churchill – the German fleet retreating and attempting to lead their opponents over a trap of submarines and mines – as a possibility which must always be guarded against. Such a manoeuvre he expected would be covered by a smoke-screen and a torpedo attack by the German destroyers which would be met by turning two or more points away from the enemy. Both this and the alternative turn towards a torpedo attack (relying on 'combing' the torpedoes by individual ships steering so that they passed between them) had been practised in pre-war tactical exercises; but although the latter manoeuvre prevented loss of touch with the enemy, the turn away was considered the safer method.

The single line-ahead battle formation, which in the eighteenth century had led to so many indecisive actions, had again become the orthodoxy of the twentieth. It had not, however, gone entirely unchallenged. In 1910–11, when Sir William May commanded the Home Fleet with Richmond as his flag-captain, the possibilities of 'divided' tactics, in which the fleet was manoeuvred in several separate squadrons with the object of concentrating on a part of the enemy's line and overwhelming it as in the days of Rodney and Nelson, had been explored in a series of exercises. When May's tenure of command ended, however, the experiments had ended with him, though Sturdee continued to advocate divided tactics, as did Richmond and others of the group of iconoclastic junior officers mentioned above. The case against such tactics was that they involved the risk that a squadron operating independently might itself be overwhelmed by a concentrated enemy; that the high speeds and greatly increased battle ranges of modern ships would make it practically impossible for a commander-in-chief to keep control of squadrons operating separately; and that these same increased ranges had made it possible to achieve the desired concentration of fire on a part of the enemy while maintaining the single line-ahead. This was especially the case if the manoeuvre of 'crossing the T', or placing a fleet in single line athwart the enemy's line of advance, could be executed. Since the line-ahead formation implied reliance on the big gun for victory and tactics were then largely dominated by gunnery officers like Jellicoe himself, it is hardly surprising that it won general approval.[12]

The third dominant idea of the battle orders, centralised control, was closely linked with that of the single line-ahead, which it was claimed was the only safe way of ensuring it. By the beginning of the twentieth century it was being carried to extremes, and the subsequent introduction of wireless telegraphy strengthened it further, at what was to prove a fatal cost in stifling the initiative of subordinates. Jellicoe himself, though the general tone of his orders stressed centralisation, still laid down that his divisional commanders had discretionary powers in certain circumstances. But the very fact that he described these circumstances carefully was significant, and may have caused them to be regarded as the only cases in which individual action would be justified. Moreover most of his subordinates had been too much schooled in the prevailing tradition of 'orders are orders' to be able to take advantage even of such decentralisation as was offered them. On the other hand the German Navy allowed and practised a greater degree of independent action, and Scheer's admirals and captains (contrary to the current and complacent British conception of their nation) had more enterprise and initiative than most of their counterparts in the Grand Fleet.

Although the battle orders exhorted destroyers and other light forces to attack at any favourable opportunity, the balance of emphasis was laid on their defensive duties; and indeed it is not too much to say that the orders relegated to an essentially defensive role everything that was not armed with the big guns to which Jellicoe and most other British admirals were pinning their faith. A good deal of initiative was thus still handed over to the enemy. It must be strongly emphasised, however, that not only was Jellicoe still under the impression that the enemy would be much stronger in destroyers than the Grand Fleet but his own destroyer flotillas had just undergone a process of reorganisation. After some eight months of discussion between himself and the Admiralty, accompanied by much chopping and changing, they had been re-grouped as five flotillas (apart from those of the Battle-Cruiser Force) with the light cruiser *Castor* as their flagship and Commodore J. R. P. Hawksley as Commodore (F). Hawksley, however, had so far had no proper opportunity of training his destroyers in combined manoeuvres or exercising them in the tasks that would devolve on them.[13]

Jellicoe's plan of battle was based on the assumption that the Germans either wanted to stand and fight or could be compelled to do so. This meant that if they did not, and could not be compelled, time and sea-room would be needed to achieve victory by means of what were then the orthodox methods, and neither of these was available at Jutland on 31 May. Even if he had been able to see clearly what had happened when the High Seas Fleet twice turned away from him on that evening, he had only two alternatives, one of which was virtually ruled out by the general acceptance of the view that immediate pursuit of a retreating enemy (in fact, the old 'stern chase') was precluded by the danger from torpedoes. The other alternative was to put himself between the enemy and his base, and that is what he did.

To give Professor Marder the last word which so rightly and richly belongs to him:

> Jellicoe had in the Grand Fleet Orders put his eggs into one basket. He would seek a decision through a formal, long-range, heavy-gun duel on parallel lines in broad daylight. As [he] would have been the first to admit, the plan of battle and the subsidiary tactics were conservative and cautious. They lacked flexibility as well as daring. . . . Yet, given the stakes, and the dangers of new and sinister underwater weapons, who can say without drawing on knowledge not available to Jellicoe that the Battle Orders were excessively cautious? And if [they] had their defects, this was to be expected. They represented, after all, the tactical ideas of the time and were based largely on academic peace-time exercises and manoeuvres. . . . It needed the gruell-ing test of battle experience (to say nothing of proper and scientific study of tactical doctrine) to suggest needed modi-fications.[14]

In the latter part of May both commanders-in-chief prepared to move again. Jellicoe planned for 2 June a sweep by light cruisers down the Kattegat, with a battle squadron in close support and the battle fleet and battle-cruisers in the background ready to pounce if the High Seas Fleet rose to the bait. But Scheer anticipated him, even though his plans had to be first postponed and then altered. Having stationed submarines off the Grand Fleet's bases in the hope of taking toll of the British ships as they emerged, he originally meant to entice them out by sending Hipper's battle-cruisers to bombard Sunderland on 17 May while he himself remained unseen in rear and his Zeppelins acted as scouts. From them he hoped to learn how much of the British fleet had come out, and so be able to decide whether to attack or withdraw. At the last moment, when his submarines were already in position, he was informed that the battle-cruiser *Seydlitz*, which had recently struck a mine, could not be repaired in time, and resolved to postpone his operation till the 29th. Since the last day on which his U-boats could remain out on patrol was 1 June, any further postponement would be virtually impossible, and he therefore made an alternative plan – that Hipper should venture up the Skaggerak to attract the attention of the British while he followed fifty miles astern with the main fleet – to be put into operation if the weather should be unfavourable for Zeppelin reconnaissance. This proved in fact to be the case, and after waiting until the last possible moment Scheer decided to implement this second plan on 31 May. He also let himself be persuaded, at the cost of reducing the speed of his fleet, to take with him the six pre-dreadnoughts of his own old battle squadron, the Second, though he had originally intended to put to sea with his sixteen dreadnoughts only.

Meanwhile the presence of an unusual number of German submarines in the northern part of the North Sea had been detected by decoding their wireless signals to their headquarters at Wilhelmshaven, and had been subsequently reported to Jellicoe. From neutral sources it had also been learnt that something was brewing in the German naval bases, and finally on the morning of the 30th a coded signal from Scheer instructing his submarines to remain at their stations was intercepted and enabled the Admiralty to warn Jellicoe at midday that there were indications that the High Seas Fleet might put to sea early on the morrow. At 5.20 p.m. he received orders to raise steam and at 7.30 he was instructed to leave harbour as soon as possible. As a result he was actually at

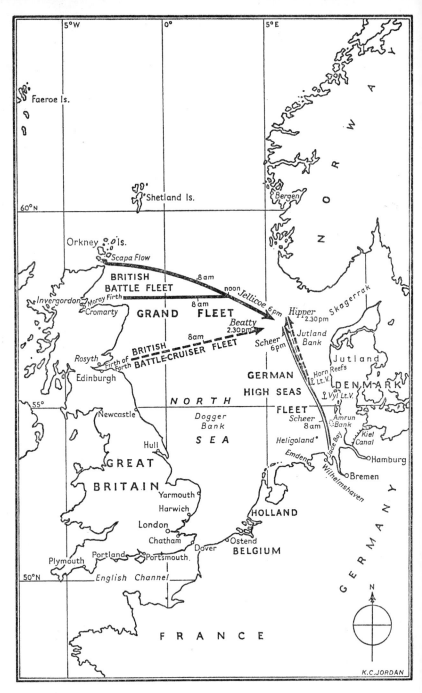

1. Map of the North Sea, 1914–18, showing the course followed by the British Grand Fleet and the German High Seas Fleet to the Battle of Jutland, 31 May 1916.

sea three and a half hours before the enemy had weighed anchor. The total force at his disposal consisted of 28 dreadnoughts (four of which were with Beatty), 9 battle-cruisers against 5, 34 armoured and light cruisers against 11, and 78 destroyers against 61. Scheer's carefully prepared submarine trap proved completely innocuous; only two U-boats sighted any British ships and only one managed to fire torpedoes, which missed their mark; while the very limited information which they were able to report was of virtually no value. About 11 o'clock on the following morning the section of the Grand Fleet which had been lying detached off Invergordon in Cromarty Firth (the Second Battle Squadron and First Cruiser Squadron under Vice-Admiral Jerram's command) made its junction with the main body, and the whole force steamed on for the rendezvous which Jellicoe had given to Beatty.

At this point what can only be called an egregious blunder was made in the Admiralty by Captain Thomas Jackson* the Director of Naval Operations. The cryptographic department which deciphered the German coded signals and was housed in Room 40 OB of the Admiralty Old Building was staffed largely by imported civilian experts who were regarded by the Operations Division and especially by Jackson as brainy interlopers whose presence was a regrettable necessity but who must be kept strictly to the most limited interpretation of their functions and could not be expected to understand anything naval outside these. Striding into Room 40 on the morning of 31 May, Jackson asked where the directional wireless placed the German call sign DK, used by Scheer's flagship *Friedrich der Grosse*. On being told, in Wilhelmshaven, he went out again and had a signal passed to Jellicoe, which he received at 12.48 p.m., that according to directional wireless the German flagship was still in the Jade River at 11.10 a.m. Had he condescended to enquire, any occupant of Room 40 could have told him that Scheer used this call-sign only when in port and that when the flagship went to sea he transferred it to a shore signal station and used another. The immediate effect on Jellicoe and Beatty (who had also received the signal) was to give them the impression that there was no likelihood of contact with the enemy for many hours to come. Jellicoe therefore reduced

* Jackson, who was promoted Rear-Admiral a week later, is often referred to by that rank in descriptions of this episode.

speed a little, partly to economise his destroyers' fuel and partly to be able to 'vet' the neutral ships he encountered and ensure that they were not enemy ships in disguise or wirelessing information to the enemy. Had he not slowed down for these reasons, he would have arrived in the battle area earlier than he did and thus have had more daylight left for fighting. The more long-term effect was to make both admirals suspicious and even sceptical of any information subsequently passed to them by the Admiralty, at least when it conflicted with what they could obtain from other sources. As Beatty put it afterwards: 'What am I to think of O.D. [Operations Division] when I get that telegram and in three hours' time meet the whole German fleet well out to sea?'[15]

This unawareness that the High Seas Fleet was much nearer than the Admiralty's signal implied also meant that Jellicoe had no reason to alter his instructions to Beatty about their rendezvous (though it is unlikely that he would have done so in any case). He had informed the Vice-Admiral that by 2 p.m. on 31 May he himself expected to reach Lat. 57°45'N., Long. 4°15'E., and had directed him to be 69 miles S.S.E. of this position at that hour. If Beatty had no news of the enemy by then, he was to turn north towards the main fleet. This separation of sixty-nine miles has been criticised as too great, and did in fact make it impossible for them to keep visual touch through their respective light forces, which contributed to the discrepancies in estimating positions that handicapped Jellicoe before the rival battle fleets made contact. On the other hand not only was this the average distance which had been maintained between the Grand Fleet and the battle-cruisers on previous excursions into the North Sea, when the Admiralty had fixed the rendezvous, but on this occasion, with Scheer's intentions unknown, the main body had to be far enough north to cover the Northern Patrol between the Orkneys and Norway against any German attempt to fall on it and raise the blockade, while the battle-cruisers had to be far enough south to guard against any raid on the east coast.

This uncertainty about the enemy's plans is not only Jellicoe's defence against this particular criticism, but goes far to explain what might otherwise be considered another of the Admiralty's contributions to the indecisiveness of Jutland – namely the handling of the Harwich force. Both in August and November 1914

Jellicoe had been assured that he could depend on it being despatched to join him in the event of a fleet action. On the evening
of 30 May, however, he was informed that it would not be sent
out until more was known about the German objectives; and
when its commander, Commodore Tyrwhitt (who was a marked
exception to the frequent lack of initiative in divisional leaders),
put to sea on his own responsibility after intercepting the signal
of the following afternoon reporting the High Seas Fleet in sight,
he was peremptorily ordered back by the Admiralty.[16] He would
of course have been too late to achieve anything by then; but had he
been unleashed twelve hours earlier and sailed by 5 a.m. he
would have reached the Commander-in-Chief by dark, and if his
flotillas had taken part in the subsequent night operations it is at
least conceivable that Scheer's movements and intentions might
not have gone uncomprehended and unreported. The Admiralty's
reason for holding him back, however, was to guard against the
possibility that under cover of Scheer's sortie a detached squadron
might come through the southern part of the North Sea and
combine with the strong German destroyer forces in the Belgian
ports to overwhelm the Dover Patrol and then raid shipping in
the Downs or the eastern part of the Channel.

At 2 p.m. on the 31st Beatty was still ten miles from the position
assigned him for that hour, and owing to an error in reckoning he
believed himself to be sixteen miles from it. He therefore continued on his course until 2.15 before turning towards the approaching Grand Fleet. Immediately afterwards the extreme
flanking units of both his and Hipper's light forces made contact
and engaged each other. Beatty promptly turned again towards
them, though it was not until 3.25 p.m. that Hipper's main force
was actually sighted by the *New Zealand*. Still believing, thanks
to the Admiralty signal, that the German battle fleet was in the
Jade or could not long have left it, Beatty then altered course once
more with the object of cutting Hipper off from the Horns Reef
and the Heligoland Bight. The German admiral, for his part, had
sighted his enemy at 3.20 (the visibility being in his favour) and
had turned about in order to fall back on Scheer, assuming correctly that he was faced by a superior force: correctly, that is, if
the Fifth Battle Squadron had been able to take a full and immediate part in the action which began at 3.47 when the battle-
cruisers of both sides opened fire practically simultaneously.

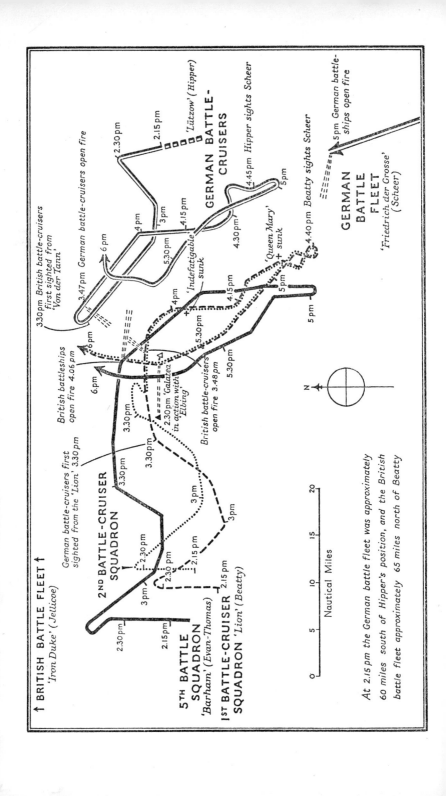

↑ BRITISH BATTLE FLEET ↑
'Iron Duke' (Jellicoe)

German battle-cruisers first
sighted from the 'Lion' 3.30 pm

2ND BATTLE-CRUISER SQUADRON

5TH BATTLE SQUADRON
'Barham' (Evan-Thomas)

1ST BATTLE-CRUISER SQUADRON 'Lion' (Beatty)

British battleships open fire 4.06 pm

2.30 pm 'Galatea'
in action with
'Elbing'

British battle-cruisers
open fire 3.48 pm

3.30 pm
3.30 pm
3.30 pm
3 pm
3 pm
3 pm
2.30 pm
2.30 pm
2.30 pm
2.15 pm
2.15 pm
2.15 pm
2.30 pm
3 pm

6 pm
6 pm

'Indefatigable'
sunk

'Queen Mary'
+ sunk

4 pm
4.15 pm
5.30 pm
5.30 pm
5 pm
5 pm
5 pm

330 pm British battle-cruisers
first sighted from
'Von der Tann'

3.47 pm German battle-cruisers open fire

2.30 pm
2.15 pm
'Lützow' (Hipper)

GERMAN BATTLE-
CRUISERS

4 pm
3 pm
4.15 pm
5.30 pm
6 pm
4.30 pm
4.45 pm Hipper sights Scheer
5 pm
5 pm

4.40 pm Beatty sights Scheer

5 pm German battle-
ships open fire

GERMAN
BATTLE
FLEET
'Friedrich der Grosse'
(Scheer)

N

0   5   10   15   20

Nautical Miles

At 2.15 pm the German battle fleet was approximately
60 miles south of Hipper's position, and the British
battle fleet approximately 65 miles north of Beatty

Rear-Admiral Hugh Evan-Thomas's squadron, however, had been so stationed as to be originally five miles further away than the battle-cruisers were from the direction in which the enemy was sighted, and these five miles were increased to ten by the fact that for reasons which are still controversial* it did not follow Beatty's first turn in that direction until some minutes had elapsed. Thus although by prodigies of steaming and by cutting corners its four great battleships – *Barham, Warspite, Malaya* and *Valiant* – managed to regain several miles and come into action with their 15-inch guns about 4.06 p.m. at the extreme range of 19,000 yards, Beatty had meanwhile begun to make the unpalatable discovery that (in his famous words of a few minutes later) there was 'something wrong with our bloody ships', and the *Indefatigable* had been sunk. What was wrong was not merely the temporarily unfavourable conditions of inferior visibility and a wind that carried the smoke of his leading ships across the range of his line, nor even shortage of firing practice, so much as the lack of anti-flash precautions for the magazines and the comparatively poor quality of the British shells.†

Soon after the Fifth Battle Squadron (which was one of the best-shooting squadrons in the Grand Fleet) opened fire it began to register hits, though the great range prevented its fire from being as effective as it might otherwise have been. On the other hand at 4.26 a plunging salvo hit the *Queen Mary* and caused explosions which blew her in two. A few minutes afterwards the *Southampton*, the flagship of Commodore Goodenough's Second Light Cruiser Squadron, which had been scouting two or three miles ahead of the *Lion*, sighted the leading ships of the German battle fleet coming up to the south-eastward. Beatty, and Hipper after him, immediately reversed course to the northward; though Goodenough disregarded the signal to turn and held on for some

* These controversies over whether and how far the failure to make full use of the power and excellent shooting of 5 BS was due to errors and omissions on Beatty's part, lack of initiative on Evan-Thomas's, bad signalling from the *Lion* (which certainly must bear some responsibility) or faulty reception in Evan-Thomas's flagship the *Barham*, have here been set aside as irrelevant to a biography of Jellicoe – except perhaps at one much later point.

† Professor Marder has shown cause to discount the 'legend' that the battle-cruisers had insufficient armour protection. *From the Dreadnought to Scapa Flow*, vol. iii: 'Jutland and After', pp. 172–4.

minutes until he had learnt fuller details of the composition, course and speed of Scheer's force, turning only when he had come under heavy fire. The Fifth Battle Squadron also did not turn for some minutes, and the responsibility for this second delay has been the subject of the same controversies as its first. What is clear, at least, is that when it was eventually ordered to turn two mistakes were made, whether by Beatty or quite possibly by his not very efficient flag-lieutenant, Ralph Seymour. It was ordered to turn in succession, which exposed each ship as it went about to a concentrated fire*, and to starboard, which placed it and its much-needed heavy guns on Beatty's disengaged quarter, increased again its distance from him, and obliged it to make a further turn to starboard to get on his engaged quarter. This last brought it closer within the German range, although this was something which cut both ways, since it took more weight off the battle-cruisers.[17]

Whatever may be said of the run to the south which had now ended, the run to the north which followed told a rather different story. The British battle-cruisers shot better, aided by the fact that visibility conditions were now in their favour. Evan-Thomas's squadron continued to deal out more than it got; and Hipper, who was now getting the worst of things in his turn, was forced round northward and then eastward, away from the approach of the Grand Fleet, of which he was thus kept in ignorance. When at this juncture (about 6 p.m.) a new enemy materialised from the north-east in the shape of Rear-Admiral Sir Horace Hood's Third Battle-Cruiser Squadron, which with four destroyers and two light cruisers in company was pressing on well in advance of Jellicoe, Hipper began to fear that he might be running into the British battle fleet, and turned further still in order to fall back again on Scheer. The German C-in-C, meanwhile, was still coming on in the continued belief that the situation was that which he had sought, namely that he had caught a detached and inferior British force at sea. Beatty in fact, despite unexpected losses due at least partly to the defects of British ships and shells, had by sticking grimly and gallantly to his opponent, and with Evan-Thomas's aid, performed his main task of bringing the whole

---

* Goodenough, it may be noted, turned his squadron together by signal.

German fleet to Jellicoe's guns without its becoming aware of its danger.

Unhappily he had not performed equally well his other task of keeping the Commander-in-Chief accurately informed of developments, and particularly of the enemy's position, formation and strength. Jellicoe in fact was bedevilled throughout the battle by widespread disregard of the emphasis which in his battle orders he had laid on the need for frequent and careful reporting. Instead, there was an almost general disposition to assume that someone else was bound to have reported; captains thought that their divisional commanders must have done so; divisional commanders, that their attendant light cruisers were doing what after all was one of their primary duties; and the light cruisers, with the shining exception of Goodenough's *Southampton*, all too often failed to discharge it. At the same time it must be pointed out that in this case both Beatty and Evan-Thomas (who sent no signals, except once in reply to an enquiry whether he was in action) had had the wireless gear of their flagships shot away, that Beatty had not had the High Seas Fleet in sight since just after five o'clock, and that the *Southampton was* reporting frequently. Even so, Jellicoe remained ignorant until virtually the last instant of the information he so urgently needed for a correct decision on deployment out of his cruising formation in parallel columns into a single line-ahead order of battle.

At 2.20 p.m., when Beatty's and Hipper's light forces had made contact, the Commander-in-Chief was still twelve miles short of the position he had intended to reach by 2 o'clock, having been delayed nearly an hour by the necessary investigation of neutral shipping which he met. Thanks to the Admiralty telegram implying that the High Seas Fleet was still in port, he had been under the impression that there was no special need for haste; but on receiving the first reports of this contact he ordered steam to be raised for full speed, although the reports did not suggest anything more than an encounter with German destroyers or light cruisers. When he later received further signals which indicated that some heavier German ships were at hand he increased speed to 18 knots (the maximum for which the fleet had steam by then) and ordered his screen of armoured cruisers to push forward till they were sixteen miles in advance of the battle fleet. They were unable, however, to manage more than six miles in advance, since they were astern of their proper station at the outset and had very little margin of speed over the battleships, especially when Jellicoe increased to 20 knots on hearing from *Lion* that the German battle-cruisers had been sighted. He also ordered Hood, who with his Third Battle-Cruiser Squadron of three *Invincibles* was twenty miles ahead of the main fleet and had in fact anticipated the order, to push on immediately to support Beatty. Hood, however, took a south-easterly course with the idea of cutting off any German ships trying to escape by the Kattegat, as a result of which he almost passed to the eastward of Hipper before turning to engage, and sent no reports. Indeed, no reports at all were received by the *Iron Duke* between 3.59 and 4.38, except Evan-Thomas's above-mentioned reply. At 4.38 came the *Southampton*'s electrifying signal: 'Have sighted enemy battle fleet, bearing approximately south-east, course of enemy north'; whereupon Jellicoe signalled to the fleet 'Enemy battle fleet is coming north' and to the Admiralty 'Fleet action is imminent'. Between 4.38 and 5 p.m. he received five reports of the German main fleet, three being from the *Southampton* and one from Beatty, relayed from the *Princess Royal* and badly garbled in transmission, which emerged as '26–30 battleships, probably hostile [!] bearing S.S.E. . . . ' This last led him to think that the Germans had every available capital ship at sea, including all (and not merely six) of their pre-dreadnoughts, and that consequently when battle was joined there would not be 'so great a discrepancy when the stakes are borne in mind'. Subsequently the combination of poor visibility with Scheer's tactics of withdrawal prevented him from ever seeing more than three or four German capital ships at one time and so gave him no opportunity of correcting this misapprehension, which may have increased his caution. Another difficulty that confused the situation further was that after long hours at sea with much zigzagging at first, many ships were a good deal out in reckoning their position, which reduced or destroyed the value of such signals as they did make. Even the *Southampton* was not exempt from error, though in her case and the *Lion*'s (as in others) it is possible that their compasses may have been affected by the heavy firing.

Between 5 and 5.40 p.m. there was a second silence in which again no reports reached the flagship. At the end of this time the two battle fleets were about thirty-two miles apart and converging

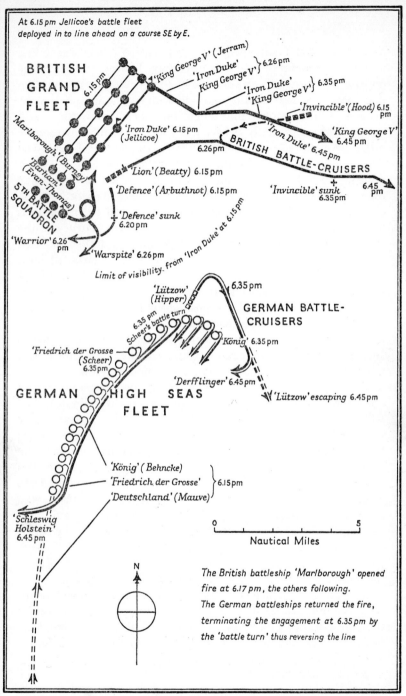

3. Map of Jutland from 6.15 to 6.45 p.m. The first clash between the battle fleets

on each other at a combined rate of 28 knots.* Scheer was in line ahead but ignorant of Jellicoe's proximity. Jellicoe was still in his cruising formation of six columns of four dreadnoughts each, in line ahead disposed abeam, and still without the information he needed for deployment into single line ahead for battle – still ignorant where precisely Scheer was and where and how soon he might be expected to appear. Between 5.40 and 6.03 he received three more signals from the *Southampton*, the last of which reported that she had lost touch with Scheer, and several vague reports from other ships of sighting gun-flashes and so forth, which caused him to remark: 'I wish somebody would tell me who is firing and what they are firing at!' But at 6 p.m. Burney in the *Marlborough*, leading the starboard column, and then at 6.01 Jellicoe himself, saw the *Lion* appearing on the starboard bow. This was disconcerting, however, because on the basis of the reports received and since there was a discrepancy of eleven miles between the estimated and true positions of the *Iron Duke* and *Lion* in relation to each other, he had placed her dead ahead and 12 miles away instead of $5\frac{1}{2}$. This meant that whereas he had expected to sight Scheer about 6.30, almost right ahead, he might now expect to sight him twenty minutes sooner, leaving only a few minutes to decide on the form and direction of his own deployment, an operation which in itself would take about twenty minutes. And still he did not know precisely *where* Scheer was and where he would appear, for when he signalled Beatty by searchlight at 6.01: 'Where is enemy's battle fleet?' the latter, who had not had it in sight since just after 5 o'clock, could only reply: 'Enemy battle-cruisers bearing S.E.' Then the mist lifted; Beatty glimpsed the head of Scheer's line and flashed by searchlight to the C-in-C., who received the message at 6.14: 'Have sighted enemy's battle fleet bearing S.S.W.' Simultaneously Evan-Thomas, whom the *Marlborough* had just reported sighting to the S.W., relayed through *Valiant*: 'Enemy battle fleet S.S.E.' Allowing 5 or 6 miles visibility, the position of the enemy's van could at last be plotted.

How then was Jellicoe to deploy? Deployment on the starboard wing column, nearest to Scheer, would have exposed the head of the line (Burney's division, composed of the oldest and least powerful dreadnoughts) to a concentrated German fire before it

* Not forty, as has sometimes been stated; they were not heading directly for each other.

could be supported by other divisions, and probably to a massed torpedo attack as well. Each successive division as it came round, blanketing the guns of those in rear, would have been pounded by the German broadsides; and the line would most likely have been forced away to port (eastward) to prevent its 'T' being crossed. Deployment on the port wing would increase the range and delay the crunch of the battle when already only two or three hours of daylight remained in which to force a decision. But it would and did have the three advantages of crossing Scheer's 'T' (and so achieving the one form of concentration which the gunnery duel in line ahead permitted), securing the better visibility, and placing the Grand Fleet squarely between Scheer and his bases, with the prospect of a whole morrow's battle if no decision was reached that evening. A third possibility, deployment on a centre column, was afterwards claimed by Churchill[18] and a few other critics of Jellicoe to have existed and to have been the best; but it demanded much more signalling, was much more complicated – too complicated at a time when the fleet was already engaged with the enemy – had not been practised in the Grand Fleet and would certainly have led to much confusion. Jellicoe scarcely hesitated a moment. Dreyer, his former protégé who was now his flag-captain, recorded later:

> I was watching the steering of the ship when I heard . . . the sharp distinctive step of the Commander-in-Chief. He looked in silence at the magnetic compass for about 20 seconds. I watched his keen, brown, weatherbeaten face, wondering what he would do. He was as cool and unmoved as ever. Then he looked up and broke the silence with the order to Commander A. R. W. Woods, the Fleet Signal Officer: 'Hoist equal speed pendant south-east.' Woods said: 'Would you make it a point to port sir, so that they will know it is on the port wing column?' Jellicoe replied: 'Very well. Hoist equal speed pendant south-east-by-east.'*[19]

* Woods was reminding Jellicoe that the code book did not contain a simple signal for deployment to south-east, and that his order would involve an unfamiliar way of signalling; whereas if the C-in-C. would deploy on a course one point to port of south-east a normal and un-ambiguous signal could be made. Cf. Lieutenant Pasco's improvement of Nelson's proposed signal before Trafalgar, 'England confides that every man will do his duty', by suggesting 'expects' instead of 'confides', since the former word was in the signal book, whereas 'confides' would have to be spelt.

Apart from the above-mentioned critics, all open to the charge of a hostile bias, the decision to deploy on the port wing has received general approval, including that of 'the ranks of Tuscany' – the German *Official History*[20] – and of the greatest British seaman of the Second World War, Admiral of the Fleet Lord Cunningham, who is quoted as saying: 'Had I been in command of the Grand Fleet at Jutland, I hope I would have been given the good sense to make the same deployment.'[21]

The deployment, however, was accompanied by several unfortunate incidents, some connected with it and some not. As Beatty came up he was obliged, in order to reach his allotted station in the van, to steam across the front of the British line as it formed, obstructing its gunfire with his smoke and causing it to reduce speed, with the result of delaying the already late deployment and producing some bunching at the rear. Evan-Thomas, whose station was also in the van, did not attempt to reach it but took up his alternative station in rear. During the turn to port which this movement required, his squadron came under heavy fire and the *Warspite*'s helm jammed, causing her to describe two complete circles before she came under control again. At 7 p.m., however, her helm once more went out of order and she was instructed to make the best of her way back to Rosyth. Meanwhile other casualties had been sustained. Rear-Admiral Arbuthnot with the First Cruiser Squadron, pressing on too boldly but apparently with the object of reconnaissance, had failed through the low visibility to realise until too late that he was rushing on to the guns of the German battle fleet, and his flagship the *Defence* had been blown to pieces with all hands, while a second ship of his squadron, the *Warrior*, was so badly damaged that she also had to be ordered home but sank before she reached port. Hood, after shooting up Hipper's light cruiser screen and leaving the *Wiesbaden* in a crippled condition to be eventually finished off by others, had taken station ahead of Beatty and was helping to engage the now badly battered German battle-cruisers when his flagship, the comparatively lightly-armoured *Invincible*, was hit by a full salvo abreast her Q turret and blew up in the same way as the *Indefatigable*, *Queen Mary* and *Defence* had already done.

On the German side Hipper's flagship the *Lützow* was so badly damaged that he ordered her back to harbour (which she also failed to reach) and shifted his flag with some difficulty to the *Moltke*, the only ship of his original five which could still be said to be fit for action. As for Scheer, the head of his line had come under heavy and accurate fire between 6.17 and 6.35 from the deploying Grand Fleet without being able to reply effectively, since owing to inferior visibility and its own drifting funnel– and gun-smoke it could see little but the flashes of the British guns. Indeed, it scored no hits on them at all. At 6.35 he ordered a *Gefechtskehrtwendung* ('battle-turn-away-together') or simultaneous 16-point turn, a manoeuvre which the High Seas Fleet had previously practised and which he covered by a destroyer attack and a smoke-screen. Five minutes later he had disappeared into the smoke and thickening mist, leaving Jellicoe, who had been unable to observe the turn-about, unaware of what had happened, since those of his ships which had seen it did not report it. At first he thought that Scheer's disappearance was due to some temporary and local thickening of the mist, but after a few minutes he began to suspect that the German admiral had made some sort of turn-away, though it was only long afterwards that he learnt precisely what had happened. He appreciated, however, that this was not the situation which he had envisaged in his memorandum of 30 October 1914 ('If, for instance, the enemy battle fleet were to turn away from an advancing fleet, I should assume that the intention was to lead us over mines and submarines, and should decline to be so drawn')[22]. That had been based on the assumption of the Germans seeking a fleet action in the first place, whereas Jellicoe knew that he had surprised them and that there was little chance of their having had time to prepare a minefield or submarine* trap. Nevertheless he thought it quite possible that their light cruisers in rear might have dropped mines, and even if they had not, a turn to follow (either by divisions or in succession) would have laid his fleet open to a torpedo attack. In clear weather and with plenty of daylight left something in the way of dividing the fleet might have been attempted, but in the prevailing conditions and so late in the day it would have been impossible to co-ordinate the movements of independent squadrons. All that remained, therefore, was to keep his position athwart the enemy's line of retreat. At 6.44 he accordingly altered course a point to S.E. by

---

* In fact, no German submarines were present at Jutland.

'Barham' (Evan-Thomas)
7.18 pm

BRITISH BATTLE FLEET

'Benbow' (Sturdee)
7.18 pm

'Orion' (Leveson)
7.18 pm

'King George V'
(Jerram)
7.18 pm

'Lion' (Beatty)
7.18 pm

7.26 pm

7.26 pm

BRITISH BATTLE-CRUISERS

7.26 pm

'Marlborough' (Burney)
7.18 pm

'Colossus' (Gaunt)
7.18 pm

7.26 pm

'Iron Duke' (Jellicoe)
7.18 pm

7.26 pm

7.26 pm

German torpedo boat attack

Smoke screen

GERMAN BATTLE-CRUISERS
7.18 pm

7.26 pm

'Derfflinger'

'Friedrich der Grosse'
(Scheer) 7.18 pm

'König' (Behncke)
7.26 pm

7.26 pm

'Deutschland' (Mauve)
7.18 pm

GERMAN BATTLE FLEET

7.26 pm

'Schleswig Holstein'

7.26 pm

N

Nautical Miles

0   5

The British battlefleet opened fire at 7.12 pm
to which the Germans replied.

The engagement was broken off when the Germans
executed the 'battle turn' away at 7.18 pm
and the British turned to avoid the torpedo attack
at 7.23 pm.

4.   Map of the second clash between the battle fleets

divisions, and at 6.55 he turned another four points to S., with his divisions now in echelon.

This move at first paid dividends. At 6.55 Scheer executed another 16-point turn and headed back eastward again in single line. Despite his own subsequent statement that his object was to deliver a surprise attack it is probable that he hoped to slip past astern (or northward) of the British fleet, which he supposed to be further to the south-east than it actually was, and to return to his bases before daylight. This time, however, his manoeuvre had been observed by Goodenough. Coming up on Evan-Thomas's quarter when the Fifth Battle Squadron made its junction with the Grand Fleet, the *Southampton* had reached her battle-station only after Scheer's first turn-away. Nevertheless the Commodore had seen what he thought was the enemy turning, though he could not be sure how many ships had turned and how much. Promptly he put his squadron about through the mists in order to investigate and, pressing in to observe the enemy's movements as closely as possible, was able at 7.04 to warn Jellicoe of what was happening. In any case Scheer had miscalculated if he hoped to pass astern of the British, and between 7.10 and 7.18 he found himself for the second time with his 'T' crossed and subjected to a tremendous and increasing cannonade to which adverse visibility left him little means of replying. From this he extricated himself by yet another simultaneous turn-away of his battleships, at the same time ordering his shattered battle-cruisers to cover it by a suicide charge (though he called it off three minutes later) and his destroyer flotillas also to attack and to raise another smoke-screen. This screen, combined with the mist and the failing light, again prevented Jellicoe from seeing what Scheer was doing, and though several of his rearward ships saw the turn-away they failed to report it. His immediate concern was the torpedo attack, which he met firstly by ordering the Fourth Light Cruiser Squadron to attack the German destroyers (in which it was joined by Commodore Hawksley on his own initiative with one flotilla), and then by turning the battle fleet away to port in two successive turns of two points each. As a result the torpedoes, which the counter-attack of the British light craft and also the fire of our nearest battleships had forced the German destroyers to fire at a range of about 7500 yards, were nearing the end of their run when they reached Jellicoe's capital ships and were therefore travelling so slowly that they were easily avoided. Avoiding action was aided, moreover, by the fact that German torpedoes showed a more visible track than did British – contrary to the information given to Jellicoe by the Director of Naval Intelligence shortly before, which had led him to expect that their approach would not be seen and may have contributed to his determination, expressed in his battle orders, to meet any such attack by turning away.

This turn-away has been called 'the most hotly debated incident of the entire Jutland action'.[23] Although hardly any German ships had yet been sunk, they had been outmanoeuvred, driven for the second time to seek safety in precipitate retreat, and were at the moment in some disorder. Jellicoe's critics have argued that if he had turned towards the torpedoes and 'combed' them, or even if he had merely turned away the tail of his line (the only part seriously threatened by a torpedo attack developing abreast of his centre) and kept his van and centre in touch with Scheer, a decisive victory might have been won that evening. Besides over-looking the fact that Jellicoe did not know that Scheer was in full retreat and was again under the impression that he had merely been hidden for the time being by mist, this minimises the danger of turning towards attacking flotillas, which lay in the possibility that they might attack in waves, with torpedoes coming from different directions. Moreover the turn-away was at that time the almost universally accepted answer to a concentrated attack, and was practised (though on a small scale) by both Beatty and Hipper on other occasions. As Lord Chatfield, who was Beatty's flag-captain at Jutland and no partisan of Jellicoe's, wrote later: 'Most experi-enced commanders would probably have acted as did Sir John Jellicoe. His was a weapon on which the world depended, and in the sudden and unexpected situation in which he found himself, of low visibility and a late hour, he was not prepared to take immeasurable risks with it.'[24] Later knowledge and especially the experience of the Second World War, may perhaps suggest that it would have been better to take those risks and turn towards the attack; but (to quote Professor Marder again) 'crystal balls were not standard issue in the Royal Navy'![25]

Since Scheer was most anxious not to be driven further from the bases to which he was trying to return, he altered course again to S.W. as soon as his returning flotillas had reported that they had seen no signs of pursuit astern, and subsequently turned south at 7.52 p.m. Meanwhile Jellicoe, equally anxious to regain contact with him but remaining unaware of his previous turn-about, had turned his own fleet back five points to starboard (one point more than he had previously turned away) at 7.35, as soon as the torpedo danger was over. That he believed Scheer to be only seven or eight miles to the westward,* just behind the thickened mist, is evident from a signal that he made at this time to the flotilla leader *Castor*, which was chasing enemy destroyers to the north-westward, not to go too near to the enemy battle fleet.[26] He also formed his own fleet, which had been in divisions before and after his turn-away, into single line ahead once more in readiness for battle. At or about 7.40 two things happened: he turned again three points more towards his invisible enemy, making his course S.W. (and therefore parallel to Scheer's, though this he could hardly know); and he received a signal from Beatty, relayed through *Princess Royal*, reporting the enemy (presumably Hipper's battle-cruisers, which were nearer to Beatty than Scheer's main fleet) in sight again, bearing N.W. by W. and ten or eleven miles distant. This signal gave no enemy course, though it did give Beatty's, who might be presumed to be steering in approximately the same direction. Actually his course, a couple of points more to the westward than the main fleet's, was one that would ultimately have converged on that of the head of the German line. Shortly afterwards he sent another signal, received by Jellicoe at 7.59, giving the German course approximately, after which he seems to have caught a glimpse of the van division of the battle fleet (Jerram's Second Battle Squadron) and seen that it was steering further to the eastward than he was. 'I shall not forget our agony of mind', he wrote later, 'seeing him [Jerram] 3 or 4 miles astern of us [actually it was more] leading his division . . . too much to the eastward while we were in touch with the enemy.'[27] There was only about an hour and a quarter of daylight left, and Beatty, burning to ensure that the last chance of intercepting Scheer should not be lost, signalled at 7.47: 'Submit van of battleships follow battle-cruisers. We can then cut off whole of enemy's battle fleet.' By the time that this had been relayed, received, deciphered and handed to Jellicoe it was about or perhaps just after 8 o'clock, and the Commander-in-Chief had either just made or was about to make a further turn of four points by divisions to a

* Scheer was actually about 15 miles away at the time.

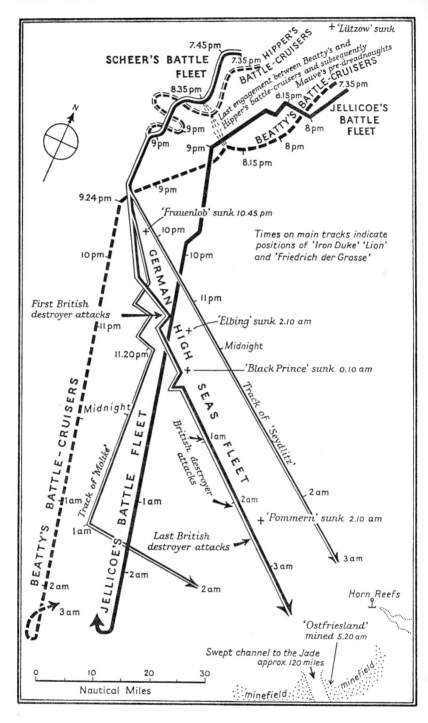

5. (Map of) the tracks of the two fleets during the night of
31 May–1 June

westerly course, with the intention of closing the enemy. The situation was still not wholly clear to him, however, and this was actually a course which would have tended to carry him across the rear of the German line; but since it seemed to him to mean that the battle fleet was now steering more in the direction of the enemy than the battle-cruisers were, and so doing all and rather more than all that Beatty was urging, he wirelessed back to him that his own course was now west, assuming that Beatty would conform and that it would then be safe for him to order Jerram to follow the battle-cruisers. This, after an interval, Jellicoe did; but as Jerram could see neither Beatty nor the enemy and did not know Beatty's exact position he could not obey the order and merely continued on the westerly course of the rest of the fleet. This passage of cross-purposes had little significance for the battle; but in the vitiated atmosphere that developed afterwards it sparked off a most regrettable and ill-founded controversy, for it became the basis of a legend, upheld by Beatty's extremer partisans and attacked by Jellicoe's, that by a refusal to follow a Nelsonian lead from the former the latter had allowed the Germans to escape.

Further contacts occurred between the leading elements of the two fleets after 8 p.m., at which hour Beatty, who had lost sight of the enemy's van, had thrown Rear-Admiral Napier's Third Light Cruiser Squadron out to the westward in order to locate it. Napier sighted the Fourth Scouting Group at 8.09, and between 8.20 and 8.32 a brisk fight developed until the Germans turned away and disappeared in the gathering darkness. Beatty meanwhile had altered course towards the sound of the guns. At 8.23 he sighted the German battle-cruisers to the north-westward, opened fire and inflicted further damage on the *Derfflinger* and *Seydlitz*. The six pre-dreadnoughts of the Second Squadron then appeared (the Germans were steaming south in two columns) and closed Beatty for long enough to enable their battle-cruisers to escape to the westward under cover of a smoke-screen, after which they followed suit. Since the other German squadrons conformed, the general result was to thrust Scheer away again to the W.S.W. and cause him to postpone his attempt to get back to his bases. Meanwhile Jellicoe in his turn had altered course to S.W. at 8.28, towards the gunfire, but saw nothing of the enemy. The same cannot be said of Jerram, who was presently responsible for one last good opportunity – a triple one – being missed. At 8.45

the light cruisers *Caroline* and *Royalist*, two miles ahead of Jerram's flagship the *King George V*, sighted dimly the leading battleships of the German First Squadron 8000 yards to the N.W. Jerram had also seen these ships at 10,000 yards, but as he was convinced that they were Beatty's battle-cruisers he did not fire and ordered the two light cruisers not to attack them (though they ignored this to the extent of firing three torpedoes which missed). Commodore Hawksley with the Eleventh Destroyer Flotilla, astern of *Caroline*, likewise saw the German ships, but decided that without Jerram's support it was inadvisable to make a torpedo attack in what was still daylight.

When darkness came down soon after 9 p.m. Jellicoe prepared his dispositions for the night. He was determined to avoid a night action as far as possible, since with less efficient searchlights, no star-shells such as the Germans had, and scarcely any director-firing gear for the battleships' secondary armament the Grand Fleet was neither equipped nor trained for it.* He therefore altered course again from S.W. to S., with the object of keeping between the German fleet and its bases until the morning light enabled him to renew the action, and formed his own fleet into night-cruising order of three columns of divisions in line ahead. Since the *Marlborough* had been struck shortly before 7 p.m. by a torpedo which reduced her speed to 17 knots her division, however, remained about three miles astern, while the three ships of the Fifth Battle Squadron still in company were five miles ahead of the main body. The Second Light Cruiser Squadron was to the westward between the rival fleets, the Fourth was scouting ahead, and the destroyers were massed about five miles astern of the battle fleet to guard against a German attempt to get back to base in that direction. Beatty was by now thirteen miles W.S.W. of the *Iron Duke* and directly ahead of Scheer's fleet, well placed to prevent him from escaping by cramming on speed and passing ahead of the British.

Three things, however, frustrated Jellicoe's plans and prevented the possibility of another Glorious First of June. First, though much the least important because without the other two it would scarcely have mattered, he miscalculated the route which Scheer

---

* Jellicoe must of course bear responsibility for his omission, as Commander-in-Chief, to train the Fleet in night action, for which he has been criticised.

Admiral Jellicoe coming on to the bridge of his flagship the Iron Duke
while Commander-in-Chief

Admiral Sir David Beatty on the quarter-deck of his flagship the
Queen Elizabeth *after his succession to the command-in-chief of the*
Grand Fleet

would take home. Out of the four possibilities as he saw them he rightly discounted the Kattegat, which was by far the longest. There remained the passage to the south-west of Horns Reef and then south between the Amrum Bank and the coast of Schleswig-Holstein, an apparently possible return through a gap in the British minefields W.N.W. of Heligoland (which the Germans had not swept and did not in fact consider using), and a southern route running along the north Frisian coast and outside its islands to the Jade.* Although it was a good deal longer than the other two, Jellicoe thought from Scheer's current course (W.S.W. as signalled to him by the *Lion* at 9.38) that this last was the most likely one for him to attempt. He therefore made for a position which would enable him to cover both this and the Heligoland route. At the same time he did not utterly neglect the Horns Reef passage, sending the minelayer *Abdiel* at 9.32 to support a rather inadequate patrol of three Harwich submarines which were lying off it by strengthening the British minefields south of their patrol line.

The German course which Beatty had reported was, however, a very temporary one, and in the meanwhile Scheer had altered to S.S.E. $\frac{1}{4}$ E., heading for Horns Reef. At 9.46 he altered again to S.S.E. $\frac{3}{4}$ E., for he had judged correctly that the British fleet was heading gradually across his bows, and that a slight eastward turn might enable him to pass, or break through, astern of it. Now came the second thing which frustrated Jellicoe – a tragic error of omission. The Admiralty, which had thrice during the previous afternoon sent him accurate but inevitably rather belated information of Scheer's position, despatched a message at 10.41 which he received, after decoding, at some time between 11.15 and 11.30. It ran: 'German battle fleet ordered home at 9.14 p.m. Battle cruisers in rear. Speed 16 knots. Course S.S.E. $\frac{3}{4}$ E.' It was in fact a conflation of three intercepted enemy messages deciphered by Room 40, one of which, passed on from Room 40 to the Operations Division at 10.10, read: 'C-in-C to Airship Detachment: Early morning reconnaissance at Horns Reef is urgently requested'. Even as it stood, the message sent to Jellicoe would

---

* There was yet another route, by a swept channel outside the Amrum Bank which emerged from the minefields about 30 miles S.W. of Horns Reef; but the Germans never used this when homeward-bound and Jellicoe does not seem to have known of its existence.

have been enough, if Scheer's reported course was plotted from his known position at 9 p.m., to tell him that the objective was Horns Reef, had not his confidence in Admiralty signals been shaken in the first place by the midday message that had placed Scheer's flagship in the Jade, and afterwards by another piece of misinformation. This was a signal of 9.58 p.m., giving the position and course of the rear ship of the German battle fleet so palpably wrongly that Jellicoe ignored it. Nevertheless if the request for airship reconnaissance had been transmitted it would have made Scheer's intentions so obvious that (as Jellicoe emphasised afterwards)[28] he would have made at once for Horns Reef and (since he was a few miles nearer and had a slight advantage of speed) got there first with a whole long summer's day before him. The early morning visibility would not in fact have been good, but it is difficult to keep the imagination from toying with the possibilities of such a situation. Instead, though the Battle of Jutland was not lost, a glorious opportunity of a decisive victory *was* lost, and lost in the Operations Room of the Admiralty by men whose fault was the very one that in their complacent self-sufficiency they attributed to the civilians of Room 40 – failure to appreciate the significance of the messages they were handling.

Yet one more chance remained, to be missed by the most surprising and most fatal of the signalling failures of the fleet itself. Between 10.15 and 2.30 Scheer forced his way home past the British rear under cover of a series of short but violent clashes which involved mainly destroyers on the British side. In these the British light forces were placed at a disadvantage not only by their inferior equipment but by the fact that the Germans had learnt part of their secret recognition signals owing to an unfortunate indiscretion. The *Lion* at 9.32 had signalled to the *Princess Royal* by flashing lamp: 'Please give me challenge and reply now in force as they have been lost', and the *Princess Royal* had complied, oblivious of the fact that German ships two miles away were able to read part of the answer. Thus in these clashes the Germans were often able momentarily to lull their enemy's suspicions while they opened fire at close range. Amazingly, neither the destroyers nor the several capital ships which realised that contact had been made with something more solid and substantial than light forces reported this all-important news to the Commander-in-Chief. For the destroyers, fighting most gallantly though in somewhat piecemeal fashion, there is much to be said in excuse; many had their wireless shot away and others were seriously damaged; moreover they had German wireless interference to contend with as well as much else. But the fact remains that under corresponding circumstances better communications and more co-ordinated control were achieved on the German side. In the penultimate encounter, indeed, Captain A. J. B. Stirling (who with his Twelfth Flotilla made the last but also the most successful attack on the escaping German fleet, blowing the pre-dreadnought battleship *Pommern* 'literally to atoms' with a torpedo) made or attempted to make three reports. But for some reason which may have been enemy jamming or damage to his own wireless neither of the first two was received by any other ship and the third only by one of his own flotilla which did not relay it. In any case, even if his first report had got through it would probably have been too late by then to head Scheer off. There is less excuse for the several British battleships which saw gun-flashes, star-shells, searchlight beams and even in at least two cases German heavy vessels, and did not report them. Some of the flashes and star-shell explosions were observed in the *Iron Duke* itself, but Jellicoe interpreted them to mean that his destroyer screen was repelling attempts of the enemy's light craft to attack from astern.

Daylight found both Jellicoe and Beatty still convinced that the enemy remained to the westward of them and that they were between him and his bases. But about 4.0 a.m. an Admiralty telegram was handed to Jellicoe which placed the High Seas Fleet only an hour's steaming from the Horns Reef lightship at 2.30. Soon afterwards came the news that it had returned to harbour. The British fleet steamed alone on the waters. After searching in vain for damaged enemy vessels and other stragglers, Jellicoe headed for Scapa Flow soon after 11 a.m. and reached it in the following afternoon.

6 After Jutland

(June–November 1916)

In the battle of Jutland the British lost three battle-cruisers, three cruisers and eight destroyers; their casualties were 6097 officers and men killed, 510 wounded and 177 taken prisoner after being picked up from the water by the enemy. The Germans lost one pre-dreadnought battleship, one battle-cruiser, four light cruisers and five destroyers; their casualties were 2551 dead and 507 wounded.[1] The balance of these losses obviously favoured them. Less obvious is the fact that if the better internal subdivision of the German capital ships and their anti-flash precautions had not made them nearly unsinkable the balance would have been appreciably different. They returned to harbour with ten heavy ships seriously damaged; the British, with eight. This meant that Jellicoe, who reported to the Admiralty at 9.45 p.m. on the day when he returned to Scapa that his battle fleet was at four hours' notice for steam and ready for action,[2] had 26 undamaged battleships and battle-cruisers; Scheer had 15. Moreover while the damaged British ships were fully repaired by the end of July, the majority of the Germans were not ready until the middle of August, and the *Seydlitz* and *Derfflinger* not until much later.

Tactically the battle was indecisive, in that neither side dealt the other a crippling blow. The High Seas Fleet had earned considerable credit (and for Hipper and his battle-cruisers scarcely any praise can be too high); with the aid of several strokes of luck it had ultimately outmanoeuvred its opponent and regained its bases. German shipbuilding, gunnery (with some limitations) and mechanical devices had come through the severest test with flying colours. But it had not achieved its original objective of obtaining parity or near-parity of forces by trapping and destroying a part of the British fleet. On the contrary Scheer's faith in further sorties of this kind as a means to victory was diminished and his conviction strengthened that only by unrestricted submarine warfare could the war be won, as he emphasised to the Emperor in his confidential report on the battle. Strategically Jutland was a British victory, or perhaps success would be a better word. The naval position remained unchanged. As Balfour put it in a message to the press in August: 'Before Jutland, as after it, the German Fleet was imprisoned; the battle was an attempt to break the bars and burst the confining gates; it failed. . . .'[3]

Unhappily that was not the first impression of a large part of the British public, to say nothing of much of the outside world. The mere fact that the High Seas Fleet had reached harbour first gave the Germans the psychological advantage of being well in advance with their version of the battle, which they presented as a German victory. To make matters worse the first British communiqué, based on a brief summary of British losses which Jellicoe had sent the Admiralty on the evening of 2 June,[4] and drafted mainly by Balfour with all his insensitiveness to public opinion,* was so bluntly honest and so tersely and unimaginatively worded[5] as to give the impression, especially to those who were prepared to read the worst between the lines, of bearing out the German claims. The British public, which had expected another Trafalgar and been encouraged by the press to expect it, leapt to the conclusion that their fleet had been defeated. Efforts were made by the Admiralty and the more sober part of the press to correct this impression, but without complete success. Much of the disappointment discharged itself against Jellicoe, who in any case had never been a very popular figure with the press. Modest and unassuming, he was totally lacking in any flair for self-advertisement and very little aware of the possible value of publicity. Newspapermen who came to Scapa, even when they brought letters of introduction from eminent persons, had found him unwilling to discuss his plans or allow them access to his ships, and adamant against any suggestion that war-correspondents might be quartered aboard the *Iron Duke* in the same way as they were accredited to armies in the field. On the other hand Beatty, the victor of Heligoland Bight and the Dogger Bank, was a colourful and even glamorous figure. A myth sprang into being that he had not been properly supported, after a long and gallant fight waged partly against the whole German fleet. An early but typical example of this distortion of the facts

---

* He apparently had the collaboration of Sir Henry Jackson and Vice-Admiral Sir Henry Oliver, the Chief of the Naval War Staff.

was the leading article of the *Weekly Despatch* for 4 June, from which the following passages are taken:

> The Germans succeeded in giving battle to a part of our fleet with their full strength . . . and then returned to their ports before our main fleet could force a decisive action. . . . We had the opportunity, had our dispositions been correct, to bring about a decisive naval battle in which the advantage, because of our superior strength, would have been on our side. Why did we fail? Why were the Germans able so to dispose their forces as to be able to attack when our battle-cruisers were unsupported, and to retire comparatively unscathed when the 15-inch guns came up?
>
> The answer is in one word – Zeppelins [an utter and ignorant error, since Scheer received no aid from Zeppelins and indeed had none with him]. The fight itself was mismanaged. . . . The battle-cruiser is a venturesome ship, and our battle-cruisers are under a venturesome commander – more power to him. But those responsible seem to have forgotten that the Germans can see where we are blind, otherwise they could never have so disposed their forces as to leave the cruisers to withstand the attack of the entire German fleet alone. We want practical seamen at the head of affairs. . . . Put Fisher in his right place at the head of the Admiralty. Bring Jellicoe down to Whitehall with the wisdom of 22 months' war, and let him advise his old chief out of his hard-earned knowledge. Give the fleet over to the younger men. Beatty would need no instruction in its handling. . . .

Jellicoe himself was deeply disappointed and cast down by the outcome of the battle. Writing to Balfour on 4 June, he expressed the hope that if his conduct of it was not considered correct the First Lord would not hesitate to order an enquiry.[6] He was further depressed by the death of Lord Kitchener, the Secretary of State for War, who was drowned on 5 June through the cruiser *Hampshire* striking a mine off the Orkneys while carrying him on a mission to Russia. For this catastrophe he considered himself in a measure responsible, since he had given the cruiser its route (though in fact its fate was due to a most unlikely combination of mischances and could not be imputed to any lack of reasonable precautions on his part). In this mood of self-reproach, which is perhaps understandable but which most would now judge need-less, he was stung by the *Despatch* article into requesting the Admiralty on 6 June to take immediate steps to prevent the future publication of such harmful misstatements. The article was referred to the Director of Public Prosecutions, but both he and the Attorney-General (F. E. Smith, later Lord Birkenhead) advised against proceedings being taken.[7] Even towards the end of the month, when he went south for a conference on 25 June in London and called in at Rosyth on the way, he was evidently still subject to fits of dejection, for Beatty told afterwards how in his cabin Jellicoe put his head between his hands and lamented that he had 'missed the greatest opportunity a man ever had'[8] – though there was perhaps a misunderstanding here and his lament may just possibly have been that he had missed it thanks to the Admiralty. Only gradually did he come round to the view, which well-informed modern opinion would endorse, that he had done about as well as was possible under the circumstances.

To the Navy also the battle was a big disappointment after the high expectations that had been entertained of the long-awaited meeting with the High Seas Fleet. Many officers and men received a shock on their return to port to find themselves at first regarded, and even sometimes reviled, as having been beaten; and though both they and most of the public gradually came round to realising that an important strategic success had been won, they could not regard it with enthusiasm. In the main fleet confidence in Jellicoe was unshaken, but the story was not quite the same in the Battle-Cruiser Fleet. Its personnel had come to regard themselves as something of a *corps d'élite*, an attitude which had tended even before Jutland to produce some mutual reservations and occasional covert criticisms between them and the rest of the Grand Fleet. Now, under the influence of heavy losses and an understandable sense of frustration after having done most of the fighting, they came to feel (and no doubt some of them must have been en-couraged by what they read in the less responsible newspapers to feel) that they had been let down by the battle fleet because Jellicoe had feared his fate too much and had not dared to

'put it to the touch, to win or lose it all.'

This feeling Beatty shared in his heart. Henceforward, accord-ing to a friend who knew him well,[9] his opinion of Jellicoe became twofold. On the one hand he continued to share his strategical and much of his tactical outlook and to appreciate his technical expertise and great qualities of character. On the other he believed with bitter regret that a tremendous opportunity had been thrown away. This ambivalence explains both a fierce outburst of criticism of which on the morrow of the battle he delivered himself in his cabin to the embarrassed Commander Dannreuther (one of the *Invincible's* few survivors)[10] and the very sympathetic letter which he wrote to Jellicoe on 9 June:

> I want to offer you my deepest sympathy in being baulked of your great victory which I felt was assured when you hove in sight. I can well understand your feelings and those of the Battle Fleet; to be so near and miss is worse than anything. The cussed weather defeats us every time. . . . Your sweep south was splendid and I made certain we should have them at daylight . . .[11]

In discussing the battle with friends in later years he was wont to emphasise that the Commander-in-Chief had adhered to the plans of manoeuvre which he had made clear beforehand that he would follow, and to close discussion with the words: 'Well, everyone did their best';[12] but his own clear and undeviating view was that for once Jellicoe should have risked some departure from those plans.

'I do hope', Beatty also wrote in the letter just quoted above, 'that you will be able to come here in *Iron Duke* soon. It would do us from top to bottom great honour to know that we have earned your approbation. . . . We are part of the Grand Fleet and would like to see our Commander-in-Chief' – a sentence which rather suggests that he was aware of the growing rift between the two parts of the Fleet and wished to close it. Jellicoe on his side was very anxious to make the Battle-Cruiser Fleet feel that it was part of a greater whole. When it visited Scapa early in August it was given a tremendous welcome, with lusty cheering. 'I have arranged', wrote Jellicoe to Jackson, 'that there shall be a good deal of social intercourse between the ships during their visit and started it last night with a dinner of BF and BCF flag officers and captains. I gather that the welcome was greatly appreciated and I think the trouble which I feared is practically already over.'[13] He was too optimistic, and probably the welcome had been too carefully arranged. It may even be suspected that here also there had been too many instructions, to the detriment of initiative and spontaneity. It seems clear that before the dinner just referred to the battle fleet element had been warned to avoid the topic of the battle, for when Rear-Admiral Pakenham (always a most uninhibited conversationalist) suddenly alluded to an episode in it there was a startled hush, followed by an outbreak of talk on various other subjects. It is hardly surprising that Beatty's suspicions, as his correspondence shows, were aroused as to the genuineness of all the warmth displayed.[14]

Naval officers generally and naval (or sometimes pseudo-naval) journalists, in their efforts to find a scapegoat for the disappointing results of the battle, had meanwhile lost little time in ranging themselves in pro-Jellicoe and pro-Beatty camps. The 'Jutland Controversy', in which their respective heroes took no public part, simmered in the background during the rest of the war; but it was only afterwards that it boiled up and over, under circumstances which must, unhappily but unavoidably, be recorded later.

A far more pleasing aftermath of Jutland was the reorganisation and reformation to which it gave rise, and to which Jellicoe had applied himself without losing an instant. On 4 June he had appointed committees of officers to examine the gunnery lessons to be learnt from the battle, and to consider and report on any suggestions for immediately increasing the protection of ships' vitals from plunging or other fire.[15] Further committees on torpedoes, wireless, anti-flame and gas, signals, searchlights, engineering and shells were soon at work. In accordance with the recommendations of the gunnery committees (one under Dreyer for the battle fleet and another under Chatfield for the battle-cruisers), the extension of the Percy Scott system of director firing to light cruisers and destroyers, and to the secondary or anti-torpedo armaments of capital ships, was pushed forward; the general system of fire control was revised and new spotting rules were laid down; range-finders were improved, and star shells introduced. It proved harder, however, to convince the Admiralty of the need for a better armour-piercing shell. Jellicoe on 25 July submitted a request that experiments should immediately be made with A.P. shell filled with trotyl and fitted with an exact copy of the German delayed-action fuse, with a view to its early introduction into the British service. He also enclosed a closely reasoned and technically detailed letter from Beatty supporting his proposal. The Admiralty replied agreeing to the experiments but stating that the German fuse was considered to have obvious defects and that it was desirable to try out other types as well.[16] In fact, it was not until Jellicoe went to the Admiralty himself as First Sea Lord, taking Dreyer with him, that the shell problem was solved. In May 1917 a new and highly efficient A.P. shell was designed, but it was only in April 1918 that it began to be issued to the Grand Fleet. In the meantime there was a prolonged period of what Chatfield recorded as 'unpleasant anxiety',[17] which no doubt contributed to the decision presently taken to pursue a still more cautious strategy.

On the other hand the Admiralty was quick to approve the introduction of anti-flash devices on the recommendation of one of the committees, and ultimately willing to accept the conviction of the senior officers of the Grand Fleet that their ships needed more armour protection. From this the Director of Naval Construction, Sir Eustace Tennyson-d'Eyncourt, dissented strongly, apparently with justification; but he was overruled and it was agreed in the autumn that additional armour should be provided.[18] In addition to these improvements in *matériel*, the intelligence arrangements were recast. The Admiralty agreed to send the Commander-in-Chief in future a daily summary of what it knew of the German forces and their probable movements; and in 1917 an important reorganisation of Room 40 took place. The Director of Naval Intelligence, Captain Reginald ('Blinker') Hall, became its head; and since he believed that the only way of getting full value from it was to make it something more than a bureau for deciphering and passing on German signals, it duly became a section of the Intelligence Division, sending in reports on the German fleet based on its extensive knowledge of that fleet and its procedures.[19] In tactics there were in some respects no changes. The new Grand Fleet Battle Orders, the chief revision of which was issued on 11 September, remained as elaborate as before.[20] Command continued to be centralised and the line-ahead formation was still the dominant principle of battle. Nevertheless there were some amendments in the direction of decentralisation and greater flexibility. In the event of the enemy combining a turn-about with a destroyer attack the flag officer leading the van was given discretionary power, if his squadron was not threatened, to press on in pursuit. For squadrons threatened by torpedo attack it was laid down that there was no absolute 'best' counter and that the appropriate action must depend on circumstances, one possibility being a turn towards the torpedoes. The turn-away, however, was still regarded as safer, other things being equal. More encouragement than before was given to destroyers to take the offensive. For the battleships a new deployment signal was introduced, to enable deployment to be carried out on the centre column if desired. The Fifth Battle Squadron was given a more advanced position in the cruising order to enable it to reach either flank of the line more easily and thus to facilitate possible 'divided' tactics. In the event of an action being interrupted by nightfall, a force was to be detailed to locate and maintain touch with the enemy battle fleet.

In strategy there was no fundamental alteration. Two main themes were discussed at the Admiralty conference on 25 June, already alluded to, which Jellicoe and Beatty attended, and the decisions taken represented Jellicoe's views. The first question considered was the necessity of not allowing the battle-cruisers to get too far away from the battle fleet, since they were not a match for their German opposite numbers. The ultimate solution was to move them to Rosyth, and it was decided that the arrangements for this should be pressed forward 'with the utmost despatch'. Meantime, where the initiative rested with us, 'the battle-cruisers should not be advanced so far from the support of the Battle Fleet as had been customary in the past', and in the event of a German raid on the east coast they were, if ordered south, 'to avoid becoming seriously entangled with superior forces until the Battle Fleet is within supporting distance, unless the Admiralty consider the circumstances sufficiently urgent to render a different course necessary, in which case Their Lordships will give instructions direct to the Vice-Admiral.' The other question discussed was whether the Fifth Battle Squadron was to be regarded as a support for the battle-cruisers, as Beatty urged, or as a fast wing division of the Grand Fleet, as Jellicoe wanted and as the Admiralty now ruled. After the German sortie of 19 August, however, Beatty was able to secure that it was stationed with him at Rosyth, on condition that both it and the battle-cruisers were to keep in visual touch with the C-in-C during joint operations and that he should control its tactical disposition. The conference of 25 June also debated the employment of the Harwich force in the event of the Germans coming out in strength, although it was not until after 19 August that it was specifically decided that if the enemy were apparently not intending to operate south of the latitude of Yarmouth it would be ordered to join Jellicoe's forces.[21]

The result of all these reforms was that within the next twelve months the Grand Fleet's efficiency was increased to an extent that would no doubt have abundantly justified Commodore Goodenough's robust comment on the morrow of Jutland: 'Well, by God, when next they come they'll rue it'. Basically, this was Jellicoe's achievement. To quote a recent authoritative assessment: 'His true greatness as a fleet commander lay in his capitalising on the lessons of Jutland.'[22]

But in the meantime strain and no doubt depression had begun to take toll of his health again. On 5 June he had written to Jackson: 'I often feel that the job is more than people over 55 [he was 56 at that time] can tackle for very long'; and at the end of July he received gratefully the First Sea Lord's suggestion that he should take some leave. 'I dislike going intensely', he wrote on the 31st, 'but I do feel quite played out. . . . It is very annoying, but I feel so constantly tired that I am afraid of not doing justice to the Fleet should we succeed in meeting the enemy.' As in the previous year, he went to Kinpurnie Castle, his father-in-law's house near Dundee, hoping for a fortnight's rest but taking a Foreign Office cipher with him and arranging for the light cruiser *Royalist* to lie at Dundee ready to take him off to rejoin the Grand Fleet if an emergency arose. In that event Jackson was to send a telegram *en clair* to Lady Jellicoe at Kinpurnie worded 'Important. He should get ready. Henry'. On the 15th he was writing that he was certainly feeling the better for the change;[23] but four days later 'Henry's' telegram came, and in half an hour he was aboard the *Royalist*, heading for a rendezvous with the Grand Fleet and hoping for a day of better fortune than at Jutland.

For a few hours on 19 August there seemed to be a fair prospect that such a day might materialise. Scheer had decided to try again to whittle down the Grand Fleet, either by catching a part of it at a disadvantage or by luring it into a submarine trap, or both. For this purpose he revived his original 'Jutland' plan of a battle-cruiser raid on Sunderland with his main fleet in support. Like

Jellicoe he had profited from the lessons of Jutland, the chief of which for him was the need of efficient reconnaissance so that he should not again be taken by surprise by the British battle fleet; and he intended to make the maximum use of airships and submarines to guard against this. One line of Zeppelins operated to the northward of his route across the North Sea and another in advance; while submarines were disposed off the British coast and on both flanks of his fleet. But as before, the interception of German signals enabled Room 40 to issue a warning early on the 18th that the High Seas Fleet intended to come out that evening, so that the Grand Fleet (temporarily under Burney till the *Royalist* joined it next morning and Jellicoe boarded the *Iron Duke*) was again at sea before it. This time the battle-cruisers were only thirty miles in advance of the main fleet and in visual touch with it through linking cruisers; the Fifth Battle Squadron was under Jellicoe's direct control; and the Harwich Force had been ordered to assemble at dawn off Brown Ridge, about fifty miles east of Yarmouth. But in the early morning of the 19th one of Scheer's submarines claimed a victim, the light cruiser *Nottingham*, which sank at 7.10. Since no trace of the submarine had been seen, it was not known at first whether the cruiser had been torpedoed or mined; and Jellicoe, thinking that he might be leading his fleet into a minefield, turned back northward 16 points until the matter was cleared up. At 9.08, having learnt that the *Nottingham* had been torpedoed, he resumed a southward course, steering about twenty-five miles to the eastward of where the attack had been made. Four hours had thus been lost, but there still remained time to bring the Germans to a decisive action.

About 2 p.m. an Admiralty signal, despatched at 1.15, was handed to Jellicoe which placed Scheer's flagship at 12.33 in Lat. 54° 32′ N., Long. 1° 42′ E. This meant that at that moment it was about sixty miles away from Beatty, with the two fleets steering on courses that converged at right angles. At 2 p.m. it would have been about forty miles distant if Scheer had continued on his course. On the assumption that he had done so, Jellicoe increased speed, turned directly towards where he supposed the enemy to be advancing, and signalled to the fleet at 2.15: 'High Seas Fleet may be sighted at any moment. I look with entire confidence on the result.' But in the meantime Scheer had received reports from the Zeppelin L13, which had sighted the Harwich Force but had

not identified its components correctly, that about sixteen destroyers with some cruisers and battleships were coming up from
the southward. Believing that his chance of destroying a smaller
and weaker detachment had come, he turned southward and
away (unknowingly) from the Grand Fleet. Shortly afterwards
the Harwich Force also turned south and steamed, equally unknowingly, away from the High Seas Fleet. Then at 1.15 Scheer
learnt by a signal from a U-boat that Jellicoe was coming south
after him, sixty-five miles away; and at 2.35 he gave up the chase
of the Harwich Force and turned for home. By 3 o'clock Jellicoe
had learnt from Admiralty messages that all hope of an action had
virtually disappeared, and at 3.53 he also turned homeward, losing
another light cruiser, the *Falmouth*, to a submarine *en route*. On
the other side of the account a British submarine had torpedoed the
German battleship *Westfalen* early in the day, but she was not
seriously damaged and was able to return to harbour.

Jellicoe has been criticised again over this affair, on the grounds
that by steering a course too close to the English coast and by
excessive caution he allowed the Germans to escape. His defenders
point out, however, that a more easterly course would have left
the east coast ports open to bombardment, which would have raised
a storm of indignation, while to have disregarded the sinking of the
Nottingham and pressed on into what might prove to be a minefield
would have been a very rash and risky action. What at any rate
is quite likely is that even had he done so Scheer would still have
been warned of his approach in time to escape, thanks to his
elaborate reconnaissance arrangements. His Zeppelins in particular
had at last come up to what Jellicoe had prophesied about them
and had served him well, even if L13 had done so only by a
blunder that had turned out to be fortunate for him. 'They
hampered us terribly . . .', wrote Jellicoe afterwards: 'One Zeppelin is worth a good many light cruisers on a suitable day'; and he
promptly enquired of the Admiralty how many British airships
were available on the east coast and whether they had orders to
co-operate with the fleet when it came within the limits of their
range. The reply, not very encouraging for the near future, was
that the current type had a very restricted range but airships more
suitable for fleet work were in course of production.[24]

It was the torpedoing of the two light cruisers, however, that
caused Jellicoe most concern. 'I much regret our losses on the

19th', he wrote to Jackson on the 23rd: 'The only way of avoiding them in future when submarines are so numerous will I fear be to screen all cruisers and light cruisers, and I am afraid the number of TBD's won't run to it. . . .'[25] On the following day he sent the Admiralty a memorandum stating that further southward movements of the Grand Fleet such as that of 19 August would almost certainly involve severe losses unless it had sufficient destroyers to screen all its other vessels. Quoting statistics to show that on the average he was 17 short of the minimum of 87 needed for this, he urged that to bridge the gap the completion of destroyers now under construction should be pushed on at the expense of all other craft except light cruisers. Their Lordships replied rather bleakly that they fully recognised the necessity of screening the ships of the Grand Fleet efficiently and had for a long time been allocating all new destroyers to it, but they had also to provide destroyers for various other theatres of naval operations, and notably for the protection of the communications of the army in France, for guarding the troopships which were bringing 30,000 men a month from Canada, and for the Mediterranean, through which ran the sea-communications of more than 300,000 troops in Egypt, Salonika and Mesopotamia. Nor could they hold out any hope, they added, of appreciably increasing the rate of production of destroyers, which had already been greatly accelerated since pre-war days. Dissatisfied with this dusty answer, Jellicoe returned to the attack with another memorandum of 13 September in which he produced no new arguments of any weight, but merely debated some of the minor points of the Admiralty's reply. This time he got no answer at all. Oliver minuted on the back of the memorandum for the benefit of his colleagues: 'This letter does not seem to call for a reply. Keeping up an argument will not provide any more destroyers', and Balfour endorsed it: 'Take no action'.[26]

The tempers of tired men at both ends of the argument were in fact becoming frayed. There had been signs of touchiness, almost of testiness, in a correspondence that Jellicoe had had with Jackson in July over improvements which the former suggested in the Admiralty's system of wireless signalling.[27] Now, in September, the Fourth Sea Lord, Captain C. F. Lambert (who had previously uttered some aspersions on Jellicoe's handling of the Jutland battle), returned from a visit to Scapa and Rosyth reporting that the Commander-in-Chief was sharply and consistently critical of the Admiralty in his conversation. This immediately provoked an explosion from Jackson, who by this time was becoming very weary and on edge.

> I regret [he wrote to Jellicoe on September 11] that he depicts your attitude as viewing everything that emanates from the Admiralty as wrong, whether it is really good, bad or indifferent. Perhaps we have tried to meet your wishes too readily during the past 15 months: that we have done so, as far as the material at our command allows, neither you nor anyone else can deny. Everything else has been starved, more or less, for the Grand Fleet. Your principal accusation seems to be 'when the Grand Fleet is ordered to sea (when the German Fleet is known to be out) that you are ordered to carry out impracticable or dangerous movements'. To this I give a flat denial. I must ask you to state definite cases to substantiate the charge...

After this opening broadside Jackson turned to a different point – Jellicoe's strong preference, which Lambert had also reported, for his brother-in-law and chief of staff Sir Charles Madden rather than any other of his subordinates as a successor in the event of his death in battle or breakdown in health (a preference to which the now reduced warmth of the relations between him and Beatty may have indirectly contributed).

> The next complaint [he continued] seems to be that your Battle Squadron Admirals are hardly up to the mark – not fit to take your place if you are knocked out. . . . We are at a very critical period of the war and personal likes and dislikes should be eradicated from all our minds. I have always had the highest opinion of your C.O.S., but to put forward the idea that he is the only man fit to take your place is I think rather strong. . . .

Then, reverting to his first point, he concluded:

> Discontent spreads rapidly, even downwards, and may react when least expected. Popularity may sometimes be dearly bought. Plain speaking is sometimes desirable and you have it above. . . . We lack the initiative [i.e., in the war at sea] and it is a bad handicap against us. That it weighs on your mind I am not surprised, but please do not let it warp your judgement to such

Jellicoe's flagship, H.M.S. Iron Duke

Sir David Beatty's flagship, while he was in command of the Battle-Cruiser Fleet, H.M.S. Lion

Vice-Admiral Sir Charles Madden, Jellicoe's Chief-of-Staff

Admiral Sir Alexander Duff, first Director of the Anti-submarine Division (a portrait painted some years afterwards)

Rear-Admiral Hugh Evan-Thomas, commanding 5th Battle Squadron. Drawing by Francis Dodd

Commodore William E. Goodenough, commanding 2nd Light Cruiser Squadron. Drawing by Francis Dodd

an extent as to make you accuse us of not giving you every support in our power or 'playing the game straightly', and putting us all down as incapables.

Jellicoe replied forcibly, especially to the first point, where he was perhaps on surer ground. After expressing his surprise at both the tone and the contents of the letter and pointing out that it would have been fairer to him if Jackson had first asked him how far Lambert's report was correct, he denied categorically that anything he had said could be interpreted as 'viewing everything that emanated from the Admiralty as wrong', and requested that Lambert should explain his statement and supply concrete examples. He also denied with equal vehemence that he had made any such accusation as that 'the Grand Fleet was ordered to carry out dangerous and impracticable movements'. As to the allegation that he considered his battle squadron admirals hardly up to the mark and not fit to take his place, this (he wrote) was apparently a misinterpretation by either Lambert or Jackson of a remark he had made to the former that undoubtedly the most capable successor to himself would be Madden. He could not, however, let the statement pass without a most definite and emphatic denial and an assurance to Jackson that he was entirely satisfied with all his flag officers in their present positions. Any suggestion to the contrary was a downright falsehood which he requested should be quashed at once. Nor had he said when discussing the question of a hypothetical successor with Lambert that Madden was the only possible man, but merely that he was the best fitted, and had added that it would nevertheless be impossible to promote him over the heads of so many seniors.

> You next say [he concluded] 'Discontent spreads rapidly.' There is no discontent here that I know of. I don't know whether the Fourth Sea Lord heard of it anywhere else [a possible allusion to Lambert's visit to Rosyth]. . . . Finally I have said nothing to [him] to the effect that 'you are not giving me all the support in your power' or 'playing the game straightly' or 'putting you all down as incapables'. . . .

In a postscript he added: 'I do not understand your remark that "Popularity may sometimes be too dearly bought." Will you kindly explain it?'

K

Since a popularity-seeker was the last thing that Jellicoe was, it is hardly surprising that Jackson made no attempt to do this. Instead, his next letter was in a much milder tone. It was not easy, he wrote, to reconcile Jellicoe's reply with the statement of Lambert, who had seen his own previous letter and affirmed that it was correct, 'except on the assumption that there was a good lot of "hot air" about', which he personally thought was the real explanation. The best plan, he suggested, was to close the subject, 'which is not well suited for correspondence. We are all apt to growl, especially at the Admiralty, and consider it the naval officer's privilege, and sometimes the air is cleared and better understandings arrived at by some plain talking.' Apropos of the hypothetical succession to the command-in-chief, he commented confidentially that he thought it highly probable that it would be offered to Beatty and that if his seniors among the squadron admirals did not like that they would have to be replaced. Madden, he pointed out, with all his good qualities, had not in virtue of the position he occupied had the responsibility of giving many final decisions, which was the real test of aptitude for command in war.

> I hope [he ended] that there is no discontent at the various bases, but rumours are rife that all is not quite so well as might be, though I cannot speak definitely on this point and it is most regrettable if such is the case and there is any intriguing prevalent. I, for one, won't countenance or take part in any. . . . I hope this explanation is clear and not to your dissatisfaction. If so, it requires no answer and we will close it for good.

Jellicoe, however, had been, in his own words, 'really surprised and a great deal hurt' by the suggestion that he was capable of denigrating his squadron commanders behind their backs, and was not prepared to accept the proffered olive branch until this had been retracted. 'I do not think', he wrote back, 'I have ever been so insulted before. . . . I can only hope that you did not mean it.' He also expressed himself strongly against Beatty as a possible successor: 'Although it appeared so extraordinary to you that I should consider Madden fitted for the post, you now suggest an officer with infinitely less experience and many years younger. So far as his seniors are concerned there is no doubt in my mind as to which officer they would prefer to serve under. However the choice is not likely to lie with me. My only reason for wishing the

Admiralty to decide the question . . . is that one might break down suddenly' – a possibility which his correspondence makes clear was often in his mind. Jackson then made a rather halting retraction and the matter dropped.[28]

It was in this not very happy atmosphere that 'one of the most important naval conferences in the war'[29] was held aboard the *Iron Duke* on 13 September between Jellicoe, Madden and Oliver, who had come north for the purpose and who also visited Beatty at Rosyth next day. The matter under discussion was the future strategy of the fleet in the light of the events of 19 and 20 August. It was agreed that this largely depended on whether the Government was prepared to face the fact that the Grand Fleet could not prevent the bombardment of east coast towns or interfere with the early stages of an enemy landing, especially if it took place well to the southward; and also on whether the fleet was to disregard submarine and mine risks and seek out the enemy whenever and wherever he was known to be at sea, or whether it was to avoid localities where he could easily lay submarine or mine traps and confine its operations to latitudes north of 55° 30' N. (corresponding roughly to a line drawn from the Farne Islands to Horns Reef). Jellicoe stated his conviction that it should not go south of that line in longitudes east of 4° 0' E., save in exceptional circumstances, since the waters beyond could not be watched by our cruisers or submarines and hence offered the enemy facilities for such traps. To the west of 4° 0' E., however, our submarine patrols could probably report by wireless whether minefields might be expected, and he therefore held that the fleet could afford to take the risks of mines in these waters if there was a really good opportunity of bringing the High Seas Fleet to action in daylight. Even so, in view of submarine risks, it should not go south of the Dogger Bank unless it had sufficient destroyers to screen all ships, which was not the case at present. At the same time he urged more constant patrolling of the North Sea by cruisers, provided that these could be screened, and pressed for the completion as soon as possible of the measures which were in train to enable the main part of the battle fleet to be based on Rosyth. He emphasised, nevertheless, that his recommendations on the fleet's policy were independent of whether Scapa or Rosyth was its base. Beatty, as Oliver reported to the Admiralty, was 'if anything more emphatic . . . than the C-in-C' that the fleet should not come far south every time the German fleet approached the east coast, but only when there was a really good chance of engaging it in daylight.[30]

Beatty in fact had written to Jellicoe a week previously:

I am very firmly of the opinion that the War has reached a stage when it behoves us [in] the Navy to move very circumspectly. The old proverb that 'When you are winning risk nothing' might well be applied now. And I think the North Sea south of Lat. 55–30 N. is a very unhealthy place for capital ships and should be left entirely to SM's who might be able to deny the use of it to the enemy except at very grave risk. If they are willing to take that risk it would surely be for an objective of great importance . . ., in which case we ought to be able to guess it and counter it. The enemy's fleet is no use to them unless they can perform some such duty as breaking up the blockade which is really now having a strangling effect and in that case they have to fight us. And in waters of our selection and not of theirs.[31]

This makes clear beyond a doubt that though Jellicoe apparently knew and resented Beatty's belief that he had not been properly supported at Jutland, and was now disposed to undervalue him as a commander, their views on strategy remained unchanged and still corresponded as closely as ever. And yet the old legend that depicts them as Fabius Cunctator* and Prince Rupert respectively dies very hard indeed, as such legends always do.

On 25 September the Admiralty notified Jellicoe that it had approved and adopted the new fleet policy which he advocated. 'The decisions embodied in [its] memorandum governed the subsequent conduct of the Grand Fleet and rank as one of the most important enunciations of naval policy issued during the war.'[32]

A few days previously Jackson had written of this change of policy, in the same letter that contained his withdrawal of the over-hasty and ill-considered insinuation that had given Jellicoe so much pain: 'It is a very defensive strategy, but is a safe one, and may tend to make them eventually take bigger risks and give you another chance of getting at them.' The reverse, however,

---

* The ultra-cautious Roman commander (for a time) in the Second Punic War against Carthage.

was the case, for on the other side of the North Sea a change of plan had also taken place. Although Scheer still saw possibilities in sorties, provided that the combination of airships with sub-marines for reconnaissance work was developed further, the German Naval Staff had come round after 19 August to the view that though such sorties might do some damage they would not have any decisive or important results. The pendulum of German naval policy therefore swung back again towards submarine warfare, which was ordered on 6 October to be resumed in accor-dance with prize rules (stipulating visit and search). Scheer had meanwhile planned another venture on the lines of 19 August, but had been compelled to cancel it because of bad weather. After this order of 6 October there were no longer any submarines at his disposal, but he could still count on Zeppelins, and he altered his plan to an advance to a point east of the Dogger Bank with ten of these in a semi-circle ahead of his fleet and destroyers on both flanks. Apparently he hoped to trap the Harwich Force or perhaps some other British detachment, but in accordance with the newly-adopted strategy the British waited on developments instead of immediately putting to sea, and he presently returned to port. Since he did not feel inclined to make further sorties without sub-marine reconnaissance, this proved to be the last time on which the High Seas Fleet ventured forth until its final abortive excursion in April 1918. A stalemate in the North Sea had set in, and the submarine war on merchant shipping soon became the decisive factor.

Meanwhile another wave of public distrust of the Admiralty surged up in the autumn of 1916 and among other results swept Jellicoe into the office of First Sea Lord. To this wave of criticism several things contributed: a couple of successful German destroyer raids into the narrows of the Channel, after the first of which Balfour proclaimed unwisely that he did not think there would be a second, but that if there was it would cost the Germans dear; a press agitation against the Admiralty's alleged mismanage-ment of the Royal Naval Air Service and its share in aerial war-fare; a cry raised, chiefly in the correspondence columns of *The Times*, that the Board was not sufficiently imbued with the offensive spirit; and above all the revived submarine campaign, which had developed in September and intensified after the German order of 6 October. An unpleasant feature of this campaign was that minelaying submarines from the Flanders ports, whose activities had so far been mainly confined to the southern part of the North Sea, were now extending them to the waters off the Clyde, the Irish Sea, the Bristol Channel, the central and western parts of the English Channel and the south coast of Ireland. The campaign as a whole led not only to a disturbing increase in the rate of sinkings but also had the indirect effect of seriously slowing down the delivery rate of cargoes through the detention of ships in port when the proximity of U-boats was reported and through their zigzagging and avoidance of dangerous areas while on voyage. An especially sinister aspect was that occasional cases began to occur of sinking without warning, in disregard of orders, which heralded the future resumption of unrestricted warfare. Unless headway could be made against all this, there was a possibility or even a prospect that neutral nations (and Norway in particular, on whose iron ore British munition factories depended) might withdraw their shipping. Already a very serious situation had arisen in the shipment of coal to France, which had been diminished or interrupted to such an extent that French factories were closing down for lack of fuel. In the Mediterranean, too, losses were heavy; and submarines of a new cruiser type were beginning to operate off the Atlantic coasts of France, Spain and Portugal, in the White Sea, and even off Iceland and the eastern coast of the United States. It was true that the ratio of losses was still small as compared with the total of voyages made and cargoes carried, and that the campaign had not so far led to any restriction of supplies comparable to that produced by the allied blockade of Germany; but on the other hand the development of anti-submarine measures was making little progress as yet. The only new devices of any importance that had recently been introduced were hydrophones, which at the moment were being fitted to naval vessels, and the decoy-ships known as Q-ships, which notwithstanding the publicity they received after the war (and which the courage of their crews richly deserved) soon ceased to achieve much. Reliance was still placed mainly on patrolling dangerous areas with small craft, and convoy was not (and for lack of escorts could hardly be) resorted to except for troop transports and certain other specially important ships. The blame for this worsening state of affairs was laid at the door of the Admiralty by a chorus of leading newspapers, naval journalists and retired admirals (to whom Fisher and Lord Charles Beresford in strange conjunction acted as fuglemen) shouting for 'new blood' and 'more salt from the sea'.

Jellicoe did not share or sympathise with the cruder and more unreflecting aspects of this agitation; but he came round to realising in October that what mattered was no longer victory over the High Seas Fleet but over the submarine menace. So completely was he persuaded of this that whereas he had previously cried out for more destroyers he was now prepared to release one of his flotillas for anti-submarine work in southern waters. He included this offer in a memorandum which he sent to Balfour on 29 October and the copy of which in the British Museum is endorsed in Sir Reginald Bacon's hand 'the letter that eventually caused Balfour to bring Jellicoe to the Admiralty'.[33] It opened starkly, realistically and (as the event proved) almost prophetically with a warning that our losses of merchant shipping, together with those of the neutral nations, might by the early summer of 1917 have such a serious effect on the importation of food and other necessities as to compel us to make a disadvantageous peace. The dwindling success of the methods of attacking submarines hitherto used he ascribed firstly to their increased size and radius of action, which enabled them to work in waters so distant as to make it increasingly difficult to trap them; secondly to the fact that they were attacking more frequently with the torpedo, which prevented the use of methods applicable to submarines that came to the surface; thirdly to the very powerful gun armament they now carried, which made them more than a match for our smaller patrol craft; and fourthly to their acquaintance by now with the anti-submarine methods in use. New methods of offence must therefore be devised, and for this purpose Jellicoe suggested the formation of a committee of younger officers who had already shown marked inventive aptitude or originality, working under a senior officer who would combine the energy to carry through promising suggestions quickly with the influence needed to overcome all difficulties that might be met with. He also urged pressing on with the completion of all merchant ships now being built in Britain and allied countries, even at the cost of retaining men for the work who would otherwise be in the Army or engaged on the making of munitions.

This memorandum impressed Balfour sufficiently for him to get the Prime Minister to read it to a meeting of the War Committee on 31 October, and to suggest that Jellicoe should be invited to attend its meeting on 2 November. At this, which Jackson and Oliver also attended, anti-submarine measures were discussed, including the convoy system, which all three admirals regarded as impracticable. Jellicoe's suggestion of a committee of experts was not raised, but was discussed by a conference at the Admiralty which he attended on the following day, after which he was asked by Balfour if he would be prepared to leave the Grand Fleet to become the head of such a committee. His first inclination was to agree, since he believed that there was now very little chance of the High Seas Fleet ever giving the Grand Fleet another opportunity to engage it. On thinking the matter over during the day and having a talk with Jackson, however, he came to the conclusion that such an arrangement would be difficult and embarrassing for both of them. No immediate action was therefore taken, though Jackson suggested that Jellicoe should become his deputy on the understanding that he would replace him in the near future. A fortnight later Balfour proposed that since the strain of trying to cope with the submarine danger was obviously wearing Jackson out, the replacement should be immediate. On 22 November, therefore, Jellicoe received a telegram offering him the post of First Sea Lord and hoping that he could take up his duties without delay. To this he replied: 'I am entirely at your disposal and if my services are required I accept the offer.' On the 28th he hauled down his flag and took leave of the Grand Fleet which he had commanded for nearly twenty-eight months of war, with a message of warm thanks to all ranks for their loyal support and of perfect confidence that should they again meet the enemy they would prove themselves more than a match for them, ship for ship, and that the issue would never be in doubt for a moment.[34] Congratulations and good wishes poured in on him from many quarters. Jackson, who had been relegated to the Presidency of the Royal Naval College at Greenwich and to whom he had written in terms that washed away all memory of their brief estrangement, replied in what Jellicoe described as a 'very fine letter':

> I am deeply touched by the kind and generous tone of your letter. . . . I have as great a confidence in your ability to do the

work in the Admiralty as you have done it in the far more oner-
ous post of Commander-in-Chief, and I have no feeling but a
sense of relief that it has now fallen into your capable hands,
and I feel convinced that your administration will achieve
success as far as human foresight and guidance can control such
operations. That Divine Guidance may assist you also is the
wish of your very sincere friend and old colleague.[35]

Fisher alone struck a discordant note, believing that Jellicoe's
appointment was a move to prop up the administration of the
Philosophic Doubter (as he called Balfour)* and thus prevent his
own appointment as First Lord. On 4 November he had written:
'If you ever allow yourself to be cajoled into leaving the command
of the Grand Fleet you will betray your country'; and on the
25th he penned what he described as the saddest letter of his life,
lamenting that Jellicoe had not listened to his entreaties: 'Your
leaving the command . . . at this juncture is absolutely parallel
to Nelson coming home to sit on an office stool the week before
Trafalgar!'[36]

Fisher, however, had long ceased to be much in touch with
reality, for Balfour's tenure of the Admiralty had little more than a
week to run. On 7 December Asquith's ministry was replaced by a
coalition government under Lloyd George, who transferred him
to the Foreign Office. Voices were heard in favour of the appointment of Fisher to succeed him, but none were very influential,
and Lloyd George would not hear of it. Instead, he appointed Sir
Edward Carson.

Meanwhile Beatty had been chosen by the Admiralty to succeed
Jellicoe in command of the Grand Fleet, despite the latter's
continued recommendation of Madden, who was made second-in-
command and commander of the First Battle Squadron. As his
Chief of Staff Beatty brought with him Rear-Admiral Sir Osmond
de B. Brock, previously commander of the First Battle-Cruiser
Squadron. Burney, who Jellicoe had insisted should go with him
to the Admiralty as Second Sea Lord, and Jerram, who was to be
relieved by Vice-Admiral Sir John de Robeck, were instructed
to haul down their flags. Sturdee, doubly hurt by the appointments
of both Beatty and Madden over his head, turned a deaf ear to
hints that he should ask to be relieved also, and stayed on to aid
Beatty loyally and well.

* In allusion to Balfour's *A Defence of Philosophic Doubt* (1879).

7 First Sea Lord (December 1916— December 1917): The Submarine Peril

WHEN Jellicoe took up his duties, after a few days' interval due to an attack of influenza, he dropped into the office of Captain Sir Douglas Brownrigg, the Chief Naval Censor. In the course of their conversation Brownrigg remarked that the new First Sea Lord had latterly had 'a bad press' and asked him if he wanted anything to be done about it. With a quizzical smile, Jellicoe replied that he was well aware what sort of press he had had and added that by the time he had told the truth about the submarine position a few times he would have a still worse one. Brownrigg asked him again if he might be allowed to see what could be done about silencing or reducing criticism and presenting a more favourable image of the Admiral to the world. No, said Jellicoe, the press must be allowed to form its own judgement, and in any case he did not expect to last twelve months and had no time to read the papers.[1] His forecasts were accurate, except that he erred a little on the pessimistic side in estimating the length of his tenure of office; but the apparent buoyancy he brought to his new task was not proof against the revelation of how true these forecasts were.

Besides stipulating that Sir Cecil Burney should be made Second Sea Lord, Jellicoe had secured the Fourth Sea Lordship for his Captain of the Fleet, Commodore Lionel Halsey. He had also expressed his intention of forming a special Anti-Submarine Division of the Naval War Staff at the Admiralty; and had asked that Rear-Admiral A. L. Duff, the second-in-command of the Fourth Battle Squadron (who had latterly been supervising at Scapa the trials of paravanes and other devices designed to protect ships from mine attack) should be made its Director, with Captain F. C. Dreyer, the former Flag-Captain of the *Iron Duke*, as his assistant. A number of other officers from the Grand Fleet were also transferred to the new department.[2] Jellicoe, in fact, brought with him to the Admiralty a considerable part of what he considered the cream of his former entourage, in order to tackle the supreme problem of the submarine menace.

He also set about reorganising the Admiralty War Staff, which was still working on the general lines introduced by Churchill when First Lord. Before that there had been no Naval Staff at all, since both Fisher and Sir Arthur Wilson, his successor as First Sea Lord, believed in keeping full control over everything connected with the administration and training of the Fleet, and the Navy War Council created in 1909 had consequently not been a true staff. At the beginning of 1912 Churchill had established a Chief of the War Staff, responsible to the First Sea Lord and having under him Operations, Intelligence and Mobilisation Divisions, each headed by a Director. Even in this organisation, however, the Chief of the Staff possessed no executive powers, and all orders affecting the movements of ships required the First Sea Lord's approval before issue. The resultant inconvenience perhaps did not matter so much during peacetime, but it became important in war, and as the war went on the Chief of the Staff came gradually to exercise executive functions, orders which were not of the first importance being issued by the Staff in accordance with the policy approved generally by the First Sea Lord. The Staff also expanded very considerably to meet war conditions, and a Trade Division dealing with all matters concerning the mercantile marine was formed. The basic anomaly of the 1912 organisation – namely that it was the First Sea Lord himself who was the true Chief of Staff and should have been recognised as such – was very apparent to Jellicoe; and after he had discussed the matter with Carson he assumed this title on 14 May and the two posts were fused. At the same time the operational work of the Staff was grouped under two departments, the first mainly concerned with operations against the enemy's surface vessels and the second with the protection of trade and with operations against the enemy's underwater warfare, whether by submarines or mines. Vice-Admiral Oliver, who now relinquished the title of Chief of the War Staff, was given the supervision of the former work under the new style of Deputy Chief of the Naval Staff, while Rear-Admiral Duff controlled the latter with the title of Assistant Chief of the Naval Staff. His place as Director of the Anti-Submarine Division was taken by Captain W. W. Fisher, who had replaced his original assistant Captain Dreyer when the latter was appointed Director of Naval Ordnance. The resultant organisation, at the time of the adoption of the convoy system in the early summer (which involved the addition of a Mercantile Movements Division), may be represented diagrammatically thus:

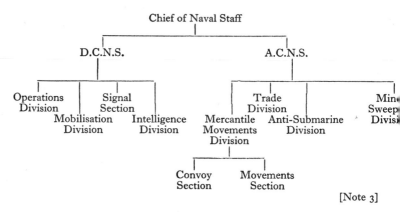

[Note 3]

The relations of the new First Lord with Jellicoe, and indeed with the whole Board, were cordial in the extreme. On the one hand Carson fully realised the urgency of the submarine peril; on the other, he lost no time in making clear that he would place himself at the disposal of his professional advisers, accepting their advice and guidance, repressing any inclination to develop his own ideas of naval strategy, and regarding his function as being to support and protect their policy against any pressure from politicians (especially the Prime Minister, between whom and himself a mutual aversion existed) or journalists. In March 1917 he made a characteristically blunt (not to say truculent) public declaration of his attitude in a speech at a luncheon gathering where the chair was occupied by the great press magnate Lord Northcliffe:

> As long as I am at the Admiralty the sailors will have full scope. They will not be interfered with by me, and I will not let anyone interfere with them.[4]

It is scarcely surprising that Jellicoe wrote afterwards: 'In him the Navy possessed indeed a true and a powerful friend'.[5]

As soon as possible after Jellicoe's advent at the Admiralty he set on foot a thorough survey of all the methods of anti-submarine warfare then in force, in order to decide future policy. These methods fell roughly into two classes: ways of attacking U-boats whenever they could be found and measures intended to give more protection to merchant shipping. Under the first head it was proposed that the patrolling of approach routes and particularly danger spots by destroyers and smaller craft, on which reliance was chiefly placed despite the meagre results hitherto achieved, should be supplemented as soon as possible by the formation of special 'hunting patrols' based on Portsmouth and Devonport for the sole purpose of harrying submarines whose approximate whereabouts was known. At that time, however, nearly the whole of the destroyers and patrol craft available in southern waters were engaged either in escorting across the Channel transports, ammunition ships and other important adjuncts of the army in France and Flanders, or in patrolling the Straits of Dover to guard the great number of merchantmen which anchored in the Downs every night; while there was also a constant demand for escorts for transports going to the Salonika and other secondary fronts. Moreover, even when it had previously been found possible to mount an intensive submarine-hunt the results had been far from encouraging. During one week in September, for example, two or at the most three U-boats had operated within an area which was watched by 49 destroyers and 48 torpedo-boats, together with 468 armed auxiliary craft. For the whole of this time they had been actively hunted by 13 destroyers and 7 Q-ships; yet they had sunk more than 30 British and neutral vessels without suffering any loss themselves. All told, British patrolling and hunting operations since January 1916 had accounted for only seven German submarines; while during the year about 100 engagements had taken place, so that even when brought to action a U-boat's chance of escape were roughly fourteen to one.[6]

Other offensive operations which were being undertaken or planned, supplementary to the work of patrolling and of hunting German submarines, included the organisation of air patrols at various points on the south coast and attempts to form ships fitted with hydrophones into special detachments which should hunt together. These hydrophone patrols became useful later on, but as yet a really satisfactory hydrophone had still to be designed. Plans were also being considered for using patrols of our own submarines against their 'opposite numbers', but here again previous experience did not hold out much prospect of success. Since the beginning of the war, British submarines on patrol had made contact with enemy boats fifty-six times; they had attacked them only on six occasions, and only three of these attacks had been successful.[7]

The measures designed to give better protection to merchant shipping comprised firstly the issue of directions as to routes to be taken. This control over routeing was, however, more rigorously exercised over outgoing then incoming traffic, since ships leaving British ports could be given more detailed instructions than those sailing from distant lands. The situation in home waters changed daily, and a line of approach which might be perfectly safe when a vessel left New York or Halifax could have become very dangerous by the time she drew near the British Isles. Hence incoming traffic was more vulnerable than the outgoing stream. Every effort was also being made to equip more merchantmen with guns; but the number of merchantmen was great and the figures showed that even those so armed were becoming less safe. Up to August 1916 the number of defensively armed merchant ships sunk by submarines had been relatively small, but after that the U-boat commanders were beginning to overcome the difficulties involved; twelve such ships were sunk in December, and in January 1917 the number rose to twenty.[8] Another measure in contemplation was a complete reorganisation of the barrage across the Straits of Dover. In the earlier part of the war an attempt had been made to bar the Straits to hostile submarines by establishing a line of drifters with indicator nets.* Vice-Admiral Sir Reginald Bacon, however, who had been appointed in April 1915 to command the defence forces at Dover, had latterly become anxious that some form of permanent barrage should be set up, and had laid a line of indicator mine nets, suspended from buoys 500 yards from each other and marked by light-buoys, between the South Goodwins and the West Dyck. This nevertheless proved no serious obstacle to the U-boats, though Bacon obstinately refused to admit the fact. A more ambitious project, urged by Beatty in particular,

---

* These were nets constructed of light material and suspended from steel hawsers each strung along a line of floats. They were either laid along the bottom or towed by drifters, and any submarine which fouled them soon revealed its presence by the disturbance it caused to the upper floats.

was the establishment of a complete mine barrage across the Heligoland Bight, but this would have required 55,000 mines, far more than were available, and in any case it was not till the autumn of 1917 that British mines became really efficient.* Instead, some half-dozen separate minefields were laid in the Bight at various times during January, though with disappointing results. All were fairly soon discovered by the enemy and channels swept through them, so that they did not cause the loss of a single outgoing or incoming submarine.[9]

Against these difficulties Rear-Admiral Duff's Anti-Submarine Division strove untiringly. Its activities in the months that followed included a great increase in the provision and use of aircraft for anti-submarine work, in close co-operation with the Royal Naval Air Service, which was presently able to bring into operation for this purpose improved types of seaplanes, aeroplanes and airships carrying heavier bombs. The number of Q-ships was very greatly increased, until their limited and diminishing value came to be realised; the use of depth-charges, of which at first there was a serious shortage, was developed and depth-charge throwers introduced; high-speed coastal motor-boats for anti-submarine operations were built in great numbers; smoke-screen apparatus and a far more effective type of shell were developed for use against submarines attacking by gunfire. But all these measures took time to develop, and Jellicoe's knowledge that it would be some months before any real benefit could be reaped from them increased his anxiety.[10]

Meanwhile, even before the resumption of unrestricted submarine warfare, British, allied and neutral shipping losses had continued to rise very seriously and in January 1917 reached a total of 368,521 tons.[11] This was a matter of grave concern. Already on 23 December Jellicoe had written to Beatty: 'The shipping situation is by far the most serious question of the day.... Drastic measures should have been taken months ago to stop unnecessary imports, ration the country and build ships. All is being started now, but ... it is nearly if not quite too late.' On the 30th he wrote again:

We are losing merchant shipping ... at the rate of about 300,000

---

* Even then, this belated efficiency was arrived at by copying the German mines exactly.

tons a month or more, and this rate will, I fear, increase during the next two to three months. My own calculations do not show that we shall add to our merchant shipping more than 500,000 to 600,000 tons in the next six months, and our allies are doing very little indeed in that direction, although something is being done by neutrals. . . . One of the greatest difficulties with which the Admiralty has to contend consists of the immense amount of shipping which is engaged in maintaining the Army in all parts of the globe, particularly . . . at Salonika. . . . In addition to these demands, our allies are becoming more and more dependent on us for shipping. . . . The shipping situation is such that to maintain our present military line of battle is a matter of the very greatest possible difficulty, and this difficulty will increase day by day as we get weaker in merchant ships.[12]

On top of this the German Government issued a declaration on 31 January that unrestricted submarine warfare would be resumed on the following day. Admiral von Holtzendorff and the Naval Staff of which he was the Chief had calculated that if their submarines could sink upwards of 350,000 tons a month when working under restrictions it was reasonable to suppose that when freed from them they could bring the rate up to 600,000 a month. His statistics showed that about $6\frac{3}{4}$ million tons of British and 3 million tons of neutral shipping had entered and cleared from British harbours during 1916, and Britain was known to have some 900,000 tons of captured enemy shipping at her disposal. She was fed and supplied, that is, by about $10\frac{3}{4}$ million tons of shipping. If the U-boats, by torpedoing at sight, could destroy 600,000 tons a month and (it was also calculated) frighten away at least two-fifths of the neutral shipping engaged in carrying supplies to Britain, at the end of five months she would have lost 39 per cent of the tonnage on which she depended, and this would be more than the country could bear. On the other side of the account it was reckoned that since the British Navy had only managed to sink 16 U-boats in the past year (besides five sunk by accident and four destroyed by the Russians) and since Germany had 111 boats operational at the moment and had arranged a programme of intensive construction, the progress of her campaign would not be affected by losses. With such a prospect the probability of a break with the United States could be accepted with equanimity.[13]

The first counter-move which the Admiralty made to meet this intensified attack was the introduction of a system of five alternative lines in each of the four areas of approach to the waters of the United Kingdom. The lines in use were changed at intervals in the hope that these switches could be made before the enemy had located the routes in current operation. An advantage claimed for this method was that the patrol craft on the line being used could thus be more numerous than if they had been scattered over the whole area. In practice, however, it was this very density of patrol craft which often gave away the line to the submarine commanders. Another counter-move was the adoption of a patrolled lane system near the British coasts, which brought merchantmen into close touch with our surface and aircraft patrols and made it more difficult for U-boats to work submerged because of the relatively shallower water. This kept down losses by gun attack in the Channel and off the Cornish and Irish coasts, but failed to meet the peril of torpedo attack.[14] The German submarines in fact surpassed Holtzendorff's calculations by sinking over two million tons of merchantmen in the first three months of their campaign (881,027 tons in April) at a cost to themselves of ten boats, two or perhaps three of which were lost through accident. In an exhaustive analysis of the position made for the British Government by Sir Leo Chiozza Money, in which he made allowance for replacements by building, repairing and buying from abroad, he came to the conclusion that at that rate the shipping in the service of Britain would probably be reduced from its current figure of 8,394,000 tons to 4,812,000 by the end of the year. The total carrying capacity of this tonnage would be between 1,600,000 and 2,030,000 tons per month, of which 1,425,000 tons would be required for food and cereals. From this it could be deduced that nothing would be left for the transport of troops, stores and munitions, and very little for the rest of the vital business of the country.[15]

Disaster was not perhaps staring the country in the face, but it was looming blackly over the horizon; and Jellicoe's realisation of the fact was not pessimism but clear-sighted realism. Holtzendorff's forecast was apparently coming true, and only a change of system could save us. But whether or how far Jellicoe had appraised correctly the change that should be made is a different question, which falls now for consideration.

His remedy at this stage, which he urged repeatedly and latterly almost desperately at those meetings of the War Cabinet which he was invited to attend, was the reduction or cancellation of the military 'sideshows' at Salonika and in Mesopotamia and East Africa that absorbed so much of our shipping resources, both mercantile and naval. Though he advocated this primarily as the only remedy which he so far saw for the darkening submarine crisis, it was a measure which also harmonised with the conviction he shared with Haig, Robertson the Chief of the Imperial General Staff and the rest of the 'Westerner' school of thought that it was on that Western Front in France that all our military effort should be concentrated. Lacking, like Kitchener before him, the oratorical and debating resources necessary to match the practised speakers with whom he sat at the War Cabinet table,* and finding it easier to marshal his arguments in carefully prepared memoranda, he also set out his views in two successive papers which were laid before that body. In the first, of 21 February, he declared that the Admiralty could hold out little hope that there would be any reduction in the rate of loss until the number of patrol vessels was largely increased, or unless the new methods which had been or were in process of being adopted resulted in the destruction of enemy submarines faster than they were being built (a remote aspiration at that moment).[16] The reduction of the number of transports and supply ships needed for overseas forces, however, would enable many light craft suitable for anti-submarine warfare and escort duties to be brought back to home waters, which would reduce the losses of merchant shipping, while the transports thus set free would considerably increase the tonnage available for the import of supplies.

> The position [he continued] is exceedingly grave, and it is a matter for the consideration of those responsible for the import of food, munitions, etc., to this country, and for the supply of necessities to our allies . . ., to determine how long we can continue to carry on the war if the losses of merchant shipping continue at the present rate. . . . In order to reduce the losses the only immediate possible remedy is to increase by

---

* 'When he found himself opposed to cabinet ministers who asked him to give a verbal opinion . . . he found it very difficult to express himself easily.' Goodenough, *Rough Record*, pp. 66–7.

every means in our power the number of patrol craft used for the protection of trade routes and approaches to land and harbours . . . [but] up to the present no complete and practicable cure for the submarine menace has been, *or is likely to be*,* discovered short of the destruction of his bases, which is obviously a military measure of great magnitude.

Two months later, on 27 April, his tone had become even more urgent, in a paper addressed in the first place to Carson, which the Board of Admiralty decided should be laid before the War Cabinet with its full support:

I feel it my duty to place before you my considered opinion that the time has arrived when it is necessary that the Government should be made to realise the very serious nature of the naval position, and it should be clearly intimated that the Admiralty can no longer accept responsibility for conducting the war on its present basis.

In my opinion the War Council fails entirely to realise the position, in spite of the repeated efforts which I have made to explain its gravity. . . . The only result so far has been the appointment of Committees to investigate various features, such as the rate at which we can build ships to replace losses, the extent to which our shipping can be reduced without starving the country, etc., etc., but I must point out with all the force at my command that all this is only playing with the situation. . . .

I have urged time after time on the War Cabinet the absolute necessity . . . for reducing the number of lines of communication which the Navy is called upon to safeguard and the necessity for increasing the protection on those . . . which remain. So far the only result . . . has been increased calls upon the Navy without any sort of reduction and with no appreciable increase of our resources. . . . It is now almost too late, but it is not quite too late.

The real fact of the matter is this. We are carrying on this war . . . as if we had the absolute command of the sea. We have not – and have not had for many months – . . . or anything approaching it. It is quite true, of course, that we are absolute masters . . . so far as surface ships are concerned, but it must be

* Author's italics.

realised . . . that all this is quite useless if the enemy's submarines paralyse, as they do now, our lines of communication. . . . *Our present policy is heading straight for disaster*,* and it is useless and dangerous in the highest degree to ignore the fact.

We must therefore so change and shape our policy as to conform with the fact that we have neither the undisputed command of the sea nor even a reasonable measure of this command. If we do not recognise this fact and shape our policy accordingly, it is my firm conviction that we shall lose the war by the starvation of this country. . . .

It is perhaps not my place to indicate the policy which should be adopted, but some considerations are perfectly evident. The first is that we must at once withdraw the whole of our force from Salonika. . . . Secondly we must realise that we cannot continue to bring reinforcements of troops into this country, unless they are conveyed in ships carrying other essentials such as food, as we cannot afford the escorting ships. Thirdly . . . the policy of importing labour must be at once abandoned for the same reason. Fourthly, the import of everything which is not essential . . . must be ruthlessly and immediately stopped. As shipping becomes available from all these sources it will be devoted entirely to the import of food until we have placed this country in a position to withstand the siege to which it is about to be subjected.

The release of the escorting and convoying vessels now devoted to the purposes named above will assist in providing protection for convoys . . . bringing . . . essentials in the way of food and munitions; but we shall be very hard put to it unless the United States help us to the utmost of their ability.

When the country is in a position to withstand a siege, then we can reconsider our future policy.[17]

With a juster appreciation of the position than of Jellicoe's standpoint, Sir William Robertson – that granite boulder of a man – had written on the previous day to Sir Douglas Haig: 'The situation at sea is very serious indeed. It has never been so bad as at present, and Jellicoe almost daily pronounces it to be hopeless.'[18]

But in the penultimate paragraph of Jellicoe's memorandum

* Jellicoe's italics.

there were some words which, more than the writer knew, carried the hope of ultimate salvation. These words were 'convoys' and 'the United States'.

Convoys on a small scale had been in operation since 1914, chiefly for troopships from Canadian and other Dominion ports. These convoys usually comprised from three to seven vessels escorted by a cruiser or armed merchant ship and taken through the danger zone by some destroyers. Similar escorts were provided for outward-bound troopships. But there were, or seemed to be, very real obstacles and objections to the adoption of a comprehensive system of convoy for merchant shipping. In the opinion of the bulk of the higher command of the Navy those of its advocates, whether naval or civilian, who based their arguments on its success in former and far-off wars were overlooking the many differences between a method used for the protection of merchant fleets that sailed perhaps twice a year and could only be attacked on the surface, and a system for the protection from underwater attack of a constant stream of trade to and from every quarter of the globe. First and foremost there was the sheer difficulty (or in Jellicoe's opinion impossibility) of finding the great number of escort vessels which would be needed. These, and especially the destroyers, would have to be taken from commands both at home and abroad which in his view were already inadequately supplied with such craft, particularly for screening purposes, and from most of which urgently worded requests for more were in fact being received.[19] Here, however, it is necessary to notice the criticism afterwards made by Vice-Admiral K. G. B. Dewar, who was then a Commander attached to the Operations Division of the Admiralty, that 'the real problem before the United States entered the war was not so much the shortage of escort vessels as the wrong use of those we had', since the system of patrolled routes to which Jellicoe pinned so much faith was absorbing many destroyers and 'an enormous number' of smaller craft, without being effective against the U-boats. Had the Admiralty really believed in convoy, he contended, 'there would have been no difficulty in providing escorts.'[20]

Jellicoe and what may be called the prevailing or orthodox school of both Royal and Merchant Navy thought also believed that merchantmen would find it impossible to keep station in the way needed for sailing in convoy. He himself based this opinion on, or was confirmed in it by, a conference with ten master mariners which he and other senior officers of the Admiralty held there on 23 February. At this meeting these merchant skippers declared that they had neither the necessary appliances in the shape of revolution indicators, telephones between bridge and engine-room and so forth, nor the necessary skilled officers since most of their best had joined the Navy or been creamed off into it as R.N.R. men.[21] It was left for later experience to show that these difficulties had been exaggerated; that sufficient appliances could be installed and training in station-keeping could be given during the relatively innocuous early stages of the first convoys, which were inward-bound. Again, it was felt that convoys would offer dangerously large and easy targets to a submarine, which (to quote an official pronouncement of the Naval Staff in January) 'could remain at a distance and fire her torpedo into the middle of a convoy with every chance of success'.[22] Moreover it was argued that the institution of a convoy system would involve loss of carrying power since vessels would make fewer voyages, and would create delays because convoys would have to travel rather below the speed of their slowest ships in order to leave a margin for station-keeping, and because the sudden influxes into our ports of masses of shipping at one time would mean congestion and slower turns-around. It was for these reasons in particular that many shipowners, better aware than other civilians of the difficulties and dangers of a convoy policy, were hostile to it or looked on it with considerable misgivings. Nor was it by any means a minor difficulty that while the United States remained neutral they might veto or raise obstacles in the way of the assembling of convoys in their ports, which would form an important part of the system.*

The possibility of convoy as a reply to the submarine menace had been mooted by Lloyd George, who favoured it, at the meeting of the War Cabinet on 2 November 1916 which Jellicoe, Jackson and Oliver had attended, but had been discounted by all three of them. At the purely naval conference which took place at the Admiralty on the following day it was not even touched on; and

---

* According to the strict law of nations, a belligerent could assemble a convoy in a neutral port; but in practice the government of a sufficiently powerful neutral might refuse to allow this on the ground that it would attract foreign combatant vessels to its waters.

in the January pronouncement of the Naval Staff referred to above Admiral Duff delivered himself of the view that 'differences of speed, loss of the safety afforded by zig-zagging, and the inevitable tendency of merchant ships to straggle at night are some of the reasons against an organised system of convoy'. Nevertheless Jellicoe in one of his early minutes to the Staff warned them that to guard the Atlantic trade against the surface raider *Moewe* which was then operating some of it might have to be placed under convoy; and endorsed the demurrer he received from Oliver with the comment that the whole question must be borne in mind and brought up again later if necessary.[23] At this stage, that is, he appears to have been somewhat withholding his judgement on the matter of convoy, though regarding it as impracticable under current conditions. 'The question of the introduction of a general convoy system', he wrote subsequently, '. . . was receiving constant consideration at the Admiralty in the early part of 1917, but the objections to it were, until a later date, far too strong to admit of its adoption.'[24] In particular, the conference with the Merchant Navy captains on 23 February seems to have strengthened his reluctance to adopt it.

Meanwhile on 13 February Lloyd George held an informal conference over one of his Downing Street breakfasts with Carson, Jellicoe and Duff in order to test what their feelings about convoy now were. Sir Maurice Hankey, who was also present, read a paper advocating it in which he began by admitting that in the earlier part of the war he had regarded the formidable objections to it as crucial. But now, he argued, circumstances had changed and it was a matter for serious consideration whether some of these objections had not lost much of their force, while others were outweighed by the failure of the methods now in use, and means might be available of overcoming the rest. The great curtailment of trade which drastic restriction of imports would bring, for example, would strike much of the force from the argument that our ports would become congested. Nor would any more time be lost than under the existing methods of devious routeing with frequent closing of ports owing to the known presence of submarines near by. The objection based on slowness could be surmounted partly by excluding the really fast vessels from the convoy system and partly by a rough grouping of vessels of approximately equal speed. Finally, the difficulty of providing escorts could probably be surmounted by carefully reorganising the existing distribution of anti-submarine craft. The two admirals were quite prepared to admit that the principles enunciated in the paper were sound; but they questioned their application to the current situation. In particular, Jellicoe declared that Hankey had disposed very lightly of the escort problem, to which he himself had devoted immense attention since he had come to the Admiralty, only to be convinced of the impossibility of finding sufficient vessels.[25]

A few days earlier, however, on 7 February and at the request of the French Government, the vessels engaged in the coal trade to northern France had been organised into rough and tentative convoys under the protection of armed trawlers. By the end of March this had produced an impressive reduction of losses, which had hitherto been high. On 3 April a conference of naval officers held at Longhope in the Orkneys to consider how the similarly heavy losses suffered by the ships employed in the Scandinavian trade could be reduced recommended unanimously that it should also be placed in convoy. This recommendation was backed by Beatty, who was a firm believer in the convoy system and was growing impatient with the Admiralty's reluctance to substitute it for the ineffective patrolling of routes. 'We have an insufficient number of ships to patrol the vast waste spaces', he had written to his wife on 28 March, 'and the Admiralty will not introduce the system of Convoy. The enemy subs are sinking ships by the score, and they will not take advice, or if they do they will not adopt it in its entirety.' The recommendation was examined at the Admiralty and endorsed by Jellicoe, who directed that it was to be put into operation experimentally with a fortnightly report on its working. It was even considered at this juncture whether the same policy could be applied to part of the Atlantic trade, but this Jellicoe felt to be too risky, since escort vessels could only be obtained by withdrawing them from patrol and other duties, with consequent losses to other trades.[26]

Westward, however, the outlook had brightened when on 6 April the United States declared war on Germany; though little could be further from the truth than to imagine that this transformed the situation in an instant. The American Navy possessed as yet only a limited number of destroyers and other craft suitable for escort duties, nor did the United States merchant marine include any great number of small vessels which could be usefully converted for this work. The American Government and naval command, moreover, had no idea of the seriousness of Britain's position. This could hardly be otherwise, since those in Britain who knew the truth were taking very good care to keep it from becoming general knowledge. Most of the newspapers, fed with misleading statistics,* were publishing optimistic statements about the German submarine campaign. Rear-Admiral William S. Sims, who had been despatched from America a few days before the declaration of war to represent his country's Navy in Britain and maintain the closest touch with the Admiralty, and who landed at Liverpool on 9 April, has recorded that till then he had no idea of the gravity of the situation. Indeed, it seemed likely to him from what he had read that the war would end in a British victory before the United States could exert any important influence on its outcome. His first few days in London were enough to show him clearly that there was no foundation for this confidence. 'The Germans, it now appeared, were not losing the war – they were winning it.' The documents shown him at the Admiralty 'disclosed the astounding fact that unless the appalling destruction of merchant tonnage which was then taking place could be materially checked, the unconditional surrender of the British Empire would inevitably take place within a few months'.

On the day after he landed Sims called on his old acquaintance Jellicoe, whom he had first met in China in 1901 and to whom he had since been drawn closer by the specialist interest in gunnery which the two men shared.†

> The admiration which I had then conceived for the Admiral's intelligence and character I have never lost [he wrote in 1920].
> ... I had known him in his own home with his wife and babies, as well as on shipboard among his men, and had observed at close hand the gracious personality which had the power to draw everyone to him and made him the idol both of his own children and the officers and jackies of the British fleet. Simplicity and directness were his two most outstanding points;
> ... success had only made him more quiet, soft spoken and

* Figures were not deliberately falsified, but the tonnage of ships sunk was not given.
† See above, p. 40.

unostentatiously dignified. . . . Of all the men I have ever met, there have been none more approachable, more frank, and more open-minded. . . . His smooth-shaven face, when I met him that morning . . . was as usual calm, smiling and imperturbable. One could never divine his thoughts by any outward display of emotion. Neither did he give any signs that he was bearing a great burden though it is not too much to say that at this moment the safety of the British Empire rested chiefly upon [his] shoulders.

After an exchange of greetings Jellicoe took from a drawer a record of tonnage losses for the last few months, showing that they were three or four times as large as those published in the press. The astounded American scanned them and voiced his consternation.

'Yes', said Jellicoe, as quietly as if he were discussing the weather. 'It is impossible for us to go on with the war if losses like this continue.'

'What are you doing about it?' asked Sims.

'Everything that we can. We are increasing our anti-submarine forces in every possible way. . . . We are building destroyers, trawlers, and other like craft as fast as we can. But the situation is very serious and we shall need all the assistance we can get.'

'It looks as though the Germans were winning the war', Sims remarked.

'They will win, unless we can stop these losses – and stop them soon.'

'Is there no solution for the problem?'

'Absolutely none that we can see now', was Jellicoe's quiet answer. He then described the work of destroyers and other anti-submarine craft, but according to Sims he showed no confidence that they would be able to control the destruction which the U-boats were wreaking.

Such at least was Sims's account of the interview.[27] According to Jellicoe fifteen years later, what he himself said was that the counter measures then being devised could not be immediately successful since time was needed for them to take effect, after which he urged Sims to do his utmost to obtain fast small craft from the United States.[28] The discrepancy is understandable where the unaided recollections in later years of two elderly men

are involved; it is also unimportant. What did matter was that
Sims, a man after Jellicoe's own heart who was at once taken
unreservedly into the Admiralty's confidence, threw himself without hesitation into the work of co-operation and of awakening
his own Government and Service chiefs to the urgent need.
Supplied by Jellicoe with the secret figures which showed the full
seriousness of the situation, he telegraphed these to the United
States and pressed the Navy Department with all his force to send
the much-wanted vessels quickly. On 13 April the Admiralty was
notified from Washington that six American destroyers would be
sent forthwith and more would follow soon. On 4 May this first
instalment of destroyers arrived at Queenstown to join Admiral
Bayly's command, but as yet they were almost literally a drop in
the ocean. The feeling prevailed that the answer to the submarine
had not been found, or did not lie among the methods favoured by
the Admiralty. Sims talked with Balfour, Carson and other
members of the Cabinet, who in assessing the situation for his
benefit repeated practically everything that Jellicoe had said. The
American Ambassador, Walter H. Page, a good friend of the
country to which he was accredited, told him sadly: 'What we are
facing is the defeat of Great Britain'. One man took an optimistic
attitude – Lloyd George. Whenever Sims, like Jellicoe before him,
tried to impress him with the gravity of the position he always
refused to acknowledge it. 'Oh yes, things are bad', he would say
with a smile and a wave of his hand. 'But we shall get the best of
the submarines – never fear!'[29]

According to Sir Maurice Hankey, Lloyd George had been convinced that convoy was the solution ever since the breakfast
gathering of 13 February to which Hankey had read his paper.
The Prime Minister, however, could not at the moment go all
out to secure its adoption, since he was at loggerheads with the
high command of the Army in the persons of Haig and Robertson
and could not afford a dispute with the Admiralty as well. He
therefore did not bring the subject up again until after the entry
of the United States into the war had raised the ultimate prospect
of a welcome reinforcement of escort vessels; though in the meantime he had learnt during a visit to the Grand Fleet that Beatty
strongly favoured a policy of convoy.[30]

During March, however, it was realised at the Admiralty that
the belief that it was impossible to provide escorts had arisen partly

from a large miscalculation of the number of voyages requiring protection in the ocean trades. In the hope of discouraging the enemy, the totals of arrivals and departures of ships given in the Admiralty's weekly statements had been made to include the repeated calls of all coasters and short sea traders of 300 tons and upwards, with the result that they appeared to average about 2500 voyages a week each way. Certain sceptical officers of the Anti-Submarine Division had now set themselves to test and revise these figures, in consultation with the new Ministry of Shipping, which produced statistics showing the actual arrivals and departures in the ocean trades to be between 120 and 140 each week.[31] This revision, placed in Admiral Duff's hands, must have played its part in the change of attitude towards convoy which now gradually took place. That a genuine blunder had been made, by which the Admiralty became hoist with its own propaganda, has been challenged and the view has been advanced* that the authorities had not wanted figures which might prove the possibility of convoying the general trade. But while it can hardly be doubted that Jellicoe's bent of mind was basically conservative and that he was not always receptive to new ideas, or old ideas revived in new circumstances, especially when they were put forward by junior officers whom he perhaps considered rather pushing or brash, the implied suggestion that he and his colleagues placed the maintenance of their collective 'face' above the salvation of the country will not perhaps commend itself to many.

Be that as it may, in the light of the amended figures the position with regard to destroyers now became that between 20 and 30 of the 70 or more needed for a really comprehensive convoy system could be found immediately. Moreover, since it was generally agreed that if it were decided to institute convoy it would have to be done by degrees, especially for the Atlantic trade, and that some months would elapse before a complete system would be in operation, this shortfall was no compelling obstacle in itself. To cover the deficit there was the promise of American assistance,† plus the fifteen or so boats that British shipyards could probably produce by the end of July, but minus any losses. The immediate call could therefore just be met, and it was conceivable

---

* By Vice-Admiral K. G. B. Dewar in *The Navy from Within*, pp. 66–7.

† By the end of July 34 American destroyers were operating in British waters.

that the total number needed could be collected as the convoy organisation expanded and developed. It was something of a gamble; but over against it stood, or appeared to stand, the certainty of defeat.

When, therefore, Lloyd George raised the convoy question again at a meeting of the War Cabinet on 23 April with Jellicoe present, and quoted Beatty's views, Jellicoe replied that the matter was under consideration but the obstacle was still the shortage of destroyers, in spite of the prospect of American aid. He added that the trial of the system which Beatty had made in the Scandinavian convoys had not so far been wholly encouraging, since two vessels in separate convoys had already been torpedoed and sunk. On the same day he also presented a memorandum whose wording implied that he was still holding to the anti-submarine measures decided on four months earlier and did not yet contemplate any fundamental change in our system of defence.[32] Nevertheless (according at any rate to Jellicoe's recollection eleven years later, confirmed by Duff in a correspondence between them in 1928) it was on an evening just about then that Duff came to his room to tell him that the shipping losses had convinced him that a general system of convoy must be tried and it was agreed that as Director of the Anti-Submarine Division he should draw up a minute recommending this in detail.[33] On the 25th the War Cabinet again discussed the question of convoy and decided that the Prime Minister should visit the Admiralty on the 30th to investigate it further.[34] On the following day, however, Duff submitted his minute in favour of the adoption of convoy to Jellicoe.[35] The latter had meanwhile written somewhat pessimistically to his friend Admiral Hamilton at Rosyth on the 25th: 'I am rather afraid the convoy system on the east coast [the Scandinavian convoys] will fail for lack of destroyers. . . . There are no destroyers at all to carry it out on the Western Approaches, but some day I may be able to carry it out, and the arrangements for doing so are being prepared.'[36] The closing words may probably be taken as referring to the minute which Duff was preparing, though the use of 'some day' implies that Jellicoe was still unenthusiastic about the adoption of convoy and did not regard it as imminent. His above-mentioned paper to Carson, dated the 27th but presumably composed during the preceding days, gives the same impression by its belated and incidental reference to convoys. On the 27th, however, he gave his approval of Duff's minute, and on the same day arrangements were begun for a trial convoy home from Gibraltar.[37]

In later years it was sometimes asserted, particularly by Lloyd George in his *War Memoirs* with what amounts to a travesty of the facts, that it was the imminent prospect or threat of the Prime Minister's descent on the Admiralty which had led to this rather abrupt decision to adopt convoy.[38] Duff, however, in the correspondence alluded to above, denied flatly and emphatically that he had been influenced by any other consideration than the escalating shipping losses, and declared that he had been completely unaware that Lloyd George's visit on 30 April had any special connection with the submarine menace, being under the impression that the Prime Minister was coming to explore the possibility of a reorganisation of Admiralty administration in general – which was in fact Lloyd George's secondary object. Jellicoe, too, denied in his *The Submarine Peril*, published in 1934 as an attempted counterblast to some sections of the *War Memoirs*, that in giving his approval to Duff's minute he had been swayed by outside pressure;[39] but it is perhaps not quite beyond the bounds of possibility that despite making that statement in all good faith sixteen or seventeen years later he may in fact have been influenced, if only subconsciously, to accelerate a step that was already under consideration by the knowledge of the Prime Minister's main purpose which he possessed though Duff did not.

However this may be, when Lloyd George arrived at the Admiralty on the 30th the utmost harmony seems to have prevailed. He was informed that it had been decided to make an immediate trial of a convoy system and (according to Hankey) 'spent the whole day there very pleasantly, lunching with Jellicoe and his wife and four little girls [and] having a great flirtation with a little girl of three'.[40]

'A few weeks ago', Hankey wrote on 29 April, 'the Admiralty scouted the idea of convoy. Now they are undertaking it on their own initiative, but apparently want weeks to organise it, though this might have been done earlier.' Although he afterwards declared that 'however cautious the Admiralty [might] have been in adopting the system, they carried it out with the utmost energy and competence',[41] it is his first comment which in retrospect seems the more apt. The interval of seven weeks between the decision to make the experiment and the formal acceptance of a full plan for it proves pretty conclusively, if proof were needed, that although the adoption of convoy had been discussed before 26 April it had not been considered so imminent as to call for extensive preliminary preparations. The Gibraltar convoy decided upon on 27 April, indeed, left the Rock on 10 May and arrived at Plymouth on the 20th, having met no submarines and station-keeping having been satisfactory on the whole, so that the success of this first trial went far to silence misgivings on that point.[42] The American Navy Department, which had hitherto taken the same unfavourable view of convoy as the British Admiralty and now only agreed to a similar experiment with the pessimistic rider that it would be inadvisable to adopt the system wholesale, was compelled by this second experiment's success to change its views. But meanwhile it was not till 17 May that a committee of naval officers, with a representative from the Ministry of Shipping, was appointed by the Admiralty to draw up a complete scheme for a general system of convoy; and it was only on 6 June that it presented its report, which was approved by Jellicoe on the 11th and by Carson on the 15th. It is difficult, therefore, to acquit the Admiralty of continuing to drag its feet in this matter. Even so, its recommendations could only be put into force by instalments, as the necessary escorting forces became available. It was first decided to run a series of convoys from Hampton Roads in Virginia at four-day intervals. Then on 22 June the system was extended to ships sailing from Canadian ports, and on 6 July to those sailing from the northern ports of the United States, which were assembled at New York. On 20 July instructions were issued for regular convoys at four-day intervals from Gibraltar, and on the 31st this measure was extended to the South Atlantic. On 11 August outward convoys were commenced; and the system was applied to the Mediterranean, outward, on 3 October, and homeward on 7 November.[43]

The adoption of convoy, therefore, did not produce any immediate and obvious transformation. The situation remained critical until after August 1917. The problem of finding sufficient escort vessels continued well into the following year, despite the building programmes that were pressed forward in both Britain and the United States. Indeed, according to Sims, 'at no time until the Armistice . . . was any escort force strong enough to ensure entire safety'.[44] By the end of October 1917, however, 99 home-ward convoys comprising 1502 steamers had been brought in with a loss of only ten vessels torpedoed while actually in their convoy and fourteen sunk after being separated from it by bad weather or other causes. At the end of November 77 convoys had been escorted outwards with losses of approximately one-half of one per cent. It is true that in addition to the losses which were incurred on the unconvoyed routes while the system was being thus gradually introduced there were still many sinkings among ships proceeding to their ports of discharge after their convoy had reached its arrival base, or after dispersal. But on the other hand not only did the advance of the system progressively reduce losses, but once it had been put into general operation it began to increase the sinkings of U-boats, by forcing them to approach convoys in order to find victims and so giving the escorts the chance to counter-attack them (a tactical point which Jellicoe and the Admiralty had failed to appreciate). Thus although at the end of the year ships were still being lost faster than they could be replaced by building, and the toll taken of the German submarines was still below (though not far below) the figures of new deliveries, the situation in both respects was reversed early in 1918. Cause for anxiety and strain, indeed, persisted until the end of Jellicoe's tenure of office.[45] But well before it closed the chief objections urged against convoy had all been demonstrated to be unfounded, the confident German forecasts had been given the lie, the crisis of the spring and early summer was over, and never again – not even, surely, in the spring of 1918 – was the enemy to come so near to victory.

Vice-Admiral Reinhard Scheer, commanding the High Seas Fleet, 1916–18

Vice-Admiral Franz Hipper, commanding the Scouting Forces, 1913–18

Lady Jellicoe, from a photograph taken on her wedding day

8 First Sea Lord: Dismissal

WHEN Jellicoe came to the Admiralty, twenty-eight months of command of the Grand Fleet had already taken a heavy toll of his constitution and nerves. Nor did he have any chance of rest and recuperation before assuming what under the circumstances was an equally or even more vitally important responsibility. On the contrary, he had immediately fallen a victim to influenza, and on his own admission had started work afterwards while still weak, feeling overwhelmed from the start by the mass of business and disregarding the efforts of his doctors to make him go slow.[1] Within a month he was laid up in bed with neuritis, where Fisher (to whom he had telephoned to come and see him) found him 'deaf as a post' and 'very seedy but indomitable'.[2] At the beginning of June he was again forced to take a short rest.[3] Unfortunately he had found at the Admiralty the same over-concern with details that was his own besetting sin, and was far from being the man to correct it.

> High officials [wrote a critic who knew it from the inside] were overwhelmed with petty tasks which deflected their energies from more important matters. An enormous number of questions were referred to [it] which should have been answered by the men on the spot. . . . The enormous number of papers and telegrams passing through the various divisions laid a very heavy burden on Jellicoe and Oliver. Jellicoe in particular minuted in his own handwriting papers on every conceivable subject, many of them dealing with comparatively trivial and unimportant matters.[4]

Coming away one evening with Hankey from a dinner to some allied mission which he had been obliged to attend, he told his companion that he had still two hours' heavy work ahead of him and that that was his nightly lot.[5] Understandably enough under these circumstances, he resented the long hours which he was

M

forced to spend with the War Cabinet, whose prolonged debates he tended to regard as a waste of time as far as he was concerned. This impatience he may not always have managed to conceal, despite his former reputation for impassivity. Indeed, he spent part of the meeting of 25 April, when convoy was one of the subjects discussed, in writing a letter to a friend,[6] which can hardly have escaped notice even if it was done while matters were under debate with which he had little or no concern. Taken in conjunction with his pessimism, or what Lloyd George and others regarded as such,* this restiveness (if it was observed) must have contributed to prejudice ministers against him.

References to this burden of work and to his frequent attendance on the War Cabinet abound in his private correspondence, especially with Beatty – 'I have found it impossible to write before owing to pressure of work every day. War Councils take up *hours* of my time' . . . 'I am overwhelmed with work at present. War Councils waste half my time' . . . 'At present I have no time at all for exercise' . . . 'Excuse frantic haste. War Council waiting for me' . . . 'I am wasting time at a War Cabinet', and so on.[7] This correspondence with Beatty was at first almost an inversion of that which he had maintained with the Admiralty while he himself was Commander-in-Chief. Now it was he who took or wanted to take cruisers and destroyers from the Grand Fleet and Beatty who grumbled or objected, though not as much as Jellicoe had formerly done. When the surface raider *Moewe* broke out into the Atlantic towards the end of 1916 he provoked a strong protest by removing four ships of the Tenth Cruiser Squadron, whose task it was to patrol the northern exit from the North Sea, in order to take part in the unsuccessful hunt for her.[8] The prolonged absence of these ships impelled Beatty to write on 27 January in a style not unlike Fisher's:

> The 10th Cruiser Squadron is the one unit that could *win* us *the war*, if up to the fullest strength. . . . There are two things that are going to win or lose this war, and nothing else will affect it a damn. . . . The real crux lies in whether we blockade

* 'In the eyes of the ministers who exercised the supreme control [Jellicoe's] worst defect was his apparent pessimism [which was very irritating to], an incorrigible optimist like the Prime Minister.' Hankey, *Supreme Command*, ii, 645.

the enemy to his knees, or whether he does the same to us. Our blockade rests on the 10th Cruiser Squadron. The Admiralty says that the vessels [detached from it] are performing essential service. But I ask for them to perform *vital* service.[9]

He also urged 'mining on the largest scale, i.e. 80,000 mines as close as can be got to Heligoland', and criticised a proposed proclamation that a large area of the North Sea was 'dangerous to shipping',* on the ground that while that was presumably intended to be taken as meaning that it was mined, in actual fact so small a part of it could be mined that the proclamation amounted to a transparent bluff at which the enemy would only laugh. Although he had also written sympathetically: 'You are up against the biggest proposition that any man has had to tackle', Beatty's letter provoked an unusually tetchy and even waspish reply which clearly reflected the state of Jellicoe's health and nerves and was peppered with such phrases as 'I cannot agree with you . . .', 'Your view that you should lay mines close in is quite incorrect . . .', 'You have too exaggerated a view of the value of mines against submarines', 'Your ideas in regard to the facility with which mines or anything else can be produced in this country at the present time are far too optimistic', 'You must take it that I am working on what I believe to be the best information' and 'In regard to your remarks about the 10th Cruiser Squadron, it is not worth discussion whether in the Admiralty reply the words "vital service" should be substituted for "essential service". I do not myself see the difference'.[10]

Beatty, however, knew the strain under which Jellicoe was labouring and how to make allowances for it. Madden, too, was at hand to play the peacemaking intermediary, writing to his brother-in-law that Beatty seemed to have regretted making 'some suggestions to you (he did not say what) at which he thought you took exception. . . . I gathered that he was sorry he had added to your worries when he hoped to have helped you'.[11] For his part Beatty now showed himself understanding and accommodating about the destroyer problem, assuring Jellicoe that he fully appreciated his

* An area bounded by a line drawn from a point four miles west of the Jutland coast due west and then south-west to within a few miles of the Yorkshire coast, then back at an acute angle to a point seven miles from the Dutch coast near Terschelling, was so proclaimed on 30 January.

difficulties in providing for everything, and that if he could not do without some of the Grand Fleet destroyers of course he must have them; though in a later letter (one of the many which show that the differences in outlook and attitude between them were less than has often been supposed) he allowed himself to wonder 'what would happen if the enemy came out with the intention of engaging us in mortal combat . . . as he certainly would have 100 submarines so disposed as to render him the utmost assistance and we have to-day 37 destroyers here [Scapa], 14 at Rosyth!!!'[12] He also strongly criticised the Admiralty in a letter to Carson after a brief visit there in April: 'The impression left on my mind . . . was that there seemed to be a lack of concrete ideas and principles, that they were meeting troubles as they came, they were not foreseen, and cut and dried plans based on sound principles were lacking. . . . I know the Admiralty dislike intensely receiving suggestions, which makes them receive them in an antagonistic spirit and if they do adopt them, do so in a modified form. . . . We are not using the brains and energy of the youth of the Service.' He was careful to add, however; 'I wish to make it quite clear that I am not attacking the individual [presumably or primarily Jellicoe], but the system which has grown up and made such a state of affairs possible.' In his letters to his wife from May onwards he was even more outspokenly critical, though still in general terms; and the anniversary of Jutland moved him to write: 'As time goes by, one realises more clearly the opportunity that was missed, an opportunity that will never recur, and what would have been easy then will be infinitely more difficult in the future. . . . However I console myself with the thought that next time, if Fate is kind and gives us a next time, the battle fleet will have their chance.' It is evident, too, that any suggestion that the battle-cruisers' gunnery at Jutland had been poor acted upon him like a red rag on a bull.[13] In fact the mental wound which the battle had left on him seemed to fester rather than heal.

Outwardly at least, the correspondence between Jellicoe and Beatty seems to have regained a little of its former warmth in the spring and early summer of this year, though in Beatty's letters to his wife a faintly patronising note began to creep into his references to his former chief. His frequent adjurations to the older man to 'keep fit, whatever you do' nevertheless suggest that he was well aware how much Jellicoe's ability to cope with his task depended on the maintenance of his physical and nervous stamina; and he placed the tennis court at his London house at the latter's disposal for this purpose, although he was only rarely able to get away from work and make use of it. Jellicoe reciprocated with equally constant expressions of good wishes; and both men voiced their wish for a meeting, either at Rosyth or in London, but were prevented by various circumstances from achieving one.[14] It is, however, significant of the mutterings and rumblings of the beginning of the 'Jutland Controversy' and of the exaggerated rumours which may have begun to circulate about the relations of the two admirals that when the King visited the Grand Fleet in June Beatty was 'very careful to explain that my relations with Jellicoe are very friendly'.[15]

They were drawn together also by a feeling of common interest against the politicians, and by Beatty's sympathy with Jellicoe as criticism and intrigues began to mount up against him. According to Lord Beaverbrook, Lloyd George 'had lost faith in Carson, Jellicoe and even his Board of Admiralty' after what he regarded as his triumph in prevailing on them* to adopt the convoy system at the end of April.[16] Undoubtedly the Prime Minister – eupeptic, intensely vital, indomitable, ruthless, gifted with an unerring sense of what the moment demanded and 'swooping upon opportunity like a hawk' – was losing patience with a tired and over-conscientious man in rather poor health who could not delegate business, constantly overworked himself and always saw the black side of things clearly. But Beaverbrook, given to over-dramatising events, was not always the most reliable of authorities, and it is possible that this loss of faith in Jellicoe was a little more gradual. Hankey at any rate gives a different account,[17] according to which Lloyd George set himself on and after his visit to the Admiralty on 30 April, with Jellicoe's cordial agreement, to relieve the First Sea Lord of as much detail as possible. In particular, he realised that it was of paramount importance that he should be freed from having to devote a large part of his energy to questions of the supply of naval material, and decided that the best way to achieve this would be to appoint a highly competent businessman to supervise the whole matter of supply. He therefore immediately appointed Sir Eric Geddes, a railway tycoon who had recently

---

* Carson seems to have been prepared to give convoy a trial earlier than the admirals were, but was determined to keep in step with them.

been engaged in organising the transport behind the British front in France and Flanders as Director-General of Transportation and had won golden opinions from Sir Douglas Haig for his success in this work, to take supreme charge of all shipbuilding, not only for the Navy but also for the mercantile marine, as Controller. This appointment was greeted with enthusiasm by Jellicoe, who had accompanied Lloyd George, Lord Robert Cecil and General Sir William Robertson to a conference in Paris on 4 May and had taken the opportunity of both meeting Geddes and consulting Haig about him.[18] According to Jellicoe's later account, Geddes told him that he was prepared to accept the appointment on the understanding that he was assured of the First Sea Lord's support.[19] His experience in his railway work in France, he said, had shown him the difficulty of taking over functions previously performed by officers, and he could not have carried this work through without the strong backing he had received from Haig. Jellicoe assured him that he would give him the same support at the Admiralty and would do his best to smooth over any difficulties that might arise with the existing Admiralty officials. It was arranged that the posts of Controller and Third Sea Lord should now be separated, the latter continuing to be held by a naval officer; and Rear-Admiral Halsey, the Fourth Sea Lord, was promoted to fill it. To Beatty, Jellicoe wrote on the 10th: 'I expect great increase in rapidity of production from the change. Geddes is a superman, an excellent fellow and has the complete whiphand of L. G.' 'I am sorry you have had to introduce a civilian as Controller', replied Beatty more soberly, 'but am glad you have got such a good one as Geddes. I assume to be able to deal with the P.M. and Politicians it is essential to go outside the Navy. I sincerely hope it will turn out all right.'[20]

One of the several ways in which it did not do so was that it had the unforeseen effect of increasing Jellicoe's burden of work still further. The new arrangement meant the creation of a very large administrative staff for the purpose of speeding up the production of ships, ordnance material, mines and so forth. Many of the new personnel had no previous experience of the work and quite a number were civilians or former civilians, circumstances that led to occasional resentment and friction, which Jellicoe according to his promise had to assuage. It meant, too, that additional accommodation had to be found, the supervision of which he regarded as also coming within the terms of his pledge. All this threw additional labour on to his shoulders, at a time when the enemy's submarine campaign was still at its height.[21]

Carson, meanwhile, was more fully aware than Jellicoe of the storm that was gathering about them both. At a luncheon on 17 May in honour of the American Navy he barked defiance, declaring that he despised his critics, and going on: 'Whenever you read criticisms of my colleague Sir John Jellicoe, try to find out what is the origin of them. But after all it does not really matter. . . . Let them grumble and growl and let us get on with our work.'[22] Despite these bold words in public, however, he was neither wholly blind to the defects in the organisation of the Admiralty nor heedless of the advisability of doing something to silence or reduce criticism by reforming them. He therefore received favourably a proposal from Lloyd George which contained the germ of the subsequent Plans Division. During the Prime Minister's visit to the Admiralty on 30 April, he had discovered that none of the directors of sections working under Sir Henry Oliver (then still Chief of the War Staff) had the specific duty of looking ahead and working out policies, plans and preparations for various contingencies.[23] Lloyd George was also alive to the criticisms now being made that the change of régime had done nothing to correct the Admiralty's lack of offensive spirit, but rather the contrary; and early in June he summoned Captain Richmond, who (in private, at least) was one of the fiercest of the critics, to London from his service with the Grand Fleet in order to hear his views. Richmond, given *carte blanche* by the Prime Minister to speak quite frankly, urged that Jellicoe should be replaced as First Sea Lord by Vice-Admiral Sir Rosslyn Wemyss, who at that moment was being considered as Naval Commander-in-Chief in the Mediterranean.[24] Lloyd George, however, was apparently not yet inclined or at any rate ready to go to these lengths, and merely proposed the formation of an 'offensive' or planning section of the Operations Division. Taking up the idea, Carson sent Jellicoe a confidential memorandum on 7 June in which he stated that he had observed

that a good deal of criticism has lately been levelled against the Admiralty on the ground that no offensive operations . . . are from time to time undertaken; and in conversation with the

P.M. and other members of the War Cabinet it is clear to my mind that this criticism has given rise to a good deal of dissatisfaction in many quarters with the present administration of the Admiralty. . . . It is clear . . . that we ought to be able to silence it by being able to state positively that the possibility of taking the offensive at sea is continually under review by the Naval Staff, and that Staff plans worked out in detail are constantly being put forward and considered. There is an idea prevalent that the Naval Staff is so fully occupied in dealing with current work that they have not sufficient time to give to initiating offensive operations. I am so impressed with the amount of labour that day-to-day events impose on the Naval Staff that I am not convinced that there may not be some truth in this idea. I therefore propose that a special Section should be formed, under the Director of Operations, which will be concerned solely with preparing plans and examining proposals for offensive naval operations. . . . I think the Section should consist of two or three Captains, with a Commander. . . .[25]

Jellicoe's reaction to this proposal was unfavourable, both on its merits (or what he regarded as its lack of merits) and because he was aware of and resented some of the outside influences behind it. He may also have been aware that it had inside support at a junior level. Commander Dewar, then a comparative newcomer to the Operations Division, had suggested a few days previously to its Director, Captain Hope, the need for such a planning section. According to Dewar himself, at his first interview with Jellicoe about this time he was told that he had a reputation for independent opinions, 'and it was evident from his tone that he did not count this unto me for righteousness'.[26] It is not impossible, then, that Jellicoe may even have suspected that this able but rather prickly and perhaps pushing young officer, who was certainly in contact with Lloyd George a little later about the project, was the commander whom Carson and perhaps the Prime Minister had in mind as a member of the proposed section. To Carson he therefore replied stiffly:

I have been informed that the Prime Minister sent for Captain Richmond (I presume in connection with this proposition) and I presume that this was done at the instigation of Colonel Hankey. I do not make any comment on this interference with Admiralty administration by Colonel Hankey. . . . I would however observe that there appears to be some misconception as to whose business it should be to *initiate** offensive operations. The proper officers for this duty are the senior officers of the War Staff, including myself, the D.C.N.S. and the Director of Operations. Obviously our experience fits us better for this purpose than the experience of more junior officers. . . . The working out of *details of a plan** is of course another matter and is one for the proposed staff.

For this subordinate function, which was not what Lloyd George or apparently Carson had intended, he suggested that Captain Richmond, whose marked abilities he at least partly recognised, and subsequently other officers of Richmond's selection should be appointed to the Operations Division,† 'leaving the D.O.O., the D.C.N.S. and myself more time to study the possibilities of offensives. At the same time', he continued,

> I would remark that I have been considering possible offensives ever since the commencement of the war and I am fairly certain that there is no possible operation . . . which has not been considered a great many times. . . . In these circumstances it would be quite useless for a comparatively junior officer without a knowledge of available vessels to put forward proposals for an offensive. It would merely waste the time of the more senior members of the War Staff in examining these proposals.[27]

To Beatty he wrote more tersely:

> The six-monthly agitation for a 'vigorous naval offensive' is beginning and the First Lord has been got hold of by the agitators and wants me to start a special staff to consider offensive operations *only.** This means that I shall get more wild schemes produced for employing the Grand Fleet in southern waters . . . and I shall have to spend time which I can't afford in checking these schemes.[28]

He repeated these views, according to Lloyd George, at a meeting of the War Cabinet on 20 June. At the same meeting, his part

---

* Jellicoe's italics.
† Captain Richmond, however, was not appointed to the Plans Section which was created in July, though Commander Dewar was.

in which probably weakened his hold on the First Sea Lordship further, he expressed himself most pessimistically (in spite of the decision taken a few days earlier to adopt a general system of convoy) about the shipping situation and the German submarine campaign. It would be impossible for Britain to continue the war in 1918, he declared, unless the Flanders offensive now being planned could capture the U-boat bases at Ostend and Zeebrugge and clear the Belgian coast of the enemy.[29] A suggestion was made, and strongly urged by Lloyd George, that these bases could be put out of action by a naval bombardment alone, without aid from the Army; but from this Jellicoe categorically dissented, all the more emphatically since Admiral Bacon, after having been repeatedly frustrated by unsuitable weather, had recently bombarded both ports with light forces from Dover and Harwich without achieving very much success. Although Lloyd George remained unconvinced and tackled Beatty about the prospects of such a bombardment when he visited Rosyth soon afterwards, he found the Commander-in-Chief (whom Jellicoe had warned) as completely opposed to the idea as the latter had been. 'What we want now is closer communication . . .', Beatty wrote to his former chief, 'and between us we can knock out any hare-brained schemes. I will come down and see you if necessary, but we must collaborate. There can be no question of any difference of opinion between us. I feel that when we meet and talk things over we always agree, and we must present a broad front to these gentlemen with wild-cat schemes.'[30]

> I am just as anxious as yourself [Jellicoe replied on 30 June] to keep in the closest touch. . . . I have got myself much disliked by the Prime Minister and others. . . . I fancy there is a scheme on foot to get rid of me. The way they are doing it is to say I am too pessimistic. That is because I point out the necessity for concentration of forces on the submarine menace and the great danger of not being able to feed the country. . . . I expect it will be done by first discrediting me in the Press. . . . I've seen signs of it already. Of course, putting aside one's duty to the country, I should be delighted to go, and have done with all politicians, but if I am of use here in the opinion of the Navy I certainly should not volunteer to go. I am not conceited, nor ambitious in the least, but I believe I *am* of use here.[31]

By return Beatty wrote again, warmly and encouragingly:

I do not think you should permit yourself to be worried by what the intriguers set themselves to do. And you must stick at all costs to your intention of not volunteering to go; that would be fatal. Do not be goaded into any step of that kind, no matter what the Press or anybody else says. . . . If you ignore entirely their insinuations and murmurings you are in a very strong position. . . . If we keep together and have plenty of opportunities to discuss the many questions I have no fear we could improve matters and defeat the manoeuvres of the intriguers. . . . Keep yourself fit and damn the papers and the critics. When they get more than you can bear send them up here.[32]

Among those who had been most unfavourably impressed by Jellicoe's pessimistic declaration at the War Cabinet meeting on 20 June was Sir Douglas Haig, the Commander-in-Chief of the British forces in France and Flanders, who had now become convinced that the Admiralty was not safe in his hands. According to a statement by Lloyd George in his *War Memoirs* it was a conversation with Haig in the early summer of this year which decided him that changes must be made there, and although this statement has been challenged and may perhaps still need some discounting it fits in well with the part which the publication of Haig's private papers has revealed him as playing during the next ten days in the moves that drove first Carson and then eventually Jellicoe out of the Admiralty. When he had met Jellicoe for the first time in December 1916 he had liked very much what he saw of him, but (strong in the citadel of his own self-confidence) had recorded in his diary even then that he would not look on him as a man of great power or decision of character. Most or all of their few subsequent contacts had occurred when both were summoned to the councils of the War Cabinet, where the gloomy tone of Jellicoe's pronouncements had led Haig to describe him privately to his wife as an old woman. After the meeting on the morning of 20 June* at which Jellicoe had struck so alarmist a note (exaggerated in the account in Haig's diary, which represents him as stating without qualification that Britain could not go on with the war), the Field-Marshal had called on Geddes at the Admiralty in the afternoon and found him 'most anxious about the state of affairs' there. According to Haig, he declared that Carson was very tired and left everything to his

* See above, p. 186.

admirals, of whom only Halsey was fit for his post, while Jellicoe was 'feeble to a degree and vacillating'. At the same time Geddes 'meant to be loyal to his colleagues', so that 'it was difficult to know how to act'. They agreed that Haig should do his best to arrange for Geddes to see Lloyd George and put before him 'the whole position of affairs'. On the 25th Haig attended another meeting of the War Cabinet, where he found opportunities of speaking separately to both Lord Curzon and the Prime Minister about 'the seriously inefficient state of the Admiralty'. 'Both', he recorded, 'seemed much perturbed already', and the latter asked him and Geddes to breakfast on the following morning. There, with no others present at first, the three discussed the state of the Admiralty, Geddes giving his views much as he had expressed them to Haig five days earlier. Lloyd George 'seemed much impressed' and 'decided something must be done at once'.[33] This impression of the Premier's reaction which Haig formed may perhaps profitably be read in the light cast by Hankey's description of Lloyd George's practice, before undertaking a difficult or invidious task, of obtaining the views of 'the most diverse people, each of whom would as likely as not be under the impression that he was the only confidant of the Prime Minister on the subject'.[34]

At this stage Lloyd George sent for Lord Milner, who as the War Cabinet Minister most directly concerned with the increase of food production at home and with those shipping priorities which fixed the amount and kind of imports that were brought into the country was already critical of Carson and the Admiralty. The replacement of Jellicoe and two or three members of the Board was then discussed, according to Haig, and Lloyd George finally announced that he was firmly decided to take some immediate action to improve matters, but uncertain as to what was the best decision to take at present. Later in the day Milner wrote to the Prime Minister advising that Geddes should be made First Lord and Carson compensated with a seat in the War Cabinet, where his gifts of counsel would make him very useful. 'In that case', Milner continued,

> with a really first-rate administrator at the head of the Board, the great requisite in the First Sea Lord would be courage and knowledge of men, and intimate acquaintance with the best

men in the Service and a determination to bring them on and put them into their right places regardless of seniority and red tape. Such a First Sea Lord can be found more easily than a naval man who is a great administrator. That quality must be imported from outside.[35]

It was perhaps not a bad description of the man who eventually succeeded Jellicoe, Sir Rosslyn Wemyss.

Milner's recommendations were supported by Curzon and Bonar Law, and the need of change was also strongly urged by the Controller of Shipping, Sir Joseph Maclay. At this juncture, with the general adoption of convoy only just being resolved on and losses still very high, Maclay was greatly perturbed by what he considered the Admiralty's failure to cope with the peril. On 28 June he wrote to the Prime Minister:

> . . . It has come to my knowledge this morning that private meetings are being held of shipmasters and others to consider the position, and there is a danger that unless something is done in connection with the Admiralty we shall have these men refusing to go to sea. . . . I am led to believe that confidence in the Admiralty has pretty well gone.[36]

It was at this point that Lloyd George's above-mentioned visit to the Fleet at Rosyth took place, in the opening days of July. It seems that he made use of this opportunity to probe for discontent with the Admiralty, and he is said* even to have sounded more than one flag officer about his willingness to take over the First Sea Lordship if offered it. A rumour (probably groundless) also somehow arose about this time that Prince Louis of Battenberg (now the Marquis of Milford Haven) might be recalled from his enforced retirement to resume the position. On his return south the Prime Minister next took the precaution of 'clearing his yardarm' by an interview on 5 July with the King's secretary, Lord Stamfordham, who reported to His Majesty that he was contemplating replacing Carson by Geddes and perhaps removing Jellicoe, since the latter was too pessimistic and 'apt to get "cold feet" if things did not go quite right'.[37] After some further days of hesitation and a prod from Milner on the 16th Lloyd George

---

* By Lord Charles Beresford in a letter of 16 August to Jellicoe. Add. MS 49037, ff. 51–4.

proceeded to implement the first part of what might with some justice be called the Milner Programme on the following day by kicking Carson upstairs into the War Cabinet and promoting Geddes into his place. Both the Premier and the new First Lord, however, seem to have baulked at the second part of the programme, feeling that it might not be advisable after all to make a clean sweep of the heads of the Admiralty by dismissing Jellicoe too, lest it should provoke an outburst of opposition that might seriously damage Geddes's prospects of a successful administration. Instead it was decided to buttress him and ease his burden by a rearrangement of offices that would also make it possible to get rid of Burney and perhaps Oliver. The first idea was to replace the former as Second Sea Lord by a younger and abler man in better health. But since the man chosen was Sir Rosslyn Wemyss, whom Captain Richmond had already urged Lloyd George to put in Jellicoe's place, it is difficult to avoid the suspicion that the Premier was now making a preliminary move that would at least facilitate his taking that advice if in due course he decided to do so. A younger son of an ancient and distinguished Scottish family, Wemyss had married the daughter of a diplomat, Sir Robert Morier, had moved much in high society, and possessed a good deal of knowledge of Europe and European politics. He had also an extensive acquaintance with the Mediterranean, where he had served in pre-war days under Lord Charles Beresford, whom he had liked and admired, though he had come later to deplore the way in which 'Charlie B.' in his feud with Fisher had dragged the Navy into politics. From this feud he had held himself aloof as far as possible, though he regarded Fisher, while recognising the value and necessity of his reforms, as otherwise a menace to the Navy because of his dictatorial methods, his ruthless bearing down of all opposition, his blatant favouritism and vindictive treatment of officers who did not see eye to eye with him. To Jellicoe, as a product – though a worthy product – of that favouritism, Wemyss could not perhaps feel closely drawn, but he was too decent and friendly a soul to regard him in consequence with any dislike, much less jealousy. Sociable, courteous, gay and talkative, known not only to his wide circle of friends but to the whole Navy as 'Rosy', he was not a great man, but he had a good deal of energy for work and some talent for organisation. During the war he had been naval commander-in-chief in the last stages of the

Dardanelles operation, and had pressed strongly, in conjunction with Commodore Roger Keyes, for a renewed attempt to force the Straits with ships. Subsequently he had held the East Indies command, from which he was just being transferred to the command-in-chief in the Mediterranean. Geddes now seized the opportunity of a visit which he made to Rosyth immediately after assuming his new office to ask Keyes (who by then was serving in the Grand Fleet as a rear-admiral) his opinion of him. Keyes replied that if Geddes wanted someone to conceive brilliant strategic enterprises he did not think that was in Sir Rosslyn's line, but if he wanted someone who would get the right sort of people about him, back them through thick and thin, accept any amount of responsibility and never get rattled or worried, Wemyss was his man.[38]

When, after other arrangements had been made for the Mediterranean command by the appointment of Vice-Admiral Gough-Calthrope, Wemyss arrived at the Admiralty in September however, he himself suggested an alternative and in his view a better arrangement. As things stood, if the First Sea Lord was absent from the Admiralty through ill-health (as Jellicoe had been, more than once) or for any other reason the whole burden of the naval war devolved automatically on the Second Sea Lord, whose duties did not allow him time to study most of the matters on which he might thus suddenly find himself called to give decisions. Wemyss therefore advised the First Lord that it would be better to leave the Second Sea Lord to his departmental duties, appointing (since Burney had already been removed)* someone junior to himself, and to make his own appointment an additional one with functions confined to staff work. The post of Deputy First Sea Lord was accordingly created for him, and Vice-Admiral Sir H. L. Heath was made Second Sea Lord.[39] 'I shall like Wemyss here', wrote Jellicoe to Beatty (after expressing his strong sympathy for his old friend Burney): 'He is such a nice fellow to work with.'[40] Oliver survived, though the event proved that both he and Jellicoe were living on borrowed time henceforward.†

Meanwhile important questions of strategy were falling to be

* He was appointed C-in-C, Rosyth (Coast of Scotland), in succession to Sir Frederick Hamilton on the latter's death in the following October.

† Vice-Admiral Oliver was transferred from the Admiralty to a seagoing command soon after Jellicoe's dismissal.

debated. The submarine menace still loomed very large. Our methods of attacking U-boats were not so far meeting with more success than before, while the adoption of convoy was as yet incomplete and its results were not fully apparent. What was under consideration was whether some bold and sweeping plan of war could be devised which would prove a final remedy and thus provide an answer to the demands from several quarters for a more offensive naval policy. Churchill, who had returned to the Government as Minister of Munitions during the Cabinet reshuffle of which Carson's removal from the Admiralty had been the main feature, once more put forward proposals for attacks on Heligoland or Borkum or Sylt, as well as for sealing up the mouths of the German North Sea rivers by sinking blockships in order to prevent the passage of submarines. Jellicoe drew up a memorandum which began by commenting adversely on these proposals. He rejected the idea of attacking the islands (as he had done twice before), and pointed out that while the sealing of the enemy's North Sea ports would certainly somewhat reduce the submarine threat by making the U-boats use Kiel and the Sound and Great Belt as their route out and home, the only complete solution would be to block this route also. This, he continued, could not be done except by maintaining a blockading force off the exits from the Baltic; which would be possible only when the High Seas Fleet had been somehow disposed of or by the use of a base in the Kattegat where a fleet could be kept that was capable of dealing with anything which might be sent against our blockading forces. All this would be an operation of great magnitude requiring the employment of a very large part of the combined naval resources of the Allies, including so many of their light forces that the convoy system would have to be dropped again. Hence if the operation failed to block the German ports on both the Baltic and North Seas Britain would be very much worse off than before. In the latter part of the memorandum, however, with a slight and not altogether consistent change of tone, he declared that his previous remarks should not be taken as meaning that Churchill's general idea of an offensive ought to be vetoed, since if the current measures against submarines failed the country would be faced by the alternatives of 'dealing with the menace at its root or concluding a peace other than we desire'. The outlines of a plan for sealing the enemy's ports, he stated, were therefore

Admiral Sir John Jellicoe at the time of his First Sea Lordship, 1917

In the nets

Golfing in New Zealand

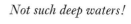

One Lord on donkey

Some of Lord Jellicoe's relaxations in later life

being prepared. Whether because of the semi-hiatus between the two parts of the paper, or the reiteration towards its close of the possibility of defeat, he was asked by Geddes not to send it to the War Cabinet.[41]

As Captain S. W. Roskill has said,* Jellicoe's minutes and papers of the latter part of 1917 'certainly show little vigour or imagination', and are clear evidence that the strain upon him was wearing down his powers. He was caught in a vicious circle; declining powers led to more criticism, and this criticism contributed further to the strain. Even his handwriting deteriorated, and it was not long after this that he produced a paper (on the reorganisation of the air services leading to the formation of the Royal Air Force†) which was so lacking in clarity that Geddes endorsed it 'Better not use this argument'.

The weakness of this latter memorandum was particularly unfortunate in view of the importance of its subject. Attempts to set up administrative machinery designed to reduce the confusion and duplication between the Royal Naval Air Service and the Royal Flying Corps (controlled respectively by the Admiralty and the War Office) and to improve their co-ordination had hitherto proved unsatisfactory. A committee created in July under the chairmanship of the South African statesman General Smuts had reported in favour of the formation of a single unified air force – a recommendation of the highest value and importance for the future, but marred by the Committee's failure to appreciate the special requirements of naval aviation. When its report came up for discussion the sea officers of the Admiralty argued (though with little aid from Jellicoe's ineffective paper) for the retention of the Royal Naval Air Service till the end of the war and the adequate recognition of these naval needs in any subsequent merger. But though Geddes spoke to the brief they provided before the War Cabinet on 23 August, the presentation of their case was handicapped by a number of largely irrelevant factors. The Admiralty's prestige had been weakened and its weight in counsel lowered by the recent lack of any spectacular success in the naval war and by its slowness in adopting convoy; the rift between its

* In his article, 'The Dismissal of Admiral Jellicoe' in *Journal of Contemporary History*, i, No. 4 (Oct. 1966), p. 72.

† 'Remarks on a Scheme of an Imperial Air Policy', 14 August 1917. Adm. 116/1806.

N

civilian and naval members was developing;* Lloyd George did not rate it high; and the whole question of a united air force had become entangled in political and strategic questions which had nothing to do with the proper development and use of the new arm. Daylight raids on London by German aeroplanes had caused consternation and alarm, and the Premier was anxious to take any step which promised to win him public support or to break the deadlock on the Western Front (under whose Commander-in-Chief a number of squadrons of the R.N.A.S. had already been placed). The result was that the War Cabinet brushed aside the Admiralty's hesitations and reservations and accepted all the Smuts Committee's main proposals. On 2 February 1918 the Royal Air Force was established by Order in Council. 'It was to take 20 years to rectify the failure . . . to convince the Smuts Committee and the War Cabinet of the specialised needs of naval aviation, and it is no exaggeration to say that its repercussions made themselves felt with most serious effect through the Second World War.'[42]

Meanwhile among those who favoured a more offensive naval policy were the American naval chiefs, Admirals Benson and Mayo, who were respectively Chief of Operations of the U.S. Navy and Commander-in-Chief of its Atlantic Fleet. Conscious of their limited war experience, however, they did not feel sufficiently sure of themselves to press the question too hard. Soon after the United States entered the war its Navy Department had sought the Admiralty's views on the possibility of establishing a mine barrage across the northern exit from the North Sea, between the Shetlands and Bergen. Such a barrage would be an obstacle to submarines using the Kattegat route as well as to those coming from the German North Sea ports. Moreover the enemy would be unable to sweep up the mines, as he was sweeping those laid in the Heligoland Bight, owing to the distance of the barrage from his bases. On the other hand the difficulties of the project were the great depth of water in which many would have to be moored, the very large number of patrol craft that would be needed to force submarines to dive into that part of the minefield which was safe for surface vessels, the problem of preventing them from evading it by passing within Norwegian territorial waters, and above all

* Geddes had just made a change in its Secretaryship, appointing Sir Oswin Murray in place of Sir Graham Green.

the immense number of mines which would be required. On the last ground particularly, and also on that of shortage of patrol craft, the Admiralty had replied that the scheme was impractciable for at least 9 to 12 months.[43] The Navy Department now asked that an inter-Allied naval conference, which was shortly to be held in London and which Admiral Mayo would attend, should consider methods of taking the offensive among other matters of mutual concern. Jellicoe's view, which Sims appears to have shared, was that the American higher command was insufficiently aware of the realities of the situation. Nevertheless he ordered a committee of the Naval Staff to examine the possibility of blocking the mouths of the German rivers, instructing it to proceed on the assumption that we intended to seal up the enemy's ports somehow and that its business was to work out how this could be done. The spirit in which he did so, however, emerges from a letter written to Beatty on 31 July:

> I have formed . . . a special committee . . . to work out a plan of blocking the Germans in. Mayo . . . is coming over here soon to a conference, and the U.S. Navy Board keep on harping on an offensive. One cannot see the difficulties clearly except by having a regular plan of the operations systematically worked out. . . . We *may* find it a feasible proposition, though I don't think we shall, but at any rate I will get it worked out. It would help greatly if you would get a committee on to the same thing.[44]

The committee of the Naval Staff reported unanimously that an attempt to block up the rivers was not to be recommended. Beatty did not appoint a committee, but asked Madden to examine both the questions of blocking the rivers and of a North Sea barrage, which he did exhaustively, producing a detailed report to the effect that the former was quite impossible and the latter impracticable under existing conditions. Beatty in a covering letter agreed with both conclusions, though he reiterated his former advocacy* of a barrage closer in across the Heligoland Bight.[45]

At the Conference which met on 4 and 5 September and was also attended by representatives of the French, Italian, Russian and Japanese navies, Admiral Mayo explained that he came with

---

* See above, p. 179.

no definite instructions, but in order to learn how the American Navy could best assist and co-operate with those of the Allies, particularly in dealing with the submarine threat. Jellicoe then set out the two alternative plans which had already been considered. The first, the immense blocking operation against all the German harbours in the North Sea and the Baltic, would, he explained, require 40 old battleships and 43 old cruisers for use as blockships. These it would not be beyond the Allies' combined power to provide, but the expenditure of so many cruisers for this purpose would hamstring the convoy system which was just being developed. Since the Allied delegates were not prepared to face this, the proposal was allowed to drop. The second alternative, the North Sea barrage, Jellicoe estimated would require 100,000 mines, which would not be available for some considerable time, even with American assistance. The conference accepted this alternative in principle but resolved that until such time as it could be implemented attention should be devoted to the improvement and extension of the existing minefields in the Heligoland Bight and the Straits of Dover.[46] On 22 September Jellicoe approached the American Navy Department for the aid that the barrage plan necessitated, and was informed generously that it was duly ordering 100,000 mines from its contractors. In the event, work on the Northern Barrage began in March 1918.

Jellicoe also took advantage of Admiral Mayo's visit to discuss with him a matter which he had already raised with Admiral Sims, the desirability of a small force of American battleships being sent to join the Grand Fleet. He took up the point again with Admiral Benson, who came to Britain in November, and as a result four American battleships under Rear-Admiral Hugh Rodman arrived in British waters for this purpose early in December. On all occasions Jellicoe's relations with the American admirals were uniformly cordial. What perhaps it would not be proper to describe as a lighter side of Mayo's visit was that he accompanied Jellicoe and Bacon in the destroyer *Broke*,* flying his flag, to witness a bombardment of Ostend by a monitor. The flag was afterwards presented to him as a souvenir of the first occasion on which an

---

* This was perhaps not the most tactful choice of ship, since her name commemorated the captain of the British frigate *Shannon*, which fought and took the American *Chesapeake* in a single-ship engagement during the Anglo-American war of 1812–14.

American admiral had been under fire in a British ship. In addition to his formal expressions of thanks he wrote privately to Jellicoe before he left Britain at the beginning of October: 'Your patience, openness, courtesy and continual kindness have impressed me very much and you may always number me among your admirers and, I trust you will permit, your devoted friends.' Benson also wrote appreciatively of 'the most open frankness on the part of yourself and the officers of your Service'. Sims, whose ideas matched Jellicoe's so closely, except that he was convinced sooner and more completely that convoy was the way of salvation, had been invited during the summer to attend the daily meetings of the naval members of the operations side of the Admiralty, where his co-operation was of great value; and Jellicoe also broached to Benson the idea that experienced American officers should come over to work in various sections of the Admiralty, where they could place the views of the Navy Department before their British colleagues and transmit back to Washington the appreciation of the situation they had gained. Benson agreed after some discussion, and the first officers seconded for this duty arrived before the end of 1917.[47]

By the time of the conference and of Mayo's visit the arrival of Wemyss to take up his duties had served as a signal for Geddes to press for a reorganisation of the Admiralty which would both improve its administration and make the newcomer's deputyship to Jellicoe an effective reality. Hitherto the new First Lord had walked rather warily, knowing little of the Navy at the outset and having had no political experience, but he now produced a memorandum expressing his opinion that the duties and responsibilities of the Naval Staff and of the Board as a whole should be more clearly defined.[48] The departmental responsibility of each member of the Board, he pointed out, was not sufficiently precise, nor was it anywhere laid down what categories of business should come to the Board as a whole for consideration. Both he and Jellicoe then proceeded to formulate schemes of reorganisation.[49] These agreed in recommending the division of the Board into two committees, for operations and *matériel* or maintenance respectively, and in proposing that the whole Board should meet at least once a week, as required, to discuss important questions affecting both sides. Each also made clear that members of one committee were by no means to be precluded from attending meetings of the other when matters affecting or interesting them were being discussed; though Geddes's memorandum went further by specifically emphasising that the Deputy First Sea Lord, besides being a member of the Operations Committee, should as far as possible make a practice of coming to the meetings of the Maintenance Committee too. In both plans the whole organisation of the Admiralty was correspondingly divided, more distinctly than before, into operational and maintenance sides under the two committees. Nor does there seem to have been any serious difference or debate over the assignment of shipbuilding, armaments, stores, works, finance, the air service and questions of personnel and discipline to the maintenance side. On the operational side there was again agreement on placing the directors of trade, mercantile movements and mine-sweeping, as well as the Anti-Submarine Division, under the superintendence of the Assistant Chief of the Naval Staff. Where the two schemes differed was that in Geddes's proposal the controversial Plans Section of the Operations Division, which had been established in July, was raised to the status of a separate division; the Intelligence Division was divided into two parts, dealing respectively with general intelligence and intelligence affecting naval operations; and a new Division of Training was introduced. Moreover (and this was the crux of the whole matter) the new Divisions of Plans and Training and the section dealing with intelligence affecting naval operations, which were to take over what Geddes described as 'the duties that have hitherto in the main fallen to the same hard-worked staff which deals daily with the immense amount of written and telegraph work involved in naval operations', were in his intention to be the special province of the newly arrived Deputy First Sea Lord, leaving only Operations, Signals and General Intelligence to constitute the jurisdiction of Oliver as Deputy Chief of the Naval Staff. In this way, Geddes concluded, Wemyss, attending both committees,

> would be daily in touch with the operations and with naval strategy and policy, and will then be able . . . to relieve the First Sea Lord on an emergency. It will be his particular duty to keep in close touch with the Maintenance Committee and also with the various Commanders-in-Chief. He will be free from daily routine work, and I hope that these new groups of

carefully selected officers [the two new departments and the sub-department which he proposed Wemyss should control] will form a body by whom new problems and solutions will be constantly under consideration.

Jellicoe's main overt objection was to the proposed separate Plans Division. In his view planning should remain under the control of the Operations Division, since he held that 'it was undesirable for a body of officers not working under the authority of those in close touch with the daily operations of the Fleet to put forward plans for operations which necessarily involved the use of the same vessels and material, as such a procedure must inevitably lead to impracticable suggestions and consequent waste of time'.[50] He cannot, however, have viewed with equanimity the proposed transfer to Wemyss of effective control over a considerable and important part of the work of the Admiralty, which was undoubtedly the First Lord's main aim. The outcome of the 'considerable discussion and some difference of opinion' which followed was that Jellicoe outwardly lost on the first issue but recovered some ground in practice, while on the second he won a pyrrhic victory. A separate Plans Division was established, but both it and the whole of Intelligence were placed with Operations and Signals under the oversight of Oliver, leaving Wemyss with only the new Training and Staff Duties Division directly under him. Jellicoe also issued instructions that the Director of the Plans Division (Wemyss's friend Rear-Admiral Keyes, who had been brought down from the Grand Fleet to the post) should be in close touch with the Director of the Operations Division (Rear-Admiral Hope) before submitting any proposals to Oliver or himself.[51]

The barbed darts of newspaper critics were now beginning to get under Jellicoe's skin. Lord Northcliffe's *Daily Mail* in particular made from August onwards something like a dead set at the Admiralty administration, and its prejudiced and vindictive attacks rose to a climax in the latter part of October after what it called 'the North Sea Affair' of the 17th of that month. In this, a convoy of twelve merchantmen bound from Bergen to Lerwick in the Shetlands with two escorting destroyers was attacked by two of the latest German cruisers, the destroyers were sunk in a hopeless battle against odds, and all but two of the merchantmen were destroyed. The *Daily Mail* declared that the Admiralty, besides not having sufficient 'intelligent initiative' to cope with the submarine menace, had shown itself incapable of using the naval forces competently enough to prevent what it described as this 'grievous humiliation', for which those responsible 'should be punished'. It went on to assert that 'the High Command ashore' stood indicted by the unanimous opinion of the country that it lacked the necessary energy of attack and that the 'overwhelming force' of the Navy was being inefficiently used. Pointing out that the officer who had commanded in the Battle of Jutland was now First Sea Lord, it compared him to General McClellan who had been removed from his command during the American Civil War for what it not quite accurately called incompetence.* These diatribes provoked Jellicoe to seek the highest legal opinion, that of the Attorney-General Sir F. E. Smith (later Lord Birkenhead), on whether official government action might not be taken. Smith, however, held that while a prosecution under the Defence of the Realm Act would probably succeed it would be highly inexpedient, in view of the need for secrecy about Admiralty war measures, to make them the subject of a case at issue in a civil court.[52] The idea of a prosecution was duly dropped, but Jellicoe received a number of letters from public personages such as Asquith and Lord Charles Beresford expressing sympathy with him over these attacks, 'If I may offer a word of advice', wrote Asquith, '. . . do not worry about the silly malignities of the worst section of the Press. I know how big they seem, and how little they really are.'[53]

The sands, however, were running out. As the *Official History of the War* puts it: 'Great as were Sir John Jellicoe's powers, and admirable as were his devotion and endurance, there was among those who met him frequently at the council table no doubt that the strain was bearing hard upon him and could not be further prolonged with justice to him or advantage to the Service'.[54] On 18 November he penned for the War Cabinet another of those papers which might be described either as pessimistic or realistic according to the point of view. In this he returned to the question of destroyers which was always one of his main preoccupations, emphasising once more the vital need of enough of these craft to screen our capital ships, and coming to the conclusion that

---

* McClellan, who was a first-rate organiser, was slow and over-cautious rather than incompetent in the field.

at the moment the demand exceeded the supply by ninety.[55] Occasions of friction with Geddes also grew frequent. Jellicoe considered that the organisation which the latter had set up when Controller for directing the building of naval and merchant vessels was failing to produce better or even as good results as the previous organisation in the hands of naval officers and Admiralty officials, and told him so on more than one occasion. Even more productive of trouble between them was Geddes's attitude to and treatment of flag-officers. The First Lords of the previous generation – Lord Spencer, Goschen, Lord Northbrook, Lord George Hamilton and others – had invariably treated the naval chiefs with the same deference and courtesy with which they themselves were treated. This tradition, a trifle damaged before the war but repaired by Balfour and in his bluff and blunt way by Carson, was alien to Geddes's experience. He was accustomed to give orders and to speak his mind, without too much concern for the courtesies and customs that smooth the asperities of life. As Jellicoe felt obliged to tell him, he regarded the Sea Lords as subordinates and not colleagues, and when any of them retorted in kind to his own brusqueness he resented it. Thus he took exception to Jellicoe's recommending Admiral Duff for a K.C.B. on the ground that he did not like his manner or the wording of some of his minutes, and was told by Jellicoe that Duff was being recommended for his services and not his manner. Again, after a disappointingly in-conclusive action in the Heligoland Bight on 17 November between cruisers and light forces on both sides, which led to Rear-Admiral Napier who commanded the British cruisers being required to explain his actions and inactions, Geddes leapt to the conclusion that Napier was at fault and that Beatty as C-in-C was shielding him. Jellicoe had to tell him that this was unjust and wrong and that he must await Napier's explanation, with which in fact the Admiralty was reasonably satisfied. Furthermore, when on 12 December a second Norwegian convoy was surprised and destroyed in circumstances which caused a good deal of comment, Geddes not only ordered a court of inquiry (in itself a reasonable proceeding) but instead of leaving the rest to Beatty in the normal way he drew up instructions that the names of the members of the court must be submitted to him and all the facts must be brought out, which carried the implication that if the inquiry was left to the Commander-in-Chief he might pack the court or cover up what had gone wrong. Jellicoe, who was partly incapacitated by being in bed with a bad cold, learnt of this in time to attempt to head Geddes off by drafting a proper and suitable official telegram to Beatty; but Geddes altered it without his knowledge to a more offensive form and despatched it, accompanied by a still more offensive personal one from himself. Jellicoe saw these for the first time when he visited Rosyth on the 22nd and found Beatty furious. On his return he told Geddes that they were both insulting. 'The First Lord', he recorded later, 'did not like my frankness.'*[56] A day or two afterwards the blow fell.

Geddes and Wemyss had both been irritated, in their several ways (and Geddes of course over a longer period), by Jellicoe's persistent reluctance or rather refusal to delegate authority. Wemyss's reaction, however, was to go and have a courteous talk with him. 'Some time in December', he recorded in the memoirs which he left unfinished at his death,

> I had a conversation with him and told him that I feared I was not of as much assistance to him as I had hoped to be. I pointed out to him that he was giving me no responsibilities and that as matters stood I was merely giving an extra opinion on dockets which could well be dispensed with, and I asked him directly whether he trusted me or not.

Jellicoe's reply, which incidentally seems to dispose of any possibility that his reluctance to give Wemyss more scope arose from regarding him as one of his ill-wishers, was

> to the effect that he entirely trusted me, but that he could see no way towards shifting any of his responsibilities on to me, since such would not be legal. My reply was that it was legally a matter for the First Lord, and that if he chose to appoint certain duties to me, the procedure would be constitutionally correct. Sir John did not agree with me and the matter dropped for the time; but I seriously began to reconsider my position, and to wonder whether it was either right or useful that I should remain under such circumstances. [However] I knew that to throw up my appointment would cause more difficulties.[57]

* After Jellicoe's dismissal Beatty took the opportunity of a visit by Geddes to the Grand Fleet to demand a letter of apology from him, got a promise of one, reminded him of the promise a few weeks later, and ultimately received a letter which he read to his assembled flag-officers.

Another point of difference between Wemyss and Jellicoe was the Dover Barrage. The former, supported strongly and even vehemently by Keyes, felt that more could be done to prevent German submarines from passing through it, which the Intelligence Department had established they were doing without much difficulty. Bacon, the architect of the Barrage, obstinately refused to believe this. Towards the end of December Wemyss therefore proposed to both Geddes and Jellicoe that Bacon should be replaced. Geddes agreed; Jellicoe, who was prone to carry loyalty to his friends almost to a fault, dissented. Wemyss left the discussion, which had taken place in the First Lord's room, feeling that nothing remained for him but to resign and was considering how to do so with as little damage to the Admiralty's prestige as possible when on the evening of 22 December he received a message from Geddes asking him to come over for a talk after dinner. When he arrived the First Lord told him that he had made up his mind to get rid of Jellicoe, and asked him if he was prepared to take his place. After some moments of doubt and hesitation, Wemyss assented, believing that under the circumstances it was his duty to do so, but by no means pleased at the manner of his sudden elevation.[58]

Geddes, however, sought no such man-to-man interview with Jellicoe as Wemyss had done. Instead, he delayed until the evening of the 24th, at 6 p.m. on which Jellicoe received a letter from him marked 'Personal and strictly private' and containing the following:

> After very careful consideration I have come to the conclusion that a change is desirable in the post of First Sea Lord. I have not, I can assure you, arrived at this view hastily or without great personal regret and reluctance. . . . I have thought that you would prefer me to convey this decision to you in writing, but should you wish to see me, I shall of course be at your disposal at any time. . . .[59]

This delay till Christmas Eve, after which no newspapers would appear for two days, has been widely ascribed to a desire to prevent public knowledge of the dismissal until it had become an irreversible *fait accompli*. Admiral Bacon, always a strong partisan of Jellicoe and obviously no neutral in this particular matter, also asserted in his biography of the latter that Geddes's purpose in marking the envelope as he did (which it must be admitted seems in itself a rather natural proceeding) was to make it difficult for Jellicoe to consult his colleagues. Had he done so, Bacon continued, 'there is little doubt that the Prime Minister, late on Christmas Eve, would have been faced with the choice of finding an entirely different lot of Sea Lords – Sir Rosslyn Wemyss excepted – or a new First Lord'.[60] Wemyss, however, stated in his memoirs that Geddes 'hated the job' of dismissing Jellicoe and 'did it in a manner which, sudden though it was, he considered the best for him and for all others concerned';[61] and Jellicoe himself in his autobiographical account of the matter affirmed that Geddes had shortly beforehand expressed a desire and even made an attempt to return to his railway work in France. 'The assumption in my mind', he wrote, 'is that Lord Northcliffe was pressing the Prime Minister to get rid of me, the Prime Minister was pressing Geddes, the latter wanted to avoid trouble and so tried to get away from the Admiralty, but failing this carried out the desire of Northcliffe'.*[62] Geddes, however, in a statement which he afterwards drafted for possible parliamentary use but of which he does not seem to have availed himself, categorically denied any outside pressure, declaring that during the whole time that he was First Lord Lloyd George had never attempted to influence his judgement of Jellicoe's fitness for his position, and that he himself had arrived independently at the conclusion that a change was needed. It should however be borne in mind that this statement of his sole responsibility was drawn up for a debate in which his chief the Prime Minister was engaged in self-justification.[63]

Shortly after he had received the letter, Jellicoe, stunned and feeling that he must speak to someone, went to see his old flag-captain Halsey, whom he told what had occurred, adding that he felt that he could hardly carry on under the circumstances and so proposed to go immediately on leave, instructing Wemyss to take over. After asking Halsey if he thought this course justified and being told that he did, Jellicoe then wrote to Geddes to this effect and received a reply that it would be the most convenient course, whereupon he left the Admiralty forthwith. Geddes, having motored to Sandringham next day to see the King, wrote

---

* Jellicoe had been told by Carson that when he was First Lord both he and Lloyd George had been frequently pressed by Northcliffe to dismiss him.

again in the evening asking to be informed before the Cabinet met on Boxing Day morning whether he would accept a peerage. The first impulse of Sir John and Lady Jellicoe was to decline it, but they changed their minds for reasons which he afterwards set out thus:

(1) For the sake of the Service which got so few honours.

(2) So that I should not sink into obscurity but have a platform from which to speak if things went wrong and foolish action was taken with the Navy.

(3) For the sake of my children, as History might never know the truth and say I was kicked out, evidently justly as no honour was conferred.

He therefore assented and after the Cabinet meeting next morning received the following letter:

Dear Sir,
    I have the honour to inform you that His Majesty has been pleased to approve of my recommendation that the dignity of a Peerage of the United Kingdom should be conferred on you.

Yours faithfully,
D. Lloyd George

He became Viscount Jellicoe of Scapa on 15 January 1918.[64]

It is difficult to escape the conclusion that Jellicoe was no longer fit to continue as First Sea Lord. In this connection words used by Churchill in 1911 in another context are surely pertinent:

The duties of the First Sea Lord are vital to the country. It is essential that he should be thoroughly fit. He must be able to transact a mass of business without being unduly fatigued. He must have sufficient health and strength to bear any sudden strain or stress. If he is not thoroughly fit it is the First Lord's duty to tell him so, to suggest his resignation, and if necessary to supersede him. No personal considerations can stand in the way of the public interest in a matter so closely connected with the public safety.[65]

Nor was it a matter of health alone. But there are a right and several wrong ways of discharging an unpalatable task, and this, to put it mildly, was one of the latter.

A multitude of letters of sympathy came pouring in on Jellicoe as soon as the news of his resignation became known. The first

was an embarrassed one from Wemyss, who of course had a
flying start in the matter of that knowledge and wrote that he
regretted more than he could say the turn matters had taken
and would have liked to write more, but found it difficult. The
situation was made easier for him afterwards, however, by the fact
that Jellicoe never showed the least resentment towards him, and
both he and Lady Jellicoe went out of their way to remain on as
friendly terms with him as ever.[66] The King wrote graciously and
warmly, as to an old friend of more than thirty years' standing,
assuring him that he had not failed in his duty and that he knew
this would be the verdict of History.[67] Beatty, to whom Jellicoe
had immediately written on Christmas Day to explain what had
happened, replied that he was completely in the dark as to the
situation, but that the manner of the dismissal seemed to him
typical of 'the usual way they have at the Admiralty of dispensing
with the services of officers who have given their whole lives to
the service of the country'. He added that he was just going to
Edinburgh to meet Geddes and Wemyss, who had lost no time in
hastening up there to see him, and would write again at more
length and leisure when he had heard what they had to say. This
however he did not do, which led Jellicoe to conclude that something had passed at the interview which had made him think it
better not to write again; but when after an interval of nearly a
month he himself voiced this supposition in a tentative letter to
Beatty he received an apology for remissness and an assurance that
nothing of the sort was the case and that he had got nothing
definite out of Geddes about the reasons for the dismissal.[68]
Many other letters, from Madden (who pleaded with him not to
take the peerage), Bacon (whose own dismissal followed in a few
days), Colville, Burney, Prince Louis of Battenberg, Mr and Mrs
Asquith and many more, expressed warm indignation as well as
sympathy; but perhaps the most moving of all was a telegram from
the ratings of the Tenth Submarine Flotilla, which ran:

> We heard with regret of your retirement and would wish to
> know what was the cause, you know of course that we have
> implicit trust in you and please do not take it lying down. We
> want you back. Don't take any notice of arm-chair critics,
> what do they know of our wants and desires? Sir, you might
> ask for a naval election, they can do it in France, why not in

the Fleet? You are our Idol and one who we would follow to
Death, you have shown us the way to possess ourselves in
patience, you have always been one with us in our sports and
you are the Man we want. Don't and I don't think you will let
our country our Sacred Island home be led to ruin by a lot of
irresponsible Naval Retired Officers who do not know what
they are talking about. Come Back is the message from the
Lower Deck to you. You quite understand how we are situated
and you know that we would not Mutiny because love of
England home and beauty comes first. But speak my Lord let
us hear your voice in the Grand Fleet for we wish to hear it and
when as I hope you will soon be back our Lord and Master
then and only then shall we be satisfied.[69]

Much of this might have been sent to Nelson, in similar circumstances, by the seamen of his day.

Meanwhile the Prime Minister had in fact come within measur-
able distance of being impaled on one horn of the dilemma later
described by Bacon – of having, that is, to find new Sea Lords.
Halsey had asked Jellicoe on the morning of the 25th whether he
might inform his colleagues of what had happened and Jellicoe
had consented, since Wemyss had now given out that he was on
leave and it was already becoming known that something grave
had taken place. At the same time he advised Halsey against a
collective resignation, since its only result would be to harm the
country.[70] Nevertheless Halsey, Heath, Oliver, Duff, Rear-
Admiral Tothill and Commodore Paine (the last two of whom
were the Fourth and Fifth Sea Lords respectively) conferred together and then descended in a body upon Wemyss, who appears
to have referred them to Geddes. On the following morning
Heath on their behalf obtained an interview with the First Lord,
who began by declaring that Jellicoe's dismissal was no concern of
the Sea Lords, being entirely a matter for the Cabinet, and that in
his official capacity he absolutely refused to give any reasons for it.
However, he continued, as man to man he would be prepared to
tell Heath what he would not tell him as First Lord. He then gave
various justifications for his action, and in particular that at a meeting
two or three months previously between himself, Lloyd George,
Balfour and Carson the two latter had declared that they did not
consider Jellicoe the best man to be First Sea Lord. He also

consented to see Heath's colleagues two at a time (perhaps to avoid any appearance of justifying himself to his Board) and repeat this unofficial explanation to them. Halsey and Tothill were then called in for that purpose, but (perhaps because of his departure with Wemyss for Rosyth) Geddes went no further. In his absence the Sea Lords held two more conferences to discuss what they had learned; the first was adjourned without coming to any decision, but at the second Duff argued strongly that the opinions of Balfour and Carson, two former First Lords who were also very eminent and experienced ministers, must carry so much weight that it would be advisable to take no further action. Nevertheless when Geddes and Wemyss returned on the 28th Duff proffered his own resignation verbally and went on leave, though Geddes gave him until 1 January to make a final decision. When he returned to the Admiralty on that day he found that Geddes was away sick and that his colleagues had gathered that Carson in a letter to Jellicoe had denied any recollection of any such meeting with the Prime Minister as had been described and had declared that he had always believed and proclaimed him to be the only possible First Sea Lord. This Carson reaffirmed emphatically to Halsey, who called on him in the afternoon to seek corroboration. Meeting again, the six officers decided to send Geddes a memorandum, which was drawn up by Oliver and despatched next morning, informing him that unless he could explain this discrepancy to their satisfaction they could not remain his colleagues. Two days elapsed before Geddes replied, during which on the one hand he lunched with Heath and alternately cajoled and threatened him, and on the other several minor intermediaries invited the Sea Lords to meet them and adjured them on patriotic grounds not to resign. Then on the 4th came a letter from Geddes which skilfully evaded the point at issue and took a high tone by declaring that he was not prepared to discuss the reasons which had led him, 'after consultation with the Prime Minister and [his own] two immediate predecessors in office', to recommend Jellicoe's retirement. He had read with amazement, he went on, the intimation that they proposed to tender their resignation unless the First Lord gave them an explanation which they considered satisfactory about a personal and private conversation that he had had with three of them on a matter in no way within the scope of their duties and which had been repeated to the other three in (he asserted) breach of confidence. 'I would remind you', he concluded magisterially, 'that at this time more than any other it is the privilege of every citizen loyally and wholeheartedly to carry out the duties assigned to him.'

Bullied on one side and appealed to from the other, and feeling that they had put themselves in the wrong by letting themselves be drawn on to the ground of seeming to claim a right of interference in the appointment or dismissal of the First Sea Lord instead of simply sticking to the position that they considered Jellicoe's removal disastrous, the Sea Lords after further prolonged discussion among themselves capitulated, and in another joint letter to Geddes disclaimed any intention of suggesting that he had deliberately misrepresented Carson. To this Geddes replied that he recognised that there had been an honest misunderstanding, and considered the incident closed.[71] Subsequently, however, an acrimonious correspondence took place between him and Carson, in which the latter repeated his denial that he had ever expressed any doubts of Jellicoe's fitness for his post, while Geddes on his part denied having told the Sea Lords that he had done so. Carson also reiterated his inability to recall any such meeting of the two of them with Lloyd George and Balfour as Geddes had alluded to. Lloyd George, to whom Geddes then appealed, confirmed to him that it had taken place; while Balfour, dragged with obvious reluctance into the argument, was vague and non-committal. He admitted that he recollected discussing the Admiralty with the Premier and Geddes but could not remember any meeting of the three of them with Carson on the subject, agreed that his memory was not of the best, firmly disclaimed ever having been a consenting party to Jellicoe's dismissal, and ended by professing willingness to accept Geddes's judgement on the need of a change.[72]

9 The Empire Mission

'How strange it must be to you', wrote Madden on 28 January 1918, 'to be able to give some time to your own affairs instead of devoting it all to your country's good, as you have done for so many years.' In the same letter he informed Jellicoe that Beatty had sent the Admiralty a memorandum, to be laid before the War Cabinet, pointing out that shortages of light cruisers, destroyers and submarines available to go to sea with the Grand Fleet would make caution necessary in accepting action with the High Seas Fleet at what might be its chosen time and place, and that considerable losses might be incurred in getting to grips with it. 'When history is written', he concluded, '[this] will be a complete vindication of your policy as Commander-in-Chief and as First Sea Lord.' In later years Jellicoe endorsed the envelope in which he had kept this letter: 'Interesting as mentioning a letter from Beatty to the Admiralty . . . stating the weakness of Grand Fleet in certain particulars. Churchill should have seen this before he wrote his books criticising me for doing the same thing!!!'[1]

Meanwhile he devoted his enforced leisure to writing, not precisely an account of his stewardship, for besides involving the use of confidential documents this would have meant too personal an approach and an attitude of self-justification which was foreign to him unless thrust upon him, but a narrative of those principal parts of the naval war in which he had played a leading role. A plain, straightforward and (as he saw things) factual account, which approached eloquence only when he was paying tribute to the behaviour of his officers and men at Jutland, it contained no word of controversy or reproach – except perhaps a hint of defensiveness in the claim that convoys 'were commenced by Admiralty direction and . . . started as soon as and extended as rapidly as the necessary protecting vessels could be provided'.[2] The first volume, entitled *The Grand Fleet, 1914–16*, and dealing with its organisation, development and work under his command-was finished by the early autumn of 1918, but had to await the end of the war before publication and appeared early in 1919. The second, *The Crisis of the Naval War*, was nearly completed by the end of 1918, but his departure on what came to be called the Empire Mission prevented the finishing touches from being put to it until his return, and it came out in 1920. Dealing with the year of his First Sea Lordship, but absolutely non-committally and with only one brief, bald and incidental reference to his 'departure from the Admiralty' (in so many words) it described the changes carried out during that year in its organisation, the submarine crisis and the various anti-submarine measures which were brought into operation, the introduction and working of the convoy system, and the great services of the minesweepers and the Dover and Harwich forces. Both these honest, meticulous and still valuable books were necessarily rather circumscribed by the limitations of the knowledge available to Jellicoe while the war was still going on and the need even after it was over to keep secret some of the methods employed and certain other details.

Several attempts were meanwhile made by Sir Eric Geddes and others to provide him with employment and make use of his services. The first and most infelicitous was the offer of the Devonport Command in succession to Admiral Sir Alexander Bethell. On discovering, however, by an immediate and direct enquiry of Admiral Bethell that the latter was being prematurely retired to make room for him, Jellicoe stiffly refused to be a party to what he castigated as a proceeding that he considered unfair to a brother officer and prejudicial to the Service.[3] A more respectable proposal made early in May 1918 was that he should be appointed Allied Naval Commander-in-Chief in the Mediterranean, where operations had previously been handicapped by the lack of any such overall commander. This appointment Jellicoe was of course prepared to accept, merely making the proviso that since Lady Jellicoe had been seriously ill after the birth of their son George*
on 4 April and was at the moment in a critical condition, he would prefer not to leave England for a month, by which time, the doctors had informed him, the outcome of her illness would be decided. Happily the outcome was favourable, but meanwhile, although the French had agreed to the proposal, the Italians had dissented on the ground that they could not entrust a foreigner with the

* The present Earl Jellicoe.

power of ordering their ships to sea, and the plan fell to the ground.[4] Next came an invitation via Churchill and Geddes to serve on a committee which was to consider the organisation of the Royal Ordnance Factories, which he turned down on finding that the committee's work would have no real connection with the war.[5] He did, however, preside in the autumn over a committee of prominent naval officers who discussed the fitting of future capital ships with bulge protection against torpedoes and reported favourably thereon.[6] By this time the war was drawing to its close and he was offered the Governor-Generalship of Australia at the next vacancy. This he declined, ostensibly on financial grounds but really because he preferred and hoped for that of New Zealand, and although he had been told that it was not available at present he wished to wait for it.[7]

When the war came to an end on 11 November Jellicoe sent Admiral Beatty the following telegram:

> I am anxious to send to you and to my old comrades in the Grand Fleet congratulations on the termination of your long and arduous task.
>
> Although the glorious victory for which you all hoped has not been vouchsafed to you, the victorious end of the war is none the less due to the work carried out by the Fleet.[8]

He was not, however, invited to witness the surrender (according to the terms of the Armistice) of the German High Seas Fleet on 21 November, and did not deem it proper to go north uninvited. ('I think you were right', wrote Burney from Rosyth).[9] Nevertheless he received telegrams and letters congratulating him on the part he had played in the victory. Of these, this from Sir Walter Runciman, the former President of the Board of Trade in Asquith's ministry, may serve as an example:

> It is because the civilised world is indebted to you more than to any man for the skill and spirit of the Fleet that I think specially of you in these victorious days. Congratulations flow naturally to you, and in sending mine let me add that they are as hearty as though your Flag were still flying at Scapa.[10]

Meanwhile a new opportunity of important and interesting service had offered itself, in the shape of the Empire Mission. At an Imperial War Conference earlier in 1918, attended by the prime ministers of the Dominions, the Admiralty had put forward a plan for a single post-war Imperial Navy, embracing all the naval forces of the Empire and controlled by a central imperial naval authority on which it was tentatively suggested that the Dominions should be represented, as and when possible, by their respective navy ministers. In each of them there would be a local navy board, working in co-operation with the central authority but directly responsible to the Dominion parliament, and controlling local naval establishments, the entry and training of personnel, and so forth. Each, moreover, would decide for itself the extent to which it would share in the total cost of the Navy. This proposal was, however, rejected by a majority of the Dominion premiers, who preferred that the young nations that they governed should develop navies of their own which could co-operate with that of Britain under one direction and command established after the outbreak of any future war. At the same time they recognised that the construction, armament, equipment, training, administration and organisation of these navies would have to correspond to those of the British Navy, and had accordingly suggested in August that as soon as possible after the conclusion of hostilities the Dominions should be visited in turn by a highly qualified representative of the Admiralty who would be thoroughly competent to advise in such matters.[11] This they presently suggested should be Lord Jellicoe, and in December he was formally deputed by the Admiralty to visit Australia, New Zealand and Canada for this purpose. The question of whether South Africa, which showed no disposition to form a navy of its own, should be included in his tour was held over till the last possible moment, and indeed it was not until he was leaving Canada, still in the expectation of at least visiting the Cape and reporting on matters of local defence there, that it was decided to omit it. On the other hand, when he had reached Suez on his outward journey he was overtaken by a telegram instructing him to begin by a visit to India.

In their instructions to Jellicoe the Admiralty made clear that it still adhered to its view that a single unitary navy would be the best naval defence of the Empire, while recognising at the same time that the main purpose of the Dominions' invitation to him was to have his guidance in establishing uniformity of organisation, training and *matériel* between their several naval forces. In the light of this it therefore deputed him to advise the Dominion authorities whether the schemes of naval organisation they had adopted or might be contemplating required reconsideration, either from the point of view of their efficiency for meeting local needs or from that of ensuring the greatest possible homogeneity and co-operation between all the naval forces of the Empire. Should these authorities, they added, wish in addition to consider how far their Dominions could take a more effective share in general Imperial naval defence, he was to assist them in drawing up a scheme for consideration.[12]

Jellicoe himself shared the Admiralty's preference for a unified Imperial Navy, but he realised the necessity of accepting with the best possible grace the determination of the peoples of the Dominions that any naval forces and establishments they paid for should be their own, and of proceeding from that as a basis. The position was that during the past ten years Australia had already taken a share in naval defence and Australian naval forces already existed; New Zealand had contributed to the British Navy the battle-cruiser of that name, in which Jellicoe made his tour; but Canada had done comparatively little owing to the question having become entangled in Canadian party politics. At home uncertainty about post-war naval policy was now prevailing in Government and Admiralty circles, with the Peace Conference as yet only assembling, the functions of the prospective League of Nations a matter of speculation and debate, and a widespread belief among the public that wars would be no more, or at least were unlikely for many years to come. Hence when Jellicoe left England on 21 February 1919, accompanied by his wife and a staff headed by his old flag-captain (now Commodore) Dreyer, he had received little or no guidance from the Admiralty as to the yardstick by which he should measure the size of Dominion navies and contributions. Left thus to form his own opinion of the naval strength needed for the Empire as a whole and to base his recommendations on this, he took as his standpoint the assumptions that Britain's pre-war naval supremacy must be maintained and that a war with Japan was a future probability. 'Information obtained from the Foreign Office, my own knowledge of the recent course of events in the Pacific, information obtained from official quarters in India and Australia of the actions and aspirations of the Japanese, and the known and oft-proclaimed policy of a "white Australia", 'he wrote in the closing summary of his report, 'pointed to Japan [as] the quarter from which possible future danger to the Empire might arise.'[13] The geographical position of this putative enemy, remote from Britain and yet well placed to attempt the invasion of other parts of the Empire, would therefore call, he concluded, for the maintenance by the Imperial Navy of a 100 per cent superiority in capital ships over the fast-expanding Japanese Navy, since nothing less would enable us to keep superior forces in the theatre of war and yet remain secure against any conceivable rivals nearer home. Even in peacetime, in view of the lengthy interval before substantial reinforcements could arrive in the East, safety demanded the building up within the next five years of a Far Eastern Fleet of 8 dreadnought battle-ships, 8 battle-cruisers, 19 light cruisers, 40 destroyers with 3 flotilla leaders, 36 submarines, 4 aircraft-carriers and appropriate numbers of other craft. To this he suggested that Australia should contribute two battle-cruisers (one of which, named after the Dominion, was already in existence), 8 light cruisers, 12 destroyers and a flotilla leader, 8 submarines and an aircraft-carrier; and New Zealand 3 light cruisers, 6 submarines and a small carrier. 75 per cent of the cost of providing and maintaining this Far Eastern Fleet should be borne by Britain, 20 per cent by Australia, and 5 per cent by New Zealand. In addition he proposed that Canada should maintain a small force of light cruisers on her western seaboard to protect her trade in those waters, and that India should provide annually a sum which would pay for the up-keep of a squadron comprising 5 light cruisers, 6 submarines, an aircraft-carrier and auxiliary craft.[14] It was within this general framework that he and his staff worked out their more detailed recommendations at each stage of the tour.

Arriving at Bombay on 11 March, they had completed their report on the naval requirements of India by 30 April.[15] During the rule of the East India Company the sub-continent had had a naval service of its own, but after the Crown's assumption of direct rule the Royal Navy had taken over the protection of commerce and the general maritime defence. Subsequently a Royal Indian Marine had been created, but this was not organised as a fighting force and its main functions, besides transport and survey work, were such as in England were carried out by Trinity House, harbour commissioners, port trusts, and various similar bodies. Placed by an Act of 1884 under the direction of the Viceroy in Council, its affairs were in practice administered by the military, and although during the war it had been brought largely under naval control and its personnel had adapted themselves creditably to their changed circumstances, war experience had shown that it was quite inadequate to meet the naval requirements of India. Jellicoe therefore recommended its replacement by a Royal Indian Navy of the dimensions mentioned above, with the addition of 3 sloops for the Persian Gulf, several river gunboats for the Tigris and Euphrates, and 20 armed escort ships for convoys. This should be officered at first partly from the Royal Navy and partly by officers of the Royal Indian Marine who had gained naval experience through their work during the war, and should be manned partly and increasingly by natives of India. Subsequently the officer entry would be kept up by the training of cadets, British, Indian and Anglo-Indian, in the naval training establishments in Britain, while training ships would be maintained in India for candidates for entry as ratings. The operations of the force would be directed from Britain, but there would be a naval board in India whose head Jellicoe recommended should be a member of the Viceroy's Executive Council.

It was in the extensive section of his report which dealt with Australia that Jellicoe set out most fully his views on the probability of ultimate war with Japan and the need to maintain a large Far Eastern Fleet which would include a considerable number of capital ships. This led him to include a disquisition on the value of such vessels in modern warfare. '*The Capital Ship*', he wrote, '*is the strongest form of engine of war which exists for operating on the seas.*'* It had so far survived the advent of the torpedo, the mine, and even (as Jellicoe, writing from the standpoint of 1919, believed) of aircraft.

> Its external bulges [he continued] . . . render it immune (in the case of the newest type now building) to torpedo attack until hit by a large number of torpedoes. . . . [It] is also usually protected against torpedo attack by escorting T.B.D.'s and in future will be assisted by various scientific devices, recently invented, which will enable it to carry out defensive or offensive tactical manoeuvres against submarines. Paravanes . . . form an efficient protection against moored mines of present type.

* The italics are Jellicoe's.

Thick armoured decks protect the vitals of the Capital Ship from bombs *dropped* by aircraft, which when dropped from the low heights necessary to give much probability of hitting have but low striking velocities and therefore only small penetrative effect. High-angle guns help to keep attacking aircraft at heights from which hitting by dropped bombs is impossible. The aircraft carried on board or in an attendant vessel serve to protect [it] against enemy airships and aeroplanes. . . . The flying and the submarine enthusiasts of today are following in the footsteps of the explosive shell, the torpedo, and the mine enthusiasts who preceded them [sc., in decrying the capital ship], whilst those who recognise [its] necessity are devising successfully means to counter each fresh menace to its existence. It behoves us therefore to be cautious in accepting the opinion of specialists in any particular arm in this matter. . . . The wise course to pursue is to continue to build Capital Ships until, *if ever*, it is shown that some other weapon has been found which permanently renders them inefficient[16].

A most serious, indeed a crucial, obstacle to the maintenance of a fleet of capital ships in Far Eastern waters, however, he emphasised, was the lack of adequate docking facilities. At the moment the docks at Hong Kong and Colombo could not accommodate a modern battleship, even of the older dreadnought type, let alone the newer vessels of the *Royal Sovereign* and *Queen Elizabeth* classes, which would be equal in power to the more recent Japanese ships. One dock at Singapore could take the *Queen Elizabeths*, but only provided that they were not fitted with bulge protection. How far the Hong Kong and Singapore docks could be enlarged Jellicoe professed himself unable to judge, but he pointed out that whereas it would be necessary to use both of these bases, as well as Colombo, in the event of war with Japan, they were at present only weakly held against a determined attack by land and sea forces. The vital importance of increasing and safeguarding dock accommodation in the Far East at the earliest possible moment was therefore obvious, and it was not easy to see how the situation could be met soon enough except by the provision of floating docks. Until adequate accommodation was provided, ships of the *Royal Sovereign* class and the latest battle-cruisers such as the *Renown* and the *Repulse* (let alone the *Hood*, which was due to be completed that year) could not be sent to the Far East except under the gravest disadvantages; and hence until this was remedied we must accept a dangerous inferiority of force to Japan. 'Placing oneself in the position of a Japanese strategist', he wrote, 'the first objective on the outbreak of hostilities . . . would seem to be an attack on [our] naval bases if weakly held. . . . An examination of the defences of Singapore and Hong Kong, and the local knowledge which I possess of these two bases, make it plain to me that the operation . . . could at the present time be carried out with comparative ease.'

In addition to ensuring the proper protection of Hong Kong and Singapore and if possible enlarging their docking facilities it would be necessary, Jellicoe underlined, to provide bases in Australia suitable for accommodating not only the Royal Australian Navy but also a reinforcing British squadron. Since the probable direction of an attack on Australia would be from the north, the forces opposing such an attack ought naturally to be based in northern Australian waters. The undeveloped state of the Northern Territory and the lack of railway communication with the rest of the Commonwealth made the establishment of a northern repairing base out of the question at present; but a temporary refuelling and storing base should be established in the Northern Territory for use in war, and for this he recommended Bynoe Harbour to the westward of Port Darwin. For a base on the west coast he advised the continuation of the development of Cockburn Sound, which already possessed a dockyard and on which a considerable sum of money had been spent; while on the east coast every consideration seemed to him to point to Port Stephens rather than to the continued use of Sydney.[17]

Jellicoe also devoted a chapter of his report to considering the general naval strategy which would be needed in Far Eastern waters during the early days of a war with Japan. He began by assuming that owing either to complications in Europe or the suddenness of the attack (since the success of the unheralded onslaught on Russia in 1904 might prompt the Japanese to a similar attempt) Britain might be unable to send any reinforcements to the Far Eastern Fleet before the outbreak of war; and that Japan's ultimate aim would be the invasion of Australia, although before this she might seize harbours in New Guinea, the Dutch East Indies or the Pacific Islands to the eastward for use as advanced bases. He likewise assumed that before or concurrently with these moves she would send strong expeditions against Singapore and Hong Kong which, he reiterated, would be successful if those bases were weakly held. If, however, steps to ensure their safety had been taken in good time, the Far Eastern Fleet could at once be so disposed as to protect our communications and prevent the landing of Japanese forces in Australia or their occupation of any of the Pacific Islands, pending the arrival of reinforcements from home strong enough to allow more offensive action to be taken. For this first defensive phase the Fleet must immediately be concentrated at a point which, while easily defensible against submarine attack, was as nearly as possible equidistant from the usual peace-time bases of its several units and at the same time well situated strategically for action against Japanese moves to the southward, either against trade or to effect a landing. These requirements, he advised, would be best met by the harbour of Manus in the Admiralty Islands to the north of New Guinea (which the Americans made into a large base in the Second World War), since it occupied a good position between the routes of hostile forces proceeding from the Japanese base at Truk either to the eastward of the Solomon Islands or the westward of New Guinea. For the reconnaissances necessary to give reasonable chances of detecting any southward enemy movement in force he proposed that aircraft should be very largely employed, assisted by submarines operating from Hong Kong to watch the northern part of the China Sea and also such of the Caroline and Pellew Islands as Japan might use as naval bases, since it was practically certain that she could not undertake any such large southern movement without her ships, or many of them, calling there to refuel. Other submarines should be employed in watching off the naval bases in Japan itself, since the moral effect alone of such action would be great. Once the main fleet had been concentrated its future movements must depend on the information received.[18]

Against the background of this discussion of the naval strategical problems affecting Australian and neighbouring waters and of the desirable strength of the Imperial Fleet in the Far East, Jellicoe set his proposals (as indicated earlier) regarding the future composition of the Australian Navy. In this connection he advanced the view that the surest method of obtaining a high standard of efficiency among the officers, which in turn was the primary means of ensuring a similar standard among the lower ratings, would be to place all officers of the Royal and Australian Navies and those of such other Dominions as followed Australia's example on one list. Under this arrangement officers from each of the other navies would serve part of their time in the British Navy, thus standardising their ideas and gaining the experience which could be obtained only in a large fleet; and their promotion to the ranks of commander and captain would be made on their records of service. Unless a uniform system of training and line of thought prevailed throughout all the naval forces of the Empire, he cautioned, they would lose much of their efficiency when brought together. At the same time as he enlarged upon the benefits to Dominion officers of a period of service in the British Navy, he emphasised that it would also be fatal to the future efficiency of a Dominion navy if any but the best type of Royal Navy officer were brought out to serve in it. 'It is a regrettable fact', he wrote, 'that quite a proportion of the British naval officers at present working for the Royal Australian Navy are distinctly not of the most efficient type. [One visualises the quiet, shrewd and swift summing-up of many of these which must have taken place.] Some are officers who have failed in the Royal Navy, others have volunteered for the Royal Australian Navy in the expectation of enjoying themselves in Australia, and not of working. Others again are R.N.R. officers of a poor type who have taken commissions in the Australian Navy.' To make it possible to send only the best class of officer to Australia, however, it must be clearly laid down that that service, far from handicapping them for promotion, would be looked upon as of great merit and entitle them to the highest consideration for future advancement.[19]

At the request of the Commonwealth Government Jellicoe included in his discussion of the training of the personnel of the Australian Navy a special chapter on the subject of discipline. The reason for this, he explained frankly, was that in his view the greatest difficulty confronting that navy at the moment was the lack of discipline. This was partly a result of the post-war reaction from which the whole world was suffering, but mainly due to the widespread idea in Australia that the Australian would not submit to it – an idea unfortunately encouraged by 'a certain class of politician'. If it could be eradicated he had no doubt that the Australian Navy would be an efficient force; otherwise it would fail.

It is impossible to believe [he wrote] that those who give expression to such an idea are really acquainted with the nature and object of the discipline which they criticise. Throughout all ages it has been accepted as an axiom that no armed force can exist without discipline. The only real difference of opinion that can exist is as to the method by which discipline is first acquired and then maintained. Many of those who cry out most vociferously against discipline are themselves inclined to enforce it by the most drastic methods to gain their ends. Accepting then that discipline is essential to armed forces, the only question that arises is the method of instilling [it] into the personnel of the Australian Navy and of maintaining it.

To achieve this, he went on to advise, officers and men should be entered at an early age and those who were to have the training of them should be selected with great care and afterwards supported by authority so long as their actions were correct. Officers and petty officers sent out from the Royal Navy would not only have to be very efficient and hardworking but must possess judgement, tact, firmness and broadmindedness in their dealings with Australian rank and file during the period required to overcome 'the wrong-headed ideas at present existing'. They would have to realise that the Australian was a different type from the British sailor, requiring somewhat different handling. Among the more detailed suggestions which he added were that officers must be taught that their first duty was to the well-being of the men under them and that they must take a great interest in their work and recreations and get to know them; that kindness and courtesy should always be shown, though without familiarity; that they must realise that the more efficient and unsparing of themselves they were in their work, the easier it was to command their men; that they should be most carefully instructed in the best methods of investigating the cases of men brought up before them on a charge, thoroughly understanding that the 'accused' was not an offender unless the charge was proved, exercising patience and restraint, and constantly bearing in mind that it must be made clear to all that they were certain of obtaining justice; and that they must set an example to their men by showing both courtesy and respect towards their superior officers and consideration towards their juniors, particularly avoiding any disparaging remarks in mess about those in authority, since these would soon become known all over a ship. 'But success', he concluded, 'must finally depend on the manner in which the efficient naval officer is backed up by the Australian Government. At present political influence is constantly brought to bear on members of the Government, and as the result the decisions of officers are sometimes overruled for purely political reasons. Discipline is undermined and encouragement given to appeal to politicians behind the backs of the governing body.'[20]

After these home truths, Jellicoe turned to the administration of the Australian Navy,[21] laying emphasis on the need to devise machinery by which the professional members of the Australian Naval Board could inform Parliament of their disagreement if their recommendations were overruled by the Navy Minister in matters of vital importance – a proposal redolent of his own past experiences. He then went on to give more technical counsel on docks, the protection of bases, air requirements, the provision of fuel and stores, intelligence, coastguard, wireless and the protection of trade in wartime.

Coming next to New Zealand on 20 August, Jellicoe found the importance of sea-power clearly recognised there, but divergent views existing on the best method of co-operation with Britain. These were reconciled, however, by the suggestion that an autonomous New Zealand Division of the Royal Navy should be formed on the same lines as the Royal Australian Navy, though on a smaller scale, starting with the immediate transfer by Britain to the Dominion of a light cruiser carrying a six-inch gun armament.* In his report he recommended that no arrangements should be made as yet for building warships in New Zealand, nor any naval dockyard contemplated for the present, repairs and refits being carried out either in private yards in the Dominion or in the Australian establishments. His other recommendations followed closely the lines of those made for Australia, including almost word for word the disquisition on the continued value of capital ships and the chapter on discipline,† and in a modified form the

---

* The *Chatham* was duly transferred.

† He commented, however, that in the matter of discipline 'the New Zealanders as a race are markedly in advance of the Australians'. It might be added that, like many British officers, he had hardly grasped that Dominion discipline, while freer than in the British services, could nevertheless be very real.

desirability of arrangements by which the Prime Minister could be made acquainted with the views of the (in this case, sole) naval member of the tiny Naval Board if he disagreed with any action about to be taken by his Minister on a technical question of vital importance.[22]

A difficulty which Jellicoe encountered in all three of the Dominions he visited was that elections or the absence or illness of leading ministers interfered with consultations or decisions. In Canada, where he arrived (at Esquimalt) on 8 November, both the Prime Minister Sir Robert Borden and Mr Ballantyne the Minister for Naval Affairs had been in poor health for some time, and in the middle of the visit Borden was ordered by his doctors to take a prolonged rest outside the country, as a result of which not only did he leave before any decision about naval policy was reached, but during the last two weeks of Jellicoe's stay most of the Canadian Cabinet's time was occupied in discussing the situation thus created.[23] In addition, although a small Royal Canadian Navy had existed since 1911 and a number of people both in and outside the Canadian Navy League favoured its enlargement, there were several factors adverse to the adoption of this policy. The chief of these was the inherent difficulty of bringing home to a country which had no likely enemy near at hand and a large part of whose population lived at a great distance from the sea the fact that its quite considerable seaborne trade and therefore its prosperity nevertheless depended on the safety of its sea communications. The question of naval policy had also been bedevilled by becoming entangled in the party politics of the Dominion and was further complicated by the circumstance that although the Admiralty had by this time decided to abandon the idea of a single unitary Imperial Navy this had not yet been made known and the memorandum which it had presented to the Imperial War Conference was still being stated in the Canadian press, and apparently believed by some members of the Canadian Government, to represent its policy. It was not until several weeks after his arrival that Jellicoe received at Ottawa an Admiralty letter of 3 November enclosing a confidential paper indicating that – as he had urged – the Dominion standpoint on this matter had been fully and finally accepted. This letter had been sent to him in New Zealand but had unfortunately arrived too late and been forwarded on. He immediately wired an enquiry on 4 December whether he might communicate this change of attitude to the Canadian Ministry and received an affirmative reply, which clarified and somewhat eased the situation.

Four days previously and before the belated Admiralty letter arrived, however, he had sent off a telegram in the following terms:

> Canadian Cabinet is discussing amount naval estimates for next few years. Decision will probably be affected by amount of British naval estimates. Desire is being evinced to bear proportionate share of naval defence of Empire. Request information by wire at earliest possible moment of probable approximate annual total British naval estimates for next two or three years for confidential information of Ministers. Decision will be reached shortly so that matter is urgent . . .

He followed this by an explanatory letter of 3 December to the First Lord in which he declared that the situation was critical, inasmuch as a fleeting opportunity (he believed) existed of persuading the Canadian Government to adopt a forward naval policy. Borden, who at that stage was still struggling to carry on, was being pressed by Ballantyne to make an immediate start and was himself in favour of doing so, although some other ministers were opposed to this for political or financial reasons. Ballantyne's own conviction was that unless the matter was settled favourably before Jellicoe left Canada nothing would be done for years, and indeed he had expressed privately to him his intention, if a serious start was not made now, to scrap the existing Canadian naval service as being a pure waste of money. 'For this reason', Jellicoe wrote, 'a very sympathetic attitude towards Canada is most desirable now. If possible modern ships should be offered as a gift.' The Admiralty wired in general terms that some surplus warships might be made available, but to the urgent telegram of 30 November no answer was ever received. The situation of course still made it difficult for Jellicoe to be given the answer for which he asked, but Long's subsequent apology – 'I am distressed to find that [this telegram] was never answered. . . . The only excuse I can offer you is that we have been through a really awful time during the last six months' – was very lame.[24]

Left thus to his own resources Jellicoe therefore proceeded, as he had done in Australia and New Zealand, to frame his report as best he could on the basis of his own views about the necessary future naval strength of the Empire.[25] Examining the question of the naval forces required by Canada in the light of her own requirements and safety, he started from the assumption that in the event of the war with Japan which he prognosticated the Japanese were unlikely to attempt a landing in Canada, not only because of the great distance which separated the two countries, but because it would involve the risk of conflict with the United States. Canadian interests in the Atlantic being unlikely to be affected at all, the injury which Japan might inflict on Canada would thus be entirely or almost entirely on her trade in the Pacific. The naval forces needed under these circumstances would therefore be such as could protect that trade and the important harbours on the west coast; and the minimum force he considered necessary to achieve this comprised 3 light cruisers, 4 destroyers, 6 submarines, 8 patrol boats, 6 flying-boats and 6 torpedo-carrying aircraft, besides minesweeping trawlers and certain small craft for training purposes. As in a war with Japan the Imperial Fleet would probably be operating from Singapore or Australia, a naval base on a considerable scale which could be used by large ships was not likely to be required at present on the Pacific coast of Canada, but it would be desirable that one should eventually be provided, and since although war between Britain and the United States was almost inconceivable the possibility should not be discounted altogether it ought to be situated as far from the American border as was practicable. This ruled out Esquimalt, except as an advanced base for small craft working in or near the Straits of Juan de Foca (the main artery of trade on this coast), and Jellicoe considered that Prince Rupert Harbour to the northward, despite some climatic disadvantages and its distance of 500 miles from the Straits, should be earmarked as the future Pacific coast base. On the Atlantic coast, since in a Japanese war it was most improbable that any operations calling for the presence of large ships would take place in this area, and since Halifax already possessed a small naval dockyard and a commercial dock capable of accommodating light cruisers, with repair facilities for these and smaller craft, no further extensions seemed necessary at present.

The recommendations which followed concerning the administration, personnel, training and technical requirements of a

P

Canadian navy of these dimensions corresponded closely to those already made for Australia and New Zealand, with the minor exception that under the heading of administration Jellicoe contented himself in this case with a cautious observation that a wise interpretation by the Minister for Naval Affairs of his powers and functions and of the degree to which he should fall in with his expert colleagues on technical questions would be necessary. The section on the value of capital ships in modern warfare was again reproduced, and so, in general terms, was that on discipline, 'as it is felt that this is a matter to which special attention is necessary at the present time in view of the general unrest throughout the world which has resulted from the strain of prolonged war'. Finally, but tentatively, Jellicoe turned to consider the possibility of Canada deciding at some future time to extend her navy in order to play a part in the general naval defence of the Empire by providing, in addition to her local defence forces, a fleet unit which could share in the main operations of any future war. Such a unit he suggested might comprise a battle-cruiser, 2 light cruisers, 6 destroyers, 4 submarines and 2 fleet minesweepers, together with auxiliary vessels. According to Admiral Trevelyan Napier, a former Grand Fleet subordinate* who paid a brief visit to Ottawa soon after Jellicoe's departure, 'all from the Governor-General downwards were much impressed' by the report. He added, however, that 'whether it was going to bear any immediate fruit seemed quite an open question'.[26] In the event it did not, and the Canadian Navy remained almost microscopic for many years.

From the Admiralty Jellicoe's report received comparatively little attention or sympathy. This is particularly true of the earlier instalments, containing his recognition of Japan as a future enemy and his assessment of the size of the fleet that would have to be maintained, which arrived home while Wemyss was still First Sea Lord. The latter, who had become decidedly critical of Jellicoe, promptly told Long that he had 'entered into a sphere never contemplated by the Admiralty and far beyond his terms of reference'. The questions he had raised, Wemyss added, had not been 'maturely considered by the Board'.[27] Subsequently a rather sharply worded telegram was sent to him, which he received at the beginning of his stay in Canada, instructing him not to communicate his views on future strategical requirements to the

* See p. 127 above.

government of that Dominion before they had been submitted to the Admiralty. Immediately afterwards, however, he received the confidential paper mentioned above,* which was in fact a memorandum that the Admiralty had recently submitted to the Committee of Imperial Defence, expressing views very like his own on both the probability of a future threat from Japan and the appropriate counter-measures.[28]

Nevertheless the basic assumptions, or rather aspirations, of the report which Jellicoe and his staff had compiled – the maintenance of Britain's pre-war naval primacy and of a fleet double the strength of the Japanese Navy in capital ships – were sheer impossibilities in the post-war world. In March 1921 the Government went so far as to announce a construction programme designed to keep the Royal Navy at least equal in strength to any other. But with the United States stepping up American naval expansion by resuming the '1916 Program' of construction which on entering the war had been modified as regards capital ships, and Japan almost tripling her expenditure on her navy between 1917 and 1921, this opened up the prospect of a new and tripartite arms race. In both Britain and America demands were being voiced for reductions in defence expenditure, and since the Japanese Government of the moment was willing to enter into talks on the limitation of naval armaments the Washington Conference was called in the same year and resulted in the treaty by which a 5:5:3 ratio (and a maximum tonnage total) for capital ships and aircraft-carriers were agreed on by the three powers. Jellicoe's tour, however, though premature in the sense that if it had taken place after the Washington Conference he could have been furnished with the information really necessary for his guidance, was by no means barren of results. In addition to its moral value as a contribution to the amity of the nations of the British Commonwealth, it had led or contributed to the formation of the New Zealand Division of the Royal Navy and (though not until 1935) of the Royal Indian Navy; the Dominions – or two of them at least – had been more fully awakened to their naval needs and obligations; and they had received a wealth of valuable suggestions for the organisation and training of their naval forces, the development and protection of their harbours and dockyards, and the defence of their coasts and local shipping in wartime.

* See p. 223.

Throughout the tour Lord and Lady Jellicoe and the whole party had been given a most cordial welcome everywhere and most hospitably entertained; almost too hospitably, indeed, since the succession of receptions, addresses, speeches to be made, luncheons, dinners, balls and other functions had ended by adding appreciably to the burden of the hard work entailed by the compilation of the report. Jellicoe, to whom speech-making did not come easily, had found himself called upon to do a good deal of it, chiefly on the subject of the importance of sea-power to the Empire. This was especially the case in Canada, where he was begged by branches of the Navy League, supported by the ministers, to make speeches in all the principal cities, so that no small part of his time was devoted to what was really propaganda work.[29] There were, however, some intervals of recreation during at least the early part of the tour, and many very pleasant episodes. Just before reaching Bombay he had been informed by the Admiralty of his promotion to the rank of Admiral of the Fleet, and had received a telegram of congratulation on behalf of the Grand Fleet from Beatty, who had been similarly honoured at the same time and to whom he replied in kind. While he was in India he and Dreyer were invited by the Maharajah of Gwalior to take part in a four-day tiger shoot, in which, both being good shots and having taken the precaution of some preliminary practice with big-game rifles, they acquitted themselves creditably. The stay in Australia unfortunately coincided with the impact on that continent of the very serious post-war influenza epidemic, which caused the cancellation of a number of functions; but it was arranged that before going on to New Zealand Jellicoe should transfer his flag temporarily to the *Suva*, a 2200-ton ship belonging to the Australian Steam Navigation Company which had been specially chartered to take the party to some of the South Pacific Islands. They accordingly visited the Solomons, on one of which Jellicoe, with a guide, led his not-too-enthusiastic staff in a pre-breakfast climb of an almost perpendicular cliff 560 feet high and arrived at the top not only first but apparently freshest. This visit to the Solomons also led him to recommend Purvis Bay strongly as a possible base in the event of war with Japan – a judgement whose soundness was demonstrated in 1942. In New Zealand during the forty days of his stay he was entertained at about 40 receptions, 15 lunches, 8 public dinners and a dozen balls, as well as making

25 speeches in nine days. Despite this strenuous programme, however, he was stirred by the beauty of some of the places he visited into declaring his wish to come back again as Governor-General and end his days in that lovely land. The voyage on to Canada included calls at the Fiji Islands, Samoa, Christmas Island and Honolulu; and he arranged that after his work in that Dominion was finished he and his wife should pay a brief visit to Admiral Sims and his family at Newport in Rhode Island. Unfortunately Lady Jellicoe developed tonsilitis and the doctor who was consulted vetoed the journey, so that this happy occasion failed to materialise.[30] Jellicoe, however, managed to visit Washington with his staff, where, although President Wilson was by then too ill to receive him, he toured the Navy Yard (strongly commending the American Navy's dockyard system as compared with the British), was warmly welcomed by the House of Representatives and attended a tea party at the home of the then Assistant Secretary to the Navy, Franklin D. Roosevelt. Having given a brief address to the cadets of the Naval Academy at Annapolis, he then went on to Key West in Florida, where he rejoined the *New Zealand*. Lady Jellicoe, meanwhile, had been obliged to return to England on account of the death of her mother, Lady Cayzer, in whose care she had left her children while she was away. After calling at Havana, Port Royal in Jamaica and Port of Spain in Trinidad, the *New Zealand* anchored at Spithead on 2 February 1920. On the following day Lady Jellicoe came on board, and on the 4th she and her husband left the ship together and Jellicoe's flag was struck for the last time.[31]

10 The Jutland Controversy and the Closing Years

JELLICOE had scarcely stepped ashore on his return to England before he became involved, much to his distaste, in what came to be known as the Jutland Controversy. The first post-war phase of this was the affair of the Harper Record. Within a few weeks of the end of the war Sir Rosslyn Wemyss, somewhat disturbed by learning that Jellicoe intended to publish a book on the Grand Fleet which he feared (unnecessarily, as the event proved) might lead to mutual recriminations, and being unable to dissuade him, had appointed a small committee consisting of Captain J. E. T. Harper (who like himself had not been present at Jutland) and four other naval officers as his assistants to prepare an authoritative account of the battle based on all the available documentary evidence, such as the reports of the Commander-in-Chief and his subordinate flag-officers and captains, ships' logs, signals and written information obtained from the Director of Naval Intelligence. This, Harper was instructed, was to be a straightforward record of the sequence of events, free from comment or criticism, and by Wemyss's direction all statements were to accord with the facts obtainable from these official documents and no oral evidence was to be accepted.[1]

While Captain Harper and his assistants worked with great care and thoroughness, he did however include in his narrative of the battle-cruiser action the following paragraph, which could certainly be regarded as a departure from his instructions to avoid comment:

> The disturbing feature of the battle-cruiser action is the fact that five German battle-cruisers engaging six British vessels of this class, supported after the first 20 minutes, although at great range, by the fire of four battleships of the *Queen Elizabeth* class, were yet able to sink the *Queen Mary* and the *Indefatigable*. It is true that the enemy suffered heavily later and that

one vessel, the *Lützow*, was undoubtedly destroyed, but even so the result cannot be other than unpalatable. The facts which contributed to the British losses were, *first*, the indifferent armour protection of our battle-cruisers, particularly as regards turret-armour and deck plating, and *second*, the disadvantage under which our vessels laboured as regards to light. . . . But it is also undoubted that the gunnery of the German battle-cruisers in the early stages was of a very high standard. They appeared to get on to their target and establish hitting within two or three minutes in almost every case, and this at very long ranges of 18,000 yards. Once we commenced hitting the German gunnery fell off, but – as was shown by the rapidity with which the *Invincible* was sunk at a later stage – their ships are still able to fire with great accuracy even when they have received severe punishment. The fact that the gunnery of the German battle-fleet when engaged with our battle-fleet did not show the same accuracy must not, I think, be taken as showing that the standard is not so high as with their battle-cruisers, as I am inclined to the opinion that we then had some advantage in the way of light, although it was very bad for both sides.

In another paragraph he quoted some critical comments which Jellicoe himself had made in his report on the battle, to this effect:

The German organisation at night is very good. Their system of recognition signals is excellent. Ours is practically nil. Their searchlights are superior to ours and they use them with great effect. Finally their method of firing at night gives excellent results. I am reluctantly compelled to the opinion that under night conditions we have a good deal to learn from them.[2]

Furthermore, while the accompanying plans and charts had been carefully compiled from all the information available and were believed to be accurate, Harper himself in his covering submission when he sent in the completed Record (as it was called) in October 1919 admitted that it had been difficult to plot the actual track followed by certain squadrons or ships, especially when they were acting independently, owing to the very meagre details given in some of the logs and reports.

It had been Wemyss's intention that the Harper Record should not be shown to either Jellicoe or Beatty – a decision with which Jellicoe heartily agreed – but on 1 November, just after it had been completed and its forthcoming publication announced in Parliament and the press, Beatty succeeded him as First Sea Lord and continued in that post until 1927. His former chief of staff Vice-Admiral Brock (as he now was) had already been made Deputy Chief of the Naval Staff, and his flag-captain Chatfield became Assistant Chief, so that, as it was put at the time, 'the battle-cruiser people took over the Admiralty'. Being now responsible for the publication of the Record, Beatty read the proofs and examined the diagrams and charts. Still suffering from the lasting wound which the bitter disappointment and frustration of the long-awaited day of Jutland had left in his mind, and which was probably aggravated by severe domestic distress, he took exception to certain passages of the narrative which did not square with his recollections or which he considered showed the Battle-Cruiser Fleet in too unfavourable a light. He therefore made a number of amendments, insertions and deletions, among these last being the two paragraphs quoted above, and returned the Record to Harper on 11 February 1920 with an order to alter it accordingly. With this Harper complied, though on some points reluctantly and only after argument in which he adduced documentary evidence in support of his version. At this stage the First Lord, Walter Long, intervened to express disapproval of Beatty's action* and temporarily secured the cancellation of his instructions to Harper. Beatty, however, returned to the attack and succeeded in re-opening the question; and in May it was decided that each of the Sea Lords should be provided with a proof copy of the Record and asked to forward in writing any proposals for alterations which he might wish to make. These would be sent to Harper for his comments and afterwards discussed by a meeting at which he would be present.[3] Both Brock and Chatfield thereupon criticised the

---

* This disapproval was shared by Captain Richmond, who had written in his diary for 15 January: '[Harper] tells me the Jutland report is held up because Beatty wants alterations made. I'm sorry. I wish Beatty would leave it alone. He has made Harper alter some things which did "injustice" to the battle-cruisers' shooting, also a part of the track which H. had put in from the evidence. But Beatty says he doesn't care about all the evidence in the world, as it can't alter "facts". . . . A pity this, as it will open the way to controversy afterwards' (Marder, *Portrait of an Admiral*, p. 361).

general tone of the Record, Brock (who was the more moderate of the two) writing:

> I dislike [it], much for the same reason that Dr Fell was disliked. It is impartial and to a great extent impersonal, but it does convey to me the impression that not only was a great battle fought between the British and German fleets, but that it was one in which we got the worst of it. Neither of these impressions is correct; a great battle was *not* fought, the opposing battle fleets never really came into action, and far from getting the worst of it the direct result of the day's fighting was to drive the German fleet ignominiously into its ports. I realise, however, that . . . if we are bound to issue an official account, then this account, with a few excisions, must be published. But I feel that it is a great pity and will do the Navy no good. . . .[4]

Chatfield, who was convinced that the shooting of the battle-cruisers at Jutland had been better than that of their German opposite numbers and that it was only the defects of the British shells that had prevented them from doing more decisive damage,* complained that the Record 'lacked the note and tone of victory'.[5]

At the meeting, held on 21 June and attended by the First Lord and all the Sea Lords, various amendments suggested by the latter were discussed and it was also decided to add a foreword proposed by Beatty to the Record.[6] Jellicoe, who on his return to England had been told by 'many people'† that the Admiralty wanted to alter the Record but had hitherto adhered to his view that he ought not to read it, now asked to see this foreword, which he found to contain the following passage:

> [This] narrative of events . . . shows that the enemy's advanced forces were reinforced by their main fleet some hours before the British main fleet was able to reach the scene of action. During this period, therefore, the British were in greatly inferior force. On hearing of the approach of the British main fleet the Germans avoided further action and returned to base.

* See his *The Navy and Defence*, p. 151 and chap. xvi, *passim*.

† One of the first of these must have been Harper, whom he met by chance at the Admiralty when he went there on 11 February to pay his official call after returning from his mission – the very day on which Harper received his formal instructions from Beatty.

Greatly disquieted by the maladroit wording of this, with its implication that the main fleet had never been in action at all, Jellicoe entered into correspondence with Long, the outcome of which was that he was asked to read and comment on the Record itself, with the alterations now proposed. Having done this, albeit still reluctantly, he was moved to dissent so strongly from some of the intended changes that although he had just been offered and accepted the Governor-Generalship of New Zealand which he had coveted for some time he told both Long and the Colonial Secretary that he could not leave England to take up this appointment without some guarantee that the Record when published would not contain the passages to which he objected. Long, who in the discussions at the Admiralty had from the outset expressed a wish that nothing should be done which might distress or injure Lord Jellicoe, promised him that no amendments would be made to Harper's original draft without having first been sent out for his approval, together with proofs of their accuracy. Satisfied with this assurance, he then departed for New Zealand with his wife and family in August 1920.[7]

The Admiralty was now in a dilemma, confronted by the impossibility of revising Harper's work to the satisfaction of both Jellicoe and Beatty, especially as the First Lord was clearly inclined to sympathise with the former. In repeated discussions within its walls various compromises were suggested and discarded, including a proposal from the harassed Harper that he should be relieved of his task and that it should be entrusted to other hands. When this was refused he requested that since it was generally known that he was the officer who had drawn up the Record it should be accompanied when published by a statement that he was not responsible for any emendations in the text or charts that were not in accordance with the documentary evidence. He had been moved to make this request by knowledge that the Admiralty was about to publish the great bulk of this documentary evidence itself, in the shape of the 'Jutland Despatches', which were made public in December. Although they were termed by one newspaper 'a vast mass of undigested facts from which the layman cannot possibly disentangle the true history of this great sea-fight', Harper felt that any naval officer or even alert landsman who compared the Record with them would be able to see the discrepancies. To his request, however, he received only a dusty answer. Meanwhile the publication of the Despatches had led to a renewal of the questions which had already been asked in Parliament as to why the long-promised Record did not appear, and rumours about the reasons for this were rife, especially in the Service Clubs.[8] The Admiralty now sought a way of escape from its impasse by asking the distinguished naval historian Sir Julian Corbett to write a preface for the Record which could be substituted for Beatty's. Corbett, however, explained that since he was engaged under the auspices of the Historical Section of the Committee of Imperial Defence in writing the volumes of the official *History of the War* which were to deal with naval operations he could not accede to this request without the consent of Messrs Longmans, the publishers of the *History*. When the latter were approached they objected that if the Record appeared before the volume of the *History* dealing with Jutland this would prejudice its sales and in fact be a violation of their contract with the Government giving them the sole right to publish an account of the battle. This protest was not only accepted but seized upon by the Admiralty as a pretext for postponing the publication of the Record indefinitely.[9]

The next phase of the Jutland controversy centred around the Naval Staff Appreciation of the battle. In November 1920 Captain Ellerton, the Director of Training and Staff Duties, asked Captain A. C. Dewar to prepare an appreciation for the use of the Staff College. Dewar, a retired officer who had read history at Oxford and done some postgraduate work there under Sir Charles Firth, was the brother of Commander (now Captain) K. G. B. Dewar, the iconoclast with a chip on his shoulder who had got on the wrong side of the conservatively-minded Jellicoe while serving in first the Operations and afterwards the Plans Division of the Admiralty, and who in consequence was strongly prejudiced against him. In view of the complexities of the task, the elder Dewar asked that his brother might be associated with him in it.[10] The Harper Record with its plans and charts was placed at their disposal, and in the opening pages of the Appreciation which they produced they declared them to have been of great assistance,[11] though in after years Captain K. G. B. Dewar was much more critical of the Record in his book *The Navy from Within*, published in 1939. In this, incidentally, he emphasised that neither Beatty nor anyone else had attempted to influence the Appreciation, and that Beatty did not even see it until it was finished. 'I had only one interview with Lord Beatty', he continued, 'when I asked him whether the Appreciation was to be confined to a plain narrative or to include comments on tactics and command. He replied that an intelligible and accurate account was the main thing, but we should endeavour to bring out [the action's] lessons.'[12]

Unfortunately, though the brothers made some pertinent and valuable observations, they interpreted this permission to pass judgements far too liberally and in a spirit hostile to Jellicoe. After they had finished the Appreciation in January 1922 Rear-Admiral W. H. Haggard, who by then had succeeded Ellerton, reported of it that 'the mental attitude of the writer [sic] was rather that of a counsel for the prosecution than of an impartial appraiser of facts' and that 'an obvious bias animates his statements throughout . . ., leading to satirical observations and a certain amount of misrepresentation'.[13] Examples of the former were such comments as 'To make effective use of a large fleet attended by scores of light craft required a great deal of concentrated thought; this thought was not available; no provision had been made for it' and 'Beyond avoidance of a night action, it is difficult to trace any definite purpose in the British movements during the night', as well as the slighting conclusion of the narrative of the action – 'The Battle Fleet which had put to sea full of hope and ardour, superior to the foe in numbers and gun-power, at least his equal in discipline, individual skill and courage, returned home with two killed and five wounded. It had never been seriously in action.' Under the heading of misrepresentation, or at best of grave inaccuracy, must be placed, for instance, the statement that the Admiralty's signal of 10.41 p.m. to Jellicoe could have left him in no doubt that the High Seas Fleet was returning home by Horns Reef, so that 'if the Commander-in-Chief really desired to intercept the German Fleet his course was now clear'.[14] Beatty referred the question of whether the Appreciation should be issued as had been intended to Keyes and Chatfield, who minuted in August:

While not approving the tone in which the book is written . . . nor [agreeing] in all respects with the criticisms of the tactics of the Commander-in-Chief, e.g. the criticism of Single Line, we are in entire agreement with the main conclusions . . ., both as regards

(i) the failure of Lord Jellicoe to seize the great opportunity before him on the afternoon of the 31st May, and

(ii) his failure to make any dispositions or give any instructions that would bring the enemy to action at dawn on the 1st June.

It is not considered, however, that any sufficient cause exists at the moment to justify the issue to the Fleet of a book that would rend the Service to its foundations. . . .[15]

Since the Dewars, as the above reference to their criticisms of the single line-ahead formation indicates, had also condemned an important part of the Navy's tactical doctrine, as well as its whole conception of centralised command, the dozen copies which had been printed and distributed to a few individuals* for their comments were therefore called in, although in fact not all were returned. Captain K. G. B. Dewar, however, was detailed to give a series of lectures to the Senior Officers War Course in 1922, in which (according to the understandably embittered Harper, who attended it) he virtually reproduced the Appreciation and was severely heckled after each lecture about the inaccuracies and wrong conclusions it contained.[16]

Unhappily further prudent counsel which Admirals Keyes and Chatfield had also given that an expurgated version of the Appreciation which had been prepared by Admiral Haggard or under his supervision† should likewise not be issued, since 'however carefully it was worded the composition of the present Naval Staff would cause it to be received with hostility and suspicion in certain quarters', was not followed.[17] Instead this 'de-venomised' version of the Dewars' *Staff Appreciation*', as it has been aptly termed by Professor Marder, survived to become known (though apparently not till its eventual publication in 1924) as the *Admiralty Narrative of Jutland*.

The controversy now passed into its next phase, in which Jellicoe

---

* Among these was Corbett, who had expressed the opinion that the presentation of the facts was so faulty that the book ought not to go out with the Admiralty imprimatur (Add. MS 49037, ff. 172–3: Corbett to Jellicoe, 10 Mar. 1922).

† The functions of the DTSD included the co-ordination into an overall picture of the views of different departments of the Admiralty in cases where there was a possibility of conflict or at least need of reconciliation.

was again involved. Since the *Admiralty Narrative*, though primarily a substitute for the *Staff Appreciation*, might be regarded (or at any rate was considered by him) as ultimately replacing the Harper Record, a draft of it was sent out to him for his comments, in accordance with Long's promise in 1920,* and reached him at the end of July. To a correspondent, Commander Oswald Frewen, who had been one of Harper's assistants but had retired from the Navy shortly afterwards, he wrote that he found it 'very full of inaccurate statements and misleading deductions, especially when it sets out to point out what the C-in-C. of the Grand Fleet "ought" . . . to have gathered from the information sent him, however contradictory it might be'. After he had finished a meticulous examination of it, prolonged by the need to check a great many of its statements against the papers which he had prudently brought out with him, he declared to Frewen that the carelessness and inaccuracy of the document were remarkable and the charts and diagrams even worse.[18] To the Admiralty he wrote on 27 November that he took exception to a great deal of the narrative and many of the diagrams, and strongly dissented from the publication of the production as it stood. Having listed his objections, he requested 'most urgently' that if the Admiralty could not agree to meet them it would at least publish them in the same volume with the *Narrative*. After an interval of ten months he received a list of amendments to which the Board was prepared to agree, together with a statement that the others he wanted could not be accepted and a request to cable as soon as possible whether he concurred in the *Narrative* as now altered. Since he was still far from satisfied, however, he found it impossible to compress his further comments into a cable message and had to content himself with cabling the more important points to which he continued to object, while offering to forward the rest of his remarks at once by steamer if the Admiralty would hold up publication until they arrived.[19] This it declined to do, however, and instead issued the *Narrative* with an appendix containing the cabled criticisms, 'to meet the wishes of Admiral of the Fleet Lord Jellicoe', but plentifully annotated with counter-criticisms and prefaced by the statement that where this appendix differed from the *Narrative* Their Lordships were

* Lord Long (as he had become) had been succeeded as First Lord by Lord Lee of Fareham in 1921.

satisfied that the latter was more in accordance with the evidence available.[20]

The point on which Jellicoe felt most strongly was one which concerned not himself but Sir Hugh Evan-Thomas, who had been Rear-Admiral Commanding the Fifth Battle Squadron at Jutland. In his view that part of the *Narrative* which dealt with the battle-cruiser action was so worded* as to cast the blame unjustly on Sir Hugh for the two occasions when the distance between the battle-cruisers and the supporting Fifth Squadron was greatly increased by the time-lag between their respective turns; whereas he himself felt (though he had hitherto kept silent on the subject) that the fault was Beatty's because of the laxity of his signalling arrangements – a laxity which was turned into inefficiency by the incompetence of his flag-lieutenant. 'I could not possibly agree', Jellicoe had written to his former subordinate and old friend while his correspondence with the Admiralty was going on, 'to the attempt to place criticism (although only insinuated) on to your shoulders. The worst features of the whole *Narrative* are contained in the insinuations.' His distress at his failure to prevail on the Admiralty to alter these passages was deepened by the fact that Sir Hugh, 'a fine, straightforward and utterly honest character . . . universally liked and admired', but accustomed throughout his

* See pp. 113–14 above. The wording in question, as regards the first turn, was:
'As the *Lion* turned, the *Barham* [Evan-Thomas's flagship] hauled away two points to port . . ., presumably to recommence her zigzag. Six minutes later, the *Lion*'s "alter course" signal having been received [which Evan-Thomas to his dying day denied was the case so far as the executive signal was concerned], the *Barham* turned back 15 points. By the time she had completed this turn [she] was over nine miles from the *Lion*, and . . . was still considerably astern of her appointed station when the action commenced.' (*Narrative of the Battle of Jutland*, p. 12.)
Of the second turn, after Scheer's main fleet had been sighted, the *Narrative* said:
'[After] the *Lion* turned at 4.41 p.m. . . . the 5th Battle Squadron, still on a southerly course, was rapidly closing Admiral Beatty's battle-cruisers. . . . The *Lion* was returning full speed on a northerly course. She was soon on the port bow of the *Barham* with a signal flying to the 5th Battle Squadron to turn 16 points in succession. She passed about 1½ miles off on the port hand and the 5th Battle Squadron turned to starboard shortly afterwards. [The] turn had been delayed, and the *Lion* was now some 3 or 4 miles off . . .' (*Ibid.*, pp. 23–4).

career to precise and uniform signalling practices such as had been the rule in the Grand Fleet, had meanwhile suffered a stroke from which his health never really recovered and which was ascribed to the frustration of his own efforts to remove what he regarded as this stain on his name by getting the *Narrative* altered.[21]

If an opinion once strongly expressed by Sir Herbert Richmond is to be credited, Admiral Evan-Thomas may not have been the only person of distinction whose end was somewhat hastened by the Jutland controversy. Sir Julian Corbett's third (Jutland) volume of the official *History of the War* had also aroused some disagreement behind the scenes. The Admiralty had from the outset claimed and exercised rights of censorship over the volumes on Naval Operations which Corbett was producing for the Historical Section of the Committee of Imperial Defence. The proofs of the first volume had been submitted in 1919 to Wemyss, who after taking the opinion of Admiral Sir Edmond Slade on them had laid down the principle that any statements of personal views must be deleted but no statements of fact were to be omitted simply because they necessarily implied criticism. Corbett had accordingly gone through the text with Slade and amended certain passages which had been blue-pencilled.[22] To the second volume hardly any exception seems to have been taken; but the third, with the new regime at the Admiralty, was another matter. Since at least the early summer of 1922 Sir Julian had been in correspondence about it with Jellicoe, to whom he sent draft passages which he sometimes modified in the light of the comments which the latter made. 'My general impression on the whole affair now', he wrote in June, 'is that nothing you could have done could have forced Scheer to decisive action except meeting him in the morning between him and his base, and this he prevented simply because the necessary information which the Admiralty had intercepted was not passed on to you.' But although, as his next letter made clear, he had 'noted specially the omission to send you the [intercept] about the air reconnaissance off Horns Riff [*sic*]' he was obliged to add that from the nature of the case he could not say as much as he would have liked on this point.[23] In fact he was forbidden by the Admiralty to quote the deciphered German signals whose gist had been passed to Jellicoe in such a mutilated form that he had disregarded them, and so, as a very distinguished naval historian of our day* has written, he 'was prevented from placing a share, and perhaps the chief share, of the responsibility for the escape of the High Seas Fleet where it properly belonged'. His Jutland chapters and in particular his account of the battle-cruiser action also met when in proof with fierce criticism from Beatty and objections almost as strong from Chatfield, Oliver (now Second Sea Lord), Rear-Admiral Sir Frederick Field the Third Sea Lord, and Captain Dudley Pound the Director of the Plans Division; while Haggard wrote more moderately that while it was an exceedingly good description of the battle it was written from the standpoint of the Commander-in-Chief of the Grand Fleet.[24] At the time of Corbett's sudden death in September 1922, which Richmond thought had been hastened by these difficulties,† he had just corrected the final proofs of the volume; and Colonel E. Y. Daniel the Secretary of the Historical Section of the Committee of Imperial Defence, who after working with him for many years had possessed his entire confidence and known exactly his views on Jutland, wrote to Jellicoe that although it contained a few errors of fact which would have to be put right it would be his own earnest endeavour to see that the dead historian's account of the battle was not otherwise interfered with. He added, however, that he expected considerable trouble with the Admiralty over certain passages.[25] This proved a true forecast, though in the end Their Lordships allowed the volume to appear in 1923 with only Daniel's minor emendations and a prefatory foreword, drafted apparently by Keyes and described by them as 'a strengthened disclaimer', to the effect that while they had given the author access to official documents during its preparation they were in no way responsible for its production or the accuracy of its statements, and found that 'some of the principles advocated, especially the tendency to minimise the importance of seeking battle and of forcing it to a conclusion, [were] directly in conflict with their views'.[26] Not surprisingly, Jellicoe on the other hand eulogised it warmly, declaring that Sir Julian had possessed a remarkable gift of getting at the truth of a situation by reading official papers and of entering into his own difficulties, intentions and actions

---

* Captain S. W. Roskill, R.N., in a letter to *Times Literary Supplement*, 17 June 1960.

† Private information.

on the day of the battle – a verdict which, or something like it, would probably be widely endorsed today.

Although Jellicoe had striven, and continued to strive, successfully to avoid taking any public part in the controversy, its development had led him to explore the possibility of a second edition of *The Grand Fleet*, for which he had set to work to write a substantial appendix on Jutland. After providing Corbett with a first draft of this, he had sent a revised version[27] on 27 November 1922 (the day on which he also returned the *Admiralty Narrative* to the Board with his criticisms) to Alexander Hurd of the editorial staff of the *Daily Telegraph*, who was a prolific writer of articles on naval topics and the author of the official *War History's* volume on the Merchant Navy, and whom Jellicoe had deputed, along with his old friend and chief Reginald McKenna, to watch his interests and act for him if necessary in the matter of publication while he was away. In this appendix he made a mild reference* (mild because at that time he was still hoping that the Admiralty might modify the relevant passage in its *Narrative*) to the responsibility of the *Lion*'s faulty signalling for Evan-Thomas's delay in following the battle-cruisers' first turn; and laid great emphasis on the handicap imposed on him when meeting the German main fleet by the combination of confused and inadequate signal reports with misty weather. 'Under the conditions existing at the time that the fleets met', he wrote, '. . . it was rare to see even four ships at once, and then so indistinctly that it was very difficult to distinguish their class'; and again, 'During the whole period from 6.14 p.m. until dark it was impossible to divine to what portion of the German Battle Fleet the ships occasionally in sight belonged, and in what formation it was steaming'. Thus at the point when Scheer turned away for the second time, at 7.15 p.m.,

> it was unfortunate that I was ignorant of [its] formation, and . . .
> as I had never seen more than 3 or 4 ships at a time from the
> *Iron Duke* it was quite impossible to gauge the situation from
> my own knowledge. The disappearance of the few ships in
> sight, covered as it was by a very thick smoke-screen, did not
> therefore indicate that the German fleet had turned away. . . .

* '. . . The signal being made by flags only, wireless not being used, was apparently not clearly distinguished.'

Had, however, I been aware of the extent of the retiring movement [he continued] and had also ignored the threat of the torpedoes it would still have been very difficult to have regained touch before dark . . . under the conditions of mist and smoke-screen.

Apropos of Beatty's much-publicised signal 'Submit van of battle-ships follow battle-cruisers. We can then cut off whole of enemy's battle fleet', he wrote:

A great deal of publicity has been given to this signal by some writers to the Press, and the insinuation has been made that Sir David Beatty was imploring a reluctant Commander-in-Chief to follow him. In order to support this suggestion it has been freely stated that the signal was made by the *Lion,* and received in the *Iron Duke,* at a much earlier time than was in fact the case. The actual time of origin of the signal was 7.50 p.m. . . . It was received in the *Iron Duke*'s wireless office (as shown by the wireless log) at 7.54 p.m., and as it was in cypher de-cyphering was necessary. It could not possibly . . . have reached the bridge before 8 p.m., and it was actually some minutes later than this.

He then proceeded to describe and explain the action he had taken, as already narrated.

On the events of the ensuing night he commented:

The information at my disposal at the time indicated that the German fleet had three routes of exit from their base, viz. – *via* the Horns Reef, the Friesland coast, and a channel to the north-westward of Heligoland. The first had recently been watched by our submarines, and of this fact Scheer would be aware and this knowledge might be expected to act as a deterrent to the use of it. However when I turned south at 9 p.m. my intention was to close the Horns Reef at daylight, provided nothing occurred during the night or on the following morning to cause a change of view. It was hoped, too, that some indication of his intended route would be given during the night.

As to this:

. . . At about 11.5 p.m. a message was received from the Admiralty . . . stating that at 10.41 p.m. the enemy was believed to be returning to its base, as its course was S.S.E., $\frac{3}{4}$ E. . . . This message was of great importance if considered alone and if taken as accurate, as it would then indicate that the High Seas Fleet was . . . intending apparently to return by the Horns Reef channel.

He then explained his reasons for discounting the message and went on:

During the next hour the glare of star shell and occasional searchlights could be seen a long way astern of the Battle Fleet. No reports of what was occurring were received, and it was assumed that engagements between our destroyers and the German destroyers and supporting light cruisers were in progress. The general impression left on my mind by these occurrences was that Scheer had pushed his light forces ahead to ascertain if the routes to the Horn Reef or via Heligoland were clear for him, and seeing that his ships had come into contact with our destroyers it appeared probable that his main fleet would have been driven to the westward or at least would have been delayed sufficiently on its southerly course to give us every chance of bringing him to action in the morning.

When approached on the subject of a second edition of *The Grand Fleet*, however, the publishers, Messrs. Cassell, replied that interest in books about the war had now waned and that therefore they did not see their way to bringing one out.

All these passages-at-arms and literary excursions, it must be borne in mind, were only a part (though a rather vexatious part) of the background to Lord Jellicoe's busy and happy life in New Zealand.[28] As Governor-General he started with the advantage of having through his visit a year previously laid the foundations of the affection with which he came to be regarded by the whole people of the Dominion by the end of his term of office. He had not been long in the country before he began in his quiet and undramatic way to get rid of many of the old out-of-date usages and formalities which had raised a barrier of exclusiveness between previous governors-general and the bulk of the community apart from the small section hitherto admitted to Government House.

This barrier [to quote an observer of the process*] Lord Jellicoe was peculiarly fitted to break down . . . by almost imperceptible degrees and without conscious effort. . . . His temperament was a mixture of humility and dignity, the complete absence of make-believe or vanity, a special brand of sane optimism and a complete human understanding which had the rare quality of imparting to others the conviction that he both understood and sympathised with them in their difficulties. . . . The majority of the population expected before he arrived (and some of his photographs seemed to justify the speculation) . . . a man stern of expression, staccato of voice and sharp of command, whose will was law and who would naturally be rather unapproachable. But when he came amongst them, here was this little man with eyes tired yet kind and wise . . ., to which a twinkle of humour came readily, who was dignified but entirely free from pompousness, who told them good stories, was more approachable than their own democratic neighbours, but seemed to inspire a deep personal attachment without encouraging familiarity.

His friendliness towards people of all classes met with a ready response, especially from the young, who were drawn to him by his 'lovable smile, with at times just a hint of roguishness'; and his fund of stories, told with a dry humour, earned him a reputation as a raconteur, though he was even more noted for his many small thoughtful actions of the sort that were fundamental to his nature.

All his life Lord Jellicoe had worked hard and played hard when leisure and opportunity offered, and he continued to do so now. 'He got through a vast amount of work without ever appearing to be hurried, and in his processes of thought was invariably calm and collected with absolute self-control. Never idle, never a time-waster, he knew when and how to relax.'[29] He took only a fortnight's pure holiday in the year, and for most of the rest of the time he was hard at work, either at Wellington during the parliamentary season or travelling to visit all parts of the islands and making an immense number of speeches as he toured around. While at Wellington for the session, which lasted from the end of June until November, he presided at least once a week over the

* Sir Cecil Day, quoted in Bacon, *Life of Earl Jellicoe*, p. 477.

meetings of the Executive Council. His relations with the Prime Minister, Mr W. F. Massey, were warm and friendly, and he was on the best of terms not only with his other ministers but with the leaders of the Opposition and members of all parties. Nor, though naturally hedged about by constitutional restrictions, was he merely a popular figurehead, for his ministers not only dutifully kept him informed of all important developments of policy, but in view of his experience of men and things and his aptitude for going straight to the root of a problem they often sought and valued his counsel in unofficial conversations. Since he was aware of the importance of strengthening good relations between the Maoris and their white compatriots, he also took every opportunity of meeting and addressing them. His favourite outdoor recreations were golf, which he played on a course near Government House when he had some free time in an afternoon, and sailing. Soon after his arrival he bought a 14-foot boat which he named the *Iron Duke* and sailed himself, frequently in races and with no small success; and both at Wellington and Auckland he was a familiar figure on the waterfront, clad in old duck trousers and a once-white pullover, a pair of canvas shoes that had seen better days and hard service, and a salt-stained cap, refusing to accept priorities and privileges and behaving like any other ordinary helpful club member. He also often played tennis and occasionally cricket, went trout-fishing and deer-stalking during his annual holiday, sometimes attended race-meetings and now and again rode to hounds. In contrast, Lady Jellicoe, a bold horsewoman, hunted regularly, and their children were also enthusiasts. As time went on, however, Lord Jellicoe came to feel that they ought to have a European education, and it was this consideration that decided him to decline the extension of office which he was offered after he had been Governor-General for a little more than four years. Leaving New Zealand in November 1924, he received the honour of an earldom in the following June in recognition of his services.

While he was still on his way home the flames of the Jutland controversy, which some had hoped were dying down, were fanned again by the appearance of Admiral Sir Reginald Bacon's *The Jutland Scandal*, a belligerently partisan book meant as a counter-blast to the *Admiralty Narrative* and almost as critical of Beatty as that had been of Jellicoe. A judicious leading article in the *Daily*

Telegraph of 9 January 1925 deplored the continuation of the controversy as injurious to the interests of both the Navy and the nation.

> The impartial historian of the Great War [it prophesied] when in years to come he attempts to digest the wealth of material which will be available, may possibly reach the conclusion that each and all of the officers of high rank concerned in operations by sea and land committed errors, as fallible beings must in engagements on so vast a scale, but that a high standard of judgement was for the most part maintained in dealing with the circumstances of the fleeting moment. . . . There is nothing but bitterness to be gained by continuing to bandy words . . . . The nation will welcome the time when the Navy can be described again with truth as the Silent Service.

In 1926, however, appeared an English translation of *Der Krieg zur See*, the German official history, whose chief concern was to prove Jutland a German victory, but which in the attempt to do so threw lights on the battle that were sometimes more favourable to Jellicoe than to Beatty. Of the *Admiralty Narrative* it observed that it had been 'characterised very rightly by Admiral Jellicoe as inaccurate on several essential points'. It also reaffirmed the superiority of German gunnery in the battle-cruiser action, praised Jellicoe's deployment on his port division when he came into contact with the High Seas Fleet as the best alternative open to him, and wrote of the second contact of the main fleets that the German battle-cruisers and the leading ships of the Third Squadron 'had received much greater damage during this phase of the battle than before'.[30]

While the two men most concerned both refrained from taking any public part in the unhappy dispute, Churchill added further fuel to it in the second and still more in the third volume of his *The World Crisis* (1923–9) by the severe and sometimes unfair criticisms which he made of Jellicoe's caution, not only at Jutland but throughout the naval war. In composing his Jutland chapters it is evident that he leant heavily on the Dewars' Staff Appreciation, to a copy of which he had evidently been given access, since the diagrams he included in support of his contention that Jellicoe should have deployed on a centre column were identical with those which they had used to back the same argument.[31] Like others of Jellicoe's armchair critics, he wrote with retrospective and comprehensive plans of the engagement before him but in bland disregard of the fact that these had not been available to the Commander-in-Chief at the time.

On the other hand when in 1927 the Harper Record, or something like it, finally emerged into publication it proved a damp squib. According to Harper's own subsequent contention it was the Admiralty's awareness of the imminent appearance of a book under the title of *The Truth about Jutland*, which he had taken advantage of having just been placed on the retired list to write, that led to its decision to publish the Record at last.[32] But despite the statement made in answer to a question in the Commons on 25 May that it would be published in its original unamended form, no copy of this could be found in the Admiralty, and instead one of the proof copies surviving from 1920, which had been subjected to fewer corrections than the others, was selected.[33] Its publication finally dispelled any lingering notion that there was some sinister mystery about the details of the battle, and helped, together with Harper's own book, to stem – though not to still – the long dispute. *The Truth about Jutland*, despite its title, was equally unsensational; and though it championed Jellicoe on the vexed questions of the deployment, the turn-away and Scheer's eventual escape, and made criticisms of Beatty some of which had not been mentioned by Bacon, its tone was quieter and more restrained than that of *The Jutland Scandal*.

Behind the scenes a possible source of further controversy was quietly but only temporarily damped down at this time. Corbett's successor Sir Henry Newbolt, continuing the official *History of the War at Sea*, was now engaged on vol. v, part of which was concerned with the anti-submarine campaign and the introduction of convoy. At the beginning of 1927 the Admiralty (where Sir Charles Madden had now succeeded Beatty as First Sea Lord) sent Jellicoe a proof of the first draft of this section, which rather disturbed him and caused him to return it with a letter in which he dissented from some of the statements it contained and asked to be shown the authority on which they had been made. Soon afterwards he found by a chance meeting with Paymaster-Rear-Admiral Sir Eldon Manisty, who as a fleet paymaster had been made Organising Manager of Convoys when the system was introduced in 1917, that he had also been sent a proof of the draft and that its misstatements had reduced him to a state of fury. Jellicoe then sought an interview with Newbolt, who told him quite frankly that in his opinion it was Lloyd George's expressed intention to visit the Admiralty which had caused Duff to recommend the adoption of the system. After rebutting this idea Jellicoe entered, in order to get confirmation of his recollections, into that correspondence with Admiral Sir Alexander Duff (as he now was) which has already been mentioned* and in which the latter, who had himself retired three years earlier, stated clearly and emphatically that he had been influenced solely by the mounting shipping losses in his change of mind over convoy. Newbolt, however, remained unconvinced for some time and Jellicoe was obliged to call on his brother-in-law Madden to exert pressure to get what he described as 'the original absurdly inaccurate chapter' revised.[34]

For a time this second controversy lay dormant, but in 1933 the *News Chronicle* announced that Lloyd George would be producing the first two volumes of his *War Memoirs* in the autumn. In an interview the publishers revealed in advance that these would contain 'a strong attack on the military mind' and in particular a statement that convoys had been 'introduced solely by the civilians against strong Admiralty opposition'.[35] Actually it was the third volume, published in September 1934, which contained a chapter on 'The Peril of the Submarines'. In this Lloyd George wrote of Jellicoe's decision (in which it will be remembered that Beatty had heartily concurred)† not to hazard the Grand Fleet south of 55° 30′ and east of 4°:

> After the Battle of Jutland,‡ Admiral Jellicoe came to the conclusion it was not safe for his imposing Armada of enormous Dreadnoughts 'to undertake prolonged operations to the south of the Dogger Bank', as the risk of mines and submarines was too formidable. They were not to enter the southern end of the North Sea unless they were forced to do so by direct challenge from the German High Seas Fleet. Meanwhile the flagship must be interned in safe creeks, the flag had to be carried on the small craft, the nimble destroyers and the weather-beaten trawlers. Here is the 'Nelson touch' up to date.

Later, after references to 'the fear-dimmed eyes of our Mall

---

* See above, p. 173.   † See above, p. 148.
‡ It was actually after Scheer's sortie of 19 August 1916. See p. 147.

admirals', 'the amazing and incomprehensible difficulties encountered in inducing the Admiralty even to try the convoy system' and 'the most implacable and prolonged resistance on the part of the Admiralty', came the following passage apropos of his proposed descent thereon:

> Apparently the prospect of being overruled in their own sanctuary galvanised the Admiralty into a fresh inquisition, and by way of anticipating the inevitable they further examined the plans and figures which Commander Henderson had prepared in consultation with Mr Norman Leslie of the Ministry of Shipping. They then for the first time began to realise . . . that protection for a convoy system was within the compass of their resources. Accordingly, when I arrived at the Admiralty I found the Board in a chastened mood.[36]

Lloyd George, that is, packed into the twenty-four hours of 25–6 April both the realisation of the mistake in the shipping figures and the preparation of Duff's minute.

Sir Alexander Duff had died on 22 November 1933 without having seen these sneering strictures; but Jellicoe had gathered the gist of them in advance, and he now set to work to write, not a polemical retort to Lloyd George whom he regarded as beneath such direct notice, but a history of the labours and achievements of the Anti-Submarine Division of the Admiralty in 1917, as an indirect and more dignified reply. This he at first intended as a supplement to a new edition of *The Crisis of the Naval War* which he hoped the interest aroused by Lloyd George's *Memoirs* would now induce the publishers to bring out; but Messrs. Cassell preferred that it should be expanded into a separate book, and it appeared in 1934 as *The Submarine Peril*.

Nevertheless it would be a distortion of the facts to exaggerate the place occupied by these controversies in the active and happy life of Lord Jellicoe's closing years. After his return from New Zealand and his transfer to the retired list which had occurred at the same time, he made his home at St Lawrence Hall* near Ventnor in the Isle of Wight, in which island his parents had latterly lived and to which he was much attached, as indeed he was to the whole county of Hampshire with which most of the

---

* This had formerly belonged to Lady Jellicoe's parents.

branches of his ancestors had been connected. One of the first activities with which he was soon prominently associated was the Boy Scout Movement, in which he became County Commissioner for London in 1925. Although for much of the year he lived out of London, he never came up there without devoting part of his time to his duties in this capacity; but on taking over the presidency of the British Legion in 1928 he felt that he could not continue to carry out the duties of both offices adequately and so was obliged to resign the former. Being immediately elected a vice-president of the London Scout Council, however, he was still able to maintain contact and show his continued interest in the movement. As President of the Legion he was the successor of its founder Earl Haig on the latter's sudden death; and he immediately plunged whole-heartedly into the duties involved and set about making himself conversant with all aspects of its work. The extent to which he succeeded in identifying himself with these and the members' deep appreciation of his activities may be judged from the tribute paid to him by the Secretariat of the Legion after his death:

> The Navy had long known, and the Legion had discovered, the immense worth of this singularly lovable man, and consequently when failing health and advancing years compelled Lord Jellicoe to relinquish the Presidency, they were determined to retain if possible his active interest and made for him the position of Vice-Patron, which he held until his death. . . . The attributes which had caused him to be trusted in the Navy and to be loved by all ranks – his thoroughness and efficiency, the simplicity and kindliness of his nature, his unbounded sympathy and thought for others – won for him a secure place in the hearts of members.

Another of his activities was his chairmanship of the National Rifle Association, his connection with which had begun in 1918. To his qualities in this capacity Lord Cottesloe, who was his vice-chairman and succeeded him in 1930, bore testimony as follows:

> Seldom can such outstanding ability have been combined with such delightful modesty. At the deliberations of the Council he was ever tactful and sagacious, patient and unhurried, taking care that all views were stated before a decision was taken. Never

failing in courtesy and consideration, with an unassuming personality that radiated friendliness and sympathy, he quickly commanded personal attachment, trust and affection from all with whom he came into contact.

Himself no mean marksman, he also fired in several matches at Bisley, notably for the Lords *v.* the Commons in 1925, 1926 and 1928.[37]

These activities and various others, together with his more personal correspondence (to say nothing of the great number of letters from societies and organisations of all kinds seeking his support or services and from individuals asking for his aid or thanking him for it) involved an immense burden of letter-writing, especially as he was most punctilious in his private correspondence, answering all of it in his own hand, irrespective of the age or social standing of the correspondent. From long days spent in London or in distant parts of the country, often on British Legion business, he would return late in the evening to St Lawrence Hall to find his table crowded with communications of all sorts, to which he would presently apply himself, working and writing late into the night, as he had done at the Admiralty in former days. There is little doubt that in spite of the exercise which he took (chiefly in the form of golf) when time permitted, these labours imposed a further strain upon his health which, coming on top of those to which it had been subjected by the great responsibilities of his active career, must have somewhat shortened his life. In 1931, after a visit to Canada in the autumn accompanied by Lady Jellicoe and his son and eldest daughter, he developed a serious and painful illness which laid him up for nearly a year and was at times thought likely to have fatal consequences. From this, however, his indomitable spirit enabled him to recover, and a visit to Madeira in 1932 gave him back much of his strength; but on 9 November 1935 he apparently caught a chill while planting poppies at a pre-Armistice Day ceremony. On Armistice Day itself, characteristically disregarding his indisposition, he laid a wreath from British ex-servicemen on the Foch Memorial at Victoria, and made another public appearance on the following day. After that it became apparent that one lung and then his heart had been affected, and on the evening of 19 November he died peacefully. On the 25th he was buried in St Paul's Cathedral, on a day of mist and damp not wholly unlike that of Jutland. So perhaps Earl Beatty may have reflected, who though lying ill with influenza had thrust aside his doctor's expostulations and insisted on attending the funeral as a pall-bearer. From the effects of this exposure, aggravated by a similar insistence on being present at the last obsequies of King George V soon afterwards, he in his turn never really recovered, dying on 11 March 1936.[38]

Jutland, indeed, stands out in the lives of both men, though more clearly in Jellicoe's. All his earlier career had led up to those few seconds of swift decision on the bridge of the *Iron Duke* at 6.14 p.m. on 31 May 1916, when against all handicaps he seized the advantage over Scheer. That was his greatest moment; the rest was a long, slow anti-climax. The odds against him at Jutland, not of ships and men but circumstances and *matériel*, were after all too great to allow the resounding victory for which the nation looked. Churchill, for all his subsequent criticisms, stated Jellicoe's case in a nutshell when he wrote that he 'could have lost the war in an afternoon';[39] and he did not. Nelson at Trafalgar, Cunningham when he accepted all risks and losses in the Mediterranean during the dark days of the spring of 1941, had neither of them the whole naval might of Britain in his keeping. Jellicoe virtually had; and if he had risked it on one turn of the wheel and thrown away this country's greatest advantage he would have been execrated as long as naval history continued to be written as the architect of Britain's ruin. Instead, he achieved the success of thrusting back the German fleet into its prison-house and closing the doors on any serious prospect of its escaping by way of surface victory.

But after Jutland neither he nor Beatty was quite the same man again. The latter had had his greatest moment too, or rather his greatest hour, not of swift and sure reflection but of sustained, indomitable and inspiring valour that had borne him outwardly unmoved through seeming disaster to recovery and the prospect of triumph. And then this triumph had failed to materialise, leaving a mark that smarted all the rest of his life and burned redly more than once, but may perhaps best be counted as one of the scars of battle. Jellicoe, save perhaps for one moment,* bore his tremendous disappointment stoically; he went on to the end of the

* See above, p. 135.

road, first preparing to do better under more favourable circumstances, and then performing the duties to which he was called with all the might and powers left in him. But the impression remains that something – a ring and snap and even perhaps a resilience that were there before – had gone out of him, and that this was not due simply and entirely to the continued strain of toil and responsibility. Yet his service of enduring value was that he had taken that strain, not once but twice, as Commander-in-Chief and as First Sea Lord, and though it had worn him down it had not broken him.

The last word might perhaps be left to come from a seemingly unlikely quarter – the sometime German Emperor, who had known and liked and admired Jellicoe and when he died sent his widow his tribute to 'the illustrious Admiral, whose sterling qualities as gallant leader, splendid seaman, chivalrous opponent and British gentleman will be for ever treasured'.[40]

Appendix

The Comparative Strengths of the Grand Fleet and the High Seas Fleet

THE relative numbers of ships of the various classes in the two fleets (counting only those which had completed their training *and were battle-worthy*) at certain periods of the war prior to the Battle of Jutland were as follows:

Date	Dread-noughts	Pre-dreadnoughts	Battle-cruisers	Cruisers	Light Cruisers	Destroyers	Airships
4 August 1914							
British	20	8	4	9	12	42	—
German	13	16	3	2	15	88	1
1 October 1914							
British	20	12	6	10	12	42	—
German	15	16	3	2	14	88*	3
1 January 1915							
British	21	8	6	14	17	44	—
German	16	16	4	1	12	88*	6
1 April 1915							
British	23	8	9	17	18	54	—
German	17	16	4	—	14	88*	6
1 October 1915							
British	25	10	10	15	25	66	—
German	17	16	4	—	15	88*	12

* Approximation only.

At the outbreak of war Britain had 54 submarines, but 37 of these (the B and C classes) were unfit for oversea work and used only for coastal defence or in the Channel, while of the remaining 17 only the 9 E-class boats were equal to the best of the 28 submarines which Germany then possessed. No British submarines were attached to the Grand Fleet until a flotilla was based on Blyth in March 1916.

Of the 20 dreadnought battleships in the Grand Fleet on 4 August 1914, ten had as their main armament ten 13·5-inch guns apiece and the rest ten 12-inch. The First Battle Squadron under Vice-Admiral Sir Lewis Bayly was composed of 7 of the older ('12-inch') dreadnoughts and the 13·5-inch-gunned *Marlborough* as his flagship; the Second under Vice-Admiral Sir George Warrender comprised 8 more of the newer ('13·5-inch') ships (the tenth being the fleet flagship, the *Iron Duke*); and the Fourth under Vice-Admiral Sir Douglas Gamble was as yet only a skeleton squadron of three of the oldest '12-inchers'. The Third Battle Squadron under Vice-Admiral E. E. Bradford had 8 pre-dreadnoughts. The Battle-Cruiser Squadron (as it was first named) was originally composed of the *Lion* (flag), *Princess Royal*, *Queen Mary* and *New Zealand* only, the first three armed with 8 13·5s and the last with 8 12-inch.

Subsequent additions of capital ships on the British side were the battle-cruiser *Inflexible* (end of August 1914); the *Agincourt*, a requisitioned and renamed battleship with 14 12-inch guns which was being built for the Turkish Navy when war broke out (7 September 1914); *Erin*, another requisitioned Turk, with 10 13·5s (17 September); *Canada*, with 10 14-inch guns, under construction for Chile and also requisitioned (15 October); the battle-cruiser *Tiger* (end of October); the battleships *Benbow* and *Emperor of India*, of the *Iron Duke* class, which joined the Grand Fleet on 10 December but had been so hurriedly completed that a great deal of fitting work was required before they were in a proper condition even to begin the several weeks of practice which all newly-joined ships had to have before they became efficient enough to join the Fleet at sea or to take part in action; the battle-cruisers *Indomitable* (December 1914), *Australia*, *Indefatigable* and *Invincible* (all February 1915). With the appearance of the *Warspite* on 13 April 1915 the *Queen Elizabeth* class of super-dreadnoughts with 8 15-inch guns began to arrive and constitute the Fifth Battle Squadron. The *Queen Elizabeth* herself, which had been sent to the Dardanelles for a work-out, joined on 26 May; the *Barham* on 2 October; the *Malaya* on 18 February 1916; and the *Valiant* on 2 March. Two super-dreadnoughts of the next (*Royal Sovereign*) class, the *Revenge* and the *Royal Oak*, with similar main armaments, arrived in time to be present at Jutland, constituting (the *Queen Elizabeth* and *Emperor of India* being absent refitting) the total of 28 British dreadnought battleships present at the battle.

On the German side four of the original 13 dreadnought battle-

ships (those of the *Nassau* class) were armed with 12 11-inch guns
apiece, 4 (the *Helgoland* class) with 12 12-inch, and 5 (the *Kaiser*
class) with 10 12-inch. One of these last, the *König Albert*, was
refitting at the time of Jutland, but by then the next (*König*) class,
also with 10 12-inch guns, had joined, making the 16 dreadnought
battleships which Scheer had there (along with the 6 pre-dreadnoughts of the Second Battle Squadron).

The Channel Fleet, originally under Vice-Admiral Burney with
his flag in the *Lord Nelson* (main armament 4 12-inch and 10 9·2-
inch guns) was composed first of 16 and then 19 of the older pre-
dreadnoughts, with 7 cruisers which were almost immediately
transferred to other duties. The Harwich Force under Commodore Tyrwhitt consisted at the outbreak of war of two flotilla-
leaders and 35 destroyers. There were also the Dover and East
Coast patrol flotillas and a Third Fleet comprising our oldest
battleships and cruisers.[1]

R

Notes

In references to documents:
  Add. MS(S)   Additional Manuscript(s) in the British Museum
  Adm.   Admiralty Papers in the Public Record Office
  HP   Harper Papers in the Royal United Service Institution

I THE MAKING OF AN ADMIRAL

1. Where no other source is specifically stated, the account of Jellicoe's early life and career down to the outbreak of the First World War is based on the autobiographical fragment (Add. MS 49038, ff. 1–253) which he composed in later life but did not complete and publish.

2. H. W. Dickinson, 'Henry Cort's Bicentenary', *Transactions of the Newcomen Society* (1940–1), pp. 31–47.

3. *Southampton Times*, 16 Apr 1861.

4. *Burke's Peerage*. Numerous entries in local newspapers, viz., *Hampshire Advertiser*, *Hampshire Independent*, *Southampton Herald*, *Southampton Times*; e.g., obituary of J. R. Keele in the last-named, 2 Feb 1856.

5. Sir W. Goodenough, *A Rough Record*, pp. 66–7.

6. Vice-Admiral K. G. B. Dewar, *The Navy from Within*, p. 358.

7. Add. MS 49044, f. 159: Captain Colin Nicholson, R.N.R. (retd) to Admiral Sir Reginald Bacon, 29 Nov 1935.

8. Ibid. 49039, f. 64.

9. Ibid., 49044, f. 13: Lt-Col. G. I. Christie to Bacon, 29 Nov 1935.

10. Quoted in Sir R. Bacon, *The Life of John Rushworth, Earl Jellicoe*, p. 83.

11. Quoted in ibid., p. 101.

12. Add. MS 49035, ff. 8–19.

13. Ibid., 48990, ff. 5–9.

2 THE COMING MAN

1. Goodenough, *Rough Record*, p. 65.
2. Add. MS 48990, ff. 16–20.
3. Ibid. 49038, ff. 203–4.
4. Ibid. 48990, ff. 21–2.
5. Quoted in Bacon, *Jellicoe*, p. 167.
6. Add. MS 49006, ff. 5–7.
7. A. J. Marder, *Fear God and Dread Nought*, ii, 418–19.
8. Ibid. p. 443.
9. Add. MS 49038, ff. 235–8.
10. Ibid. 49012, ff. 2–16.
11. Ibid. 48990, ff. 131–6.
12. Sir Winston Churchill, *The World Crisis* (1938 edn), p. 137.
13. Add. MS 49035, ff. 47–8.
14. Ibid. 48993, ff. 85–93.
15. A. J. Marder, *From the Dreadnought to Scapa Flow*, i, 371.
16. Adm. 137/995, ff. 14–24.
17. Churchill, *World Crisis*, p. 153.
18. Hamilton MSS: Jellicoe to Hamilton, 17 June 1914.
19. Add. MS 48990, ff. 149–51.
20. Hamilton MSS: Jellicoe to Hamilton, 7 Aug 1914.
21. Add. MS 49037, f. 281.

3 'RESPONSIBILITY IS THE DEVIL'

1. Capt. G. Bennett, *The Battle of Jutland*, p. 33.
2. Marder, *Dreadnought to Scapa*, ii, 3–6.
3. Adm. 137/1940, ff. 33–70.
4. Add. MS 48990, f. 153. Adm. 137/1940, f. 70.
5. Marder, *Dreadnought to Scapa*, ii, 53.
6. Earl Jellicoe, *The Grand Fleet*, pp. 142–3.
7. Ibid. pp. 16–18.
8. Ibid. pp. 18–21.
9. Ibid. pp. 27–8, 72–82, 116–19, 144 *et seq.*
10. Ibid. pp. 64 *et seq.*
11. Add. MS 48990, f. 153.
12. Adm. 137/1940, f. 70.
13. Ibid. 137/996, ff. 178–80.
14. Ibid. 137/288, ff. 1–39.
15. Add. MS 48992, ff. 165–9.
16. Adm. 137/1937, ff. 13–16.
17. Add. MSS 49012, ff. 17–19, and 48992, ff. 158–63.
18. Ibid. 49012, ff. 23–5 and 29.
19. Ibid. ff. 31–6.

20. Lennoxlove MSS; Jellicoe to Fisher, 10 and 11 Nov 1914.
21. Beatty MSS: Jellicoe to Beatty, 12 Nov 1914.
22. Add. MS 49006, ff. 43–4.
23. Ibid. 48992, ff. 165–9.
24. Adm. 137/995, ff. 193–202.
25. Add MS 49006, ff. 45–8.
26. Adm. 137/995, ff. 207–10.
27. Ibid. ff. 211 and 214.
28. Ibid. ff. 68–70 and 77–9.
29. Churchill, *World Crisis*, pp. 442–4.
30. Add. MS 48990, ff. 175–7 and 183–4.
31. Ibid. 49006, ff. 74–8.
32. Adm. 137/1943, ff. 336–48.
33. Add. MS 49008, ff. 8–10.
34. Lennoxlove MSS: Jellicoe to Fisher, 2 Dec 1914.
35. Beatty MSS.
36. Add. MS 49008, ff. 15–17.
37. Ibid. ff. 39–40.
38. Add. MS 48990, ff. 175–82 and 191–3.
39. Beatty MSS. Add. MS 49008, ff. 12–18. Hamilton MSS.

4 THE LONG HAUL

1. Adm. 137/1945, ff. 233–6.
2. Ibid. 137/1937, ff. 206–9. Jackson MSS: Jellicoe to Jackson, 24 June 1915.
3. Add. MSS 49006, ff. 94–5.
4. Ibid. 49007, ff. 45–8.
5. Lord Hankey, *The Supreme Command*, ii, 317.
6. Hamilton MSS: Jellicoe to Hamilton, 9 Nov 1915.
7. Add. MS 49006, f. 140: Jellicoe to Fisher, 7 Feb 1915.
8. Jackson MSS: Jellicoe to Jackson, 16 June 1915.
9. Beatty MSS. Add. MS 49008, ff. 61–9.
10. Ibid. 48990, ff. 209–15.
11. Ibid. 48992, ff. 1–3 and 6–13.
12. Adm. 137/1953, ff. 9–10.
13. Hamilton MSS: Jellicoe to Hamilton, 16 Apr 1916. Jellicoe, *Grand Fleet*, pp. 85–7. Bacon, *Jellicoe*, pp. 204–7.
14. Add. MS 49008, ff. 61–4.
15. Hamilton MSS: Jellicoe to Hamilton, 12 and 17 Sept 1915. Jackson MSS: Jellicoe to Jackson, 22 and 30 Sept 1915.
16. Hamilton MSS: Jellicoe to Hamilton, 26 Apr 1915.
17. Add. MS 49008, ff. 36–7.
18. Lennoxlove MSS.
19. Add. MS 48992, ff. 4–5.
20. Beatty MSS: Jellicoe to Beatty, 29 Jan 1916.

21. Lennoxlove MSS.

22. Add. MS 49008, ff. 80–5.

23. Beatty MSS: Jellicoe to Beatty, 20 Feb 1916. Lennoxlove MSS: Jellicoe to Fisher, 22 Feb 1916.

24. Add. MS 49009, ff. 28–9.

25. Jackson MSS: Jellicoe to Jackson, 5 Mar 1916.

26. Adm. 137/835, ff. 42 *et seq.*, 60–72, 100–10, 117–18. Beatty MSS: Jellicoe to Beatty, 29 Jan 1916.

27. Marder, *Dreadnought to Scapa*, iii, 72–3.

28. Beatty MSS: Jellicoe to Beatty, 18 and 23 Nov and 12 Dec 1915. Add. MS 49008, ff. 67–9.

5 JUTLAND

1. A. J. Marder, *Portrait of an Admiral*, p. 201.

2. Beatty MSS: Jellicoe to Beatty, 11 Apr 1916. Add. MS 49008, ff. 92–6.

3. Jackson MSS: Jellicoe to Jackson, 13 Apr 1916.

4. Add. MS 49012, ff. 40–4.

5. Ibid. 49008, ff. 92–6.

6. Jackson MSS: Jellicoe to Jackson, 8 and 9 Mar and 26 Apr 1916. Add. MS 49009, ff. 34–5.

7. Marder, *Dreadnought to Scapa*, ii, 433.

8. Jackson MSS.

9. Sir J. S. Corbett, *History of the Great War: Naval Operations*, iii, 318.

10. Add. MS 49014, ff. 1–70.

11. Marder, *Dreadnought to Scapa*, iii, 5.

12. Ibid. pp. 12–15.

13. Cmdr J. Irving, *The Smoke-Screen of Jutland*, p. 24.

14. Marder, *Dreadnought to Scapa*, iii, 32.

15. Account by W. F. Clarke in Roskill MSS.

16. Add. MS 49014, ff. 40–58.

17. Ibid. 52505 (Evan-Thomas Papers).

18. Churchill, *World Crisis*, pp. 1046–7.

19. Admiral Sir F. Dreyer, *The Sea Heritage*, p. 146.

20. Lt-Cmdr W. T. Bagot, trans. of German official account of the Battle of Jutland, from O. Gross, *Der Krieg zur See*, v, 99.

21. Quoted in Marder, *Dreadnought to Scapa*, iii, 91.

22. Add. MS 49012, ff. 23–5.

23. Marder, *Dreadnought to Scapa*, iii, 116.

24. Lord Chatfield, *The Navy and Defence*, p. 148.

25. Marder, *Dreadnought to Scapa*, iii, 117.

26. Irving, *Smoke-Screen*, p. 176.

27. Adm. 116/2067: 'Some Remarks on Certain Paragraphs' [in the draft of the Jutland chapters of Sir J. S. Corbett's *Naval Operations*, iii].

28. Add. MS 49014, f. 278 ('Errors made in Jutland Battle').

6 AFTER JUTLAND

1. Bennett, *Jutland*, pp. 155–6.
2. Add. MS 49014, f. 61.
3. Quoted in Marder, *Dreadnought to Scapa*, iii, 188.
4. Add. MS 49014, f. 61.
5. Bacon, *Jellicoe*, pp. 327–9, which gives the text in full.
6. Jackson MSS: Jellicoe to Jackson, 5 June 1916.
7. Add. MS 49017, ff. 143, 145–6.
8. L. S. Amery, *My Political Life*, ii, 258; also private information.
9. Sir S. Leslie, *Long Shadows*, pp. 213–14.
10. Marder, *Dreadnought to Scapa*, iii, 192–3.
11. Add. MS 49008, ff. 112–14.
12. Leslie, *Shadows*, p. 216.
13. Jackson MSS: Jellicoe to Jackson, 7 Aug 1916.
14. Beatty MSS: Beatty to Lady Beatty, 8 Aug 1916.
15. Adm. 137/2027, f. 143.
16. Ibid. ff. 245–7 and 255–6.
17. Chatfield, *Navy and Defence*, p. 157.
18. Marder, *Dreadnought to Scapa*, iii, 217–18.
19. Ibid. p. 220.
20. Add. MS 49011, ff. 1–169.
21. Adm. 137/1937, *passim*.
22. Marder, *Dreadnought to Scapa*, iii, 285.
23. Jackson MSS: Jellicoe to Jackson, 5 June, 31 July, 7, 10 and 15 Aug. 1916.
24. Marder, *Dreadnought to Scapa*, iii, 248.
25. Jackson MSS: Jellicoe to Jackson, 23 Aug 1916.
26. Adm. 137/1937, ff. 44–50, 54–5 and 120–33.
27. Jackson MSS: Jellicoe to Jackson, 9 and 12 July 1916. Add. MSS 49009, ff. 58–60.
28. Jackson MSS.
29. Marder, *Dreadnought to Scapa*, iii, 250.
30. Add. MS 49008, ff. 125–30.
31. Ibid. ff. 121–3.
32. Marder, *Dreadnought to Scapa*, iii, 253.
33. Add. MS 48992, ff. 61–74.
34. Ibid. 49035, f. 169.
35. Ibid. 49009, f. 78.
36. Ibid. 49007, ff. 170–1 and 177–81.

7 FIRST SEA LORD: THE SUBMARINE PERIL

1. Rear-Admiral Sir D. E. R. Brownrigg, *Indiscretions of the Naval Censor*, pp. 67–8.

2. Earl Jellicoe, *The Crisis of the Naval War*, pp. 6–7, and *The Submarine Peril*, pp. 35–7.

3. Jellicoe, *Crisis*, pp. 8–13, and *Submarine Peril*, p. 38.

4. Lord Beaverbrook, *Men and Power*, pp. 151 *et seq.*

5. Jellicoe, *Crisis*, p. 7.

6. Ibid. chap. ii, *passim*. Sir H. Newbolt, *History of the Great War: Naval Operations*, iv, 323 *et seq.*

7. Ibid. pp. 326–7.

8. Ibid. pp. 331 and 341.

9. Ibid. pp. 331–2 and 342–3.

10. Jellicoe, *Submarine Peril*, pp. 10–13.

11. Newbolt, *Great War*, iv, 349.

12. Beatty MSS.

13. Newbolt, *Great War*, iv, 350–1.

14. Jellicoe, *Submarine Peril*, pp. 16–17.

15. Newbolt, *Great War*, iv, 385.

16. Adm. 1/8480.

17. Ibid.

18. R. Blake (ed.), *The Private Papers of Douglas Haig*, p. 221.

19. Jellicoe, *Submarine Peril*, pp. 96–102.

20. Dewar, *Navy from Within*, p. 220.

21. Bellairs Papers.

22. Quoted in Newbolt, *Great War*, v, 5.

23. Jellicoe, *Submarine Peril*, p. 111.

24. Ibid. p. 96.

25. Ibid. pp. 112–13. Hankey, *Supreme Command*, pp. 646–7. Newbolt, *Great War*, v, 10–15.

26. Ibid. pp. 15–16. Jellicoe, *Submarine Peril*, pp. 104–6. Rear-Admiral W. S. Chalmers, *Life and Letters of David, Earl Beatty*, pp. 291–292

27. Vice-Admiral W. S. Sims, *The Victory at Sea*, pp. 5–7.

28. Jellicoe, *Submarine Peril*, pp. 70–1.

29. Sims, *Victory at Sea*, pp. 8 and 12.

30. Hankey, *Supreme Command*, pp. 648–9.

31. P. Guinn, *British Strategy and Politics, 1914–18*, p. 228. Newbolt, *Great War*, v, 18.

32. Newbolt, *Great War*, v, p. 198. Hankey, *Supreme Command*, p. 650.

33. Duff MSS: Jellicoe to Duff, 13 Aug, and Duff to Jellicoe, 15 Aug 1928.

34. Newbolt, *Great War*, v, 19.

35. Jellicoe, *Submarine Peril*, pp. 124–8.

36. Hamilton MSS.

37. Jellicoe, *Submarine Peril*, p. 128.

38. D. Lloyd George, *War Memoirs*, iii, 1162–3.

39. Jellicoe, *Submarine Peril*, pp. 130–1.

40. Hankey, *Supreme Command*, p. 650.

41. Ibid.

42. Jellicoe, *Submarine Peril*, p. 129.

43. Ibid. pp. 130 *et seq.* Jellicoe, *Crisis*, pp. 132–3. Newbolt, *Great War*, v, 44–5, 48–54, 81–2, 99–106, 112–18, 134–42 and 160–4.

44. Quoted in Jellicoe, *Submarine Peril,* p. 116.
45. Ibid. pp. 216–17.

8 FIRST SEA LORD: DISMISSAL

1. Add. MS 49008, ff. 125–6. Beatty MSS: Jellicoe to Beatty, 13 Dec 1916.
2. Marder, *Fear God,* iii, 416.
3. Beatty MSS: Jellicoe to Beatty, 2 June 1917.
4. Dewar, *Navy from Within,* p. 227.
5. Hankey, *Supreme Command,* p. 658.
6. Hamilton MSS: Jellicoe to Hamilton, 25 Apr 1917.
7. Beatty MSS: Jellicoe to Beatty, 13, 20, 23 and 28 Dec 1916; 4 and 25 Jan 1917.
8. Ibid.: Jellicoe to Beatty, 4 Jan 1917.
9. Add. MS 49008, ff. 135–9.
10. Ibid. ff. 140–3.
11. Add. MS 49009, ff. 90–2.
12. Ibid. 49008, ff. 150–5.
13. Correspondence quoted in Chalmers, *Beatty,* pp. 313–17.
14. Add. MS 49008, ff. 135–56. Beatty MSS: Jellicoe to Beatty, 24 Mar, 12 Apr and 1 May 1917.
15. Beatty to Lady Beatty, 24 June 1917, quoted in Chalmers, *Beatty.* p. 319.
16. Beaverbrook, *Men and Power,* p. 161.
17. Hankey, *Supreme Command,* pp. 652–3.
18. Beatty MSS: Jellicoe to Beatty, 10 May 1917.
19. Jellicoe, *Crisis,* pp. 232–3.
20. Add. MS 49008, f. 156.
21. Jellicoe, *Crisis,* p. 235.
22. Beaverbrook, *Men and Power,* p. 162.
23. Hankey, *Supreme Command,* pp. 652–3.
24. Marder, *Portrait,* pp. 253–60.
25. Adm. 1/8489.
26. Dewar, *Navy from Within,* pp. 213, 229–30.
27. Adm. 1/8489.
28. Beatty MSS: Jellicoe to Beatty, 8 June 1917.
29. Lloyd George, *Memoirs,* p. 1174. Dewar, *Navy from Within,* p. 230.
30. Newbolt, *Great War,* v, 38–41, 45–8 and 160–2. Add. MSS 49008, ff. 160–2.
31. Beatty MSS: Jellicoe to Beatty, 30 June 1917.
32. Add. MS 49008, ff. 158–9.
33. Beaverbrook, *Men and Power,* pp. 163–6. Blake, *Haig,* pp. 186, 221, 229 and 240–2.
34. Hankey, *Supreme Command,* p. 651.

35. Beaverbrook, *Men and Power*, pp. 163–9. Blake, *Haig*, p. 242. A. M. Gollin, *Proconsul in Politics: A Study of Lord Milner*, p. 424.
36. Quoted in Beaverbrook, *Men and Power*, pp. 169–70.
37. Ibid. p. 170.
38. Lord Keyes, *Naval Memoirs*, ii, 108–9.
39. Lady Wester Wemyss, *Life and Letters of Lord Wester Wemyss*, pp. 362–3.
40. Beatty MSS: Jellicoe to Beatty, 4 Aug 1917.
41. Add. MS 48992, ff. 97–106.
42. Capt. S. W. Roskill, R.N., *Naval Policy Between the Wars*, i, 234–41.
43. Jellicoe, *Crisis*, pp. 166–7.
44. Beatty MSS: Jellicoe to Beatty, 31 July 1917.
45. Add. MS 49008, ff. 170–3.
46. Ibid. 49034, ff. 1–55.
47. Ibid. 49037, ff. 58–63 and 66–9. Jellicoe, *Crisis*, pp. 162–4.
48. Add. MS 48992, ff. 149–51.
49. Jellicoe, *Crisis*, pp. 15–20.
50. Ibid. p. 17.
51. Adm. 1/8524, f. 166.
52. Adm. 116/1805.
53. Add. MS 49037, ff. 72–3.
54. Quoted in Bacon, *Jellicoe*, p. 385.
55. Adm. 116/1768.
56. Add. MS 49009, ff. 1–9.
57. Lady Wemyss, *Wemyss*, p. 367.
58. Ibid. pp. 365–6.
59. Adm. 116/1807.
60. Bacon, *Jellicoe*, p. 379.
61. Lady Wemyss, *Wemyss*, p. 367.
62. Add. MS 49039, ff. 1–9.
63. Adm. 116/1807.
64. Ibid. Add MS 49039, ff. 1–9.
65. *Hansard*, xlv, 1897.
66. Add. MS 49049, f. 52. Lady Wemyss, *Wemyss*, p. 367.
67. Add. MS 49039, ff. 77–9.
68. Ibid. 49008, ff. 224–5. Beatty MSS: Jellicoe to Beatty, 25 Dec 1917 and 24 Jan 1918.
69. Add. MS 49039, ff. 39–40.
70. Ibid. ff. 1–9.
71. Adm. 116/1807. Duff MSS: 'Notes on the Dismissal of Sir John Jellicoe'.
72. Adm. 116/1807.

9 THE EMPIRE MISSION

1. Add. MS 49009, ff. 139–41.

2. Jellicoe, *Crisis*, p. 115.

3. Bethell MSS: Jellicoe to Admiral Bethell, 10 and 21 Apr 1918; Bethell to Jellicoe, 12 Apr 1918. Add. MS 49037, ff. 51–88.

4. Ibid. ff. 89–105.

5. Ibid. ff. 107–8.

6. Adm. 116/1428.

7. Add. MS 49037, ff. 113 and 117. Private information.

8. Add. MS 49008, f. 227.

9. Ibid. 49037, f. 121.

10. Ibid. ff. 115–16.

11. Ibid. 49045, ff. 58–9.

12. Ibid. ff. 35–44 and 92.

13. Ibid. ff. 220 *et seq.*

14. Ibid. 49048, ff. 14–24.

15. Ibid. 49046–7, *passim.*

16. Ibid. 49048, ff. 25–30.

17. Ibid. 49050, ff. 165 *et seq.*, and 49051, ff. 221 *et seq.*

18. Ibid. ff. 231 *et seq.*

19. Ibid. 49045, ff. 116–24.

20. Ibid. 49048, ff. 1–13 and 107 *et seq.*

21. Ibid. ff. 31–60.

22. Ibid. 49052–4, *passim.*

23. Ibid. 49045, ff. 219 *et seq.*

24. Ibid. ff. 200 *et seq.*

25. Ibid. 49055–7, *passim.*

26. Ibid. 49045, ff. 249–50.

27. Roskill, *Naval Policy*, pp. 279–80.

28. Add. MS 49035, f. 182.

29. Ibid. f. 200.

30. Sims MSS.

31. Except where otherwise stated, this paragraph is based on Bacon, *Jellicoe*, pp. 391–433.

10 THE JUTLAND CONTROVERSY AND THE CLOSING YEARS

1. HP 5.

2. HP 1.

3. HP 5.

4. Adm. 116/2067.

5. Ibid.

6. HP 5.

7. Add. MS 49041, ff. 114–6. Adm. 116/2067. HP 5.

8. Ibid.

9. Add. MS 49037, ff. 186–7: Sir Julian Corbett to Jellicoe, 20 Aug 1922.

10. Dewar, *Navy from Within*, pp. 265–6.
11. A. C. and K.G.B. Dewar, *Naval Staff Appreciation*, pp. 8–9.
12. Dewar, *Navy from Within*, p. 267.
13. Adm. 1/8564.
14. Dewars, *Appreciation*, pp. 106–7, 125, 129, 131.
15. Beatty MSS: Keyes and Chatfield to Beatty, 14 Aug 1922.
16. HP 5.
17. Beatty MSS: Keyes and Chatfield to Beatty, 14 Aug 1922.
18. Add. MS 53738, Jellicoe to Oswald Frewen, 25 Aug and 6 Nov 1922.
19. Add. MS 49041, ff. 118–20.
20. *Narrative of the Battle of Jutland*, p. 106.
21. Add. MS 52505: Jellicoe to Sir Hugh Evan-Thomas, 8 and 29 Oct 1923; 10 Feb and 3 Aug 1924.
22. Information supplied by Captain S. W. Roskill, R.N.
23. Add. MS 49037, ff. 177–9, 183.
24. Adm. 116/2067.
25. Add. MS 49037, ff. 189–90.
26. Adm. 116/2067. Corbett, *Great War*, iii, prefatory 'Note by the Lords Commissioners of the Admiralty'.
27. Add. MS 49040, ff. 5–146.
28. The survey of Lord Jellicoe's governor-generalship is based on Bacon, *Jellicoe*, pp. 451–84.
29. Sir Cecil Day, quoted in Bacon, *Jellicoe*, p. 477.
30. Bagot, *German Official Account*, pp. vi, 58–9, 99, 142.
31. I am indebted to Captain S. W. Roskill for pointing this out.
32. HP 5.
33. Adm. 167/67–8.
34. Duff MSS: Jellicoe to Duff, 14 and 24 Nov 1927, and 13 and 21 Aug 1928; Duff to Jellicoe 27 Nov 1927 and an undated draft; Jellicoe to Lady Duff 10 Feb 1934.
35. Ibid.: Jellicoe to Duff 28 Apr, 8 and 21 May and 28 Sept 1933.
36. Lloyd George, *Memoirs*, iii, 1134, 1136, 1138, 1162–3.
37. Bacon, *Jellicoe*, pp. 487–501.
38. Ibid. pp. 502–4, 526–7. Chalmers, *Beatty*, p. 427.
39. Churchill, *World Crisis*, p. 1015.
40. Add. MS 49037, f. 282.

APPENDIX

1. Jellicoe, *Grand Fleet*, pp. 7–11, 31, 170, and 174. Marder, *Dreadnought to Scapa*, i, 439–41.

Bibliography

A. *Manuscripts*

Admiralty Papers	(Public Record Office)
Bellairs Papers	(Public Record Office)
Bethell MSS	(Mrs A. H. Marsden-Smedley)
Duff MSS	(National Maritime Museum)
Evan-Thomas MSS ⎫ Frewen MSS ⎭	(British Museum Manuscript Department)
Hamilton MSS	(National Maritime Museum)
Harper Papers	(Royal United Service Institution)
Jellicoe MSS	(British Museum)
Keyes MSS	(Churchill College, Cambridge)
Lennoxlove MSS	(The Duke of Hamilton)
McKenna MSS	(Churchill College)
Roskill MSS	(Captain S. W. Roskill, R.N.)
Sims MSS	(Naval Historical Foundation, Washington)
Sturdee MSS	(Captain W. D. M. Staveley, R.N.)

B. *Books*

Amery, L. S., *My Political Life*. vol. ii, *War and Peace, 1914–20* (London, 1953).

Arthur, Sir G., *Life of Lord Kitchener* (London, 1940)

Aspinall-Oglander, C. F., *Roger Keyes* (London, 1951)

Bacon, Admiral Sir R., *The Life of John Rushworth, Earl Jellicoe* (London, 1936)

— *The Jutland Scandal* (London, 1925)

Bagot, Lt-Cmdr W. T., Translation (London 1926) of the German Official Account of the Battle of Jutland, from O. Gross, *Der Krieg zur See, 1914–18*, vol. v

Barnett, Correlli, *The Swordbearers: Studies in Supreme Command in the First World War* (London, 1963)

Beaverbrook, Lord, *Men and Power, 1917–18* (London, 1956)

Bellairs, Cmdr C., *The Battle of Jutland: the Sowing and the Reaping* (London, 1920)

Bennett, Captain G., R.N., '*Charlie B.*': *The Life of Lord Charles Beresford* (London, 1968)

— *The Battle of Jutland* (London, 1964)

Blake, R. (ed.), *The Private Papers of Douglas Haig, 1914–1919* (London, 1952).

Bond, B. (ed.), *Victorian Military Campaigns* (London, 1967)

Bradford, Admiral Sir E. E., *Life of Admiral of the Fleet Sir A. K. Wilson* (London, 1923)

Brownrigg, Rear-Adml Sir D. E. R., *Indiscretions of the Naval Censor* (London, 1920)

Chatfield, Lord, *The Navy and Defence* (London, 1942)

Chalmers, Rear-Adml W. S., *Life and Letters of David, Earl Beatty* (London, 1951)

Churchill, Sir Winston *The World Crisis, 1911–1918* (London, 1923–9)

Corbett, Sir J. S., *History of the Great War: Naval Operations*, vols. i–iii (London, 1921–3)

Cruttwell, C. R. M. F., *History of the Great War, 1914–1918* (2nd ed., London, 1936)

Dewar, Vice-Adml K. G. B., *The Navy from Within* (London, 1939)

Dreyer, Admiral Sir F., *The Sea Heritage* (London, 1955)

Falls, C., *The Great War* (New York, 1961)

Frost, Cmdr H. (U.S. Navy), *The Battle of Jutland* (London, 1936)

Gibson, L., and Harper, Vice-Adml J. E. T., *The Riddle of Jutland* (London, 1934)

Gollin, A. M., *Proconsul in Politics: A Study of Lord Milner* (London, 1964)

Goodenough, Admiral Sir W., *A Rough Record* (London, 1943)

Gretton, Vice-Adml Sir P., *Convoy Escort Commander* (London, 1964)

Guinn, P., *British Strategy and Politics, 1914 to 1918* (Oxford 1965)

Hankey, Lord, *The Supreme Command, 1914–18* (London, 1961)

Harper, Vice-Adml J. E. T., *The Truth about Jutland* (London, 1927)

Hase, Captain G. von, *Kiel and Jutland* (London, 1930)

Hurd, A., *The British Fleet in the Great War* (London, 1918)

Irving, Cmdr J., *The Smoke-Screen of Jutland* (London, 1966)

Jameson, Rear-Adml Sir W., *The Most Formidable Thing: The Story of the Submarine to the End of World War I* (London, 1967)

Jellicoe, Earl, *The Grand Fleet, 1914–16* (London, 1919)

— *The Crisis of the Naval War* (London, 1920)

— *The Submarine Peril* (London, 1934)

Keyes, Adml of the Fleet Lord, *Naval Memoirs, 1910–18* (London, 1934–1935)

Kipling, Rudyard, *Sea Warfare* (London, 1916)

Leslie, Sir J. R. Shane, *Long Shadows* (London, 1966)

Liddell Hart, Sir B. H., *History of the World War, 1914–1918* (London, 1934)

Lloyd, C., *The Nation and the Navy* (London, 1954)

Lloyd George, D., *War Memoirs*, vol. iii (London, 1934)

Macintyre, Captain D., R.N., *Jutland* (London, 1960)

Magnus, Sir P., *Kitchener: Portrait of an Imperialist* (London, 1938)

Marder, Arthur J., *Fear God and Dread Nought: the Correspondence of Admiral of the Fleet Lord Fisher*, 3 vols (London, 1952–9)

— *From the Dreadnought to Scapa Flow*
  1: *The Road to War, 1904–14* (London, 1961)

II: *The War Years to the Eve of Jutland* (London, 1965)

III: *Jutland and After, May 1916–December 1916* (London, 1966)

— *Portrait of an Admiral* (London, 1952)

Newbolt, Sir H., *History of the Great War: Naval Operations*, vols. iv–v (London, 1928 and 1931)

Onwe, F., *Tempestuous Journey: Lloyd George, his Life and Times* (New York, 1955)

Pollen, A. H., *The Navy in Battle* (London, 1918)

Repington, Lt-Col. C., *The First World War, 1914–18. Personal Experiences*, 2 vols (London, 1920)

Richmond, Admiral Sir H., *Sea Power in the Modern World* (London, 1934)

— *Statesmen and Sea Power* (Oxford, 1946)

Roskill, Captain S. W., R.N., *Naval Policy between the Wars*, vol. (London, 1968)

Scheer, Admiral R., *Germany's High Seas Fleet in the World War* (London, 1920)

Sims, Vice-Adml W. S., *The Victory at Sea* (London, 1920)

Spears, Sir E. L., *Prelude to Victory* (London, 1939)

Terraine, J., *Douglas Haig: the Educated Soldier* (London, 1963)

Vansittart, Lord, *The Mist Procession* (London, 1958)

Wemyss, Lady V. Wester, *Life and Letters of Lord Wester Wemyss* (London, 1935)

C. *Articles*

Buist, Cmdr C., 'Lessons from Jutland', in *National Review*, Apr 1919.

Dickinson, H. W., 'Henry Cort's Bicentenary', in *Transactions of the Newcomen Society*, vol. xxi (1940–1)

Frothingham, Captain T. G., 'The Test of Fact against Fiction in the Battle of Jutland', in *U.S. Naval Institute Proceedings*, vol. liv, no. 3 (Annapolis, 1928)

Leighton, J., 'The Historical Perspective of Jutland', in *Journal of the Royal United Service Institution*, Feb–Nov 1924

Roskill, Captain S. W., R.N., 'The Dismissal of Admiral Jellicoe', in *Journal of Contemporary History*, vol. i, no. 4, Oct 1966

Index

NOTE: *Since the ranks held by many of the officers who have been referred to changed during the time covered by the references, they have been indexed with the rank held at the period to which the majority of these references apply. The same principle has been followed with regard to the titles of political and other public figures.*

Admiralty: dissatisfaction with, 92–3, 97; inadequate signal to Jellicoe during Battle of Jutland, 129–30, 236, 240–1, 243–4; Plans Section (later Division) of, 149–51, 183–5, 198–9, 235; reorganisation of, by Jellicoe, 155–6; by Geddes, 197–9

Admiralty Narrative of the Battle of Jutland, 237–40, 242, 246, 247

Agadir Crisis, 46

Alexandria, bombardment of, 20

American Navy, 31, 168–9, 172 n., 175, 183, 194–7

Anti-flash precautions: British lack of, 113, and adoption of, 138: German, 80

Anti-submarine measures, 83, 156–9, 161, 192–3

Arabic, S.S., sinking of, 84

Arabi Pasha, revolt of, 20–1

Arbuthnot, Rear-Admiral Sir Robert, 120

Asquith, H. H., 95, 96, 153, 200, 206

Asquith, Mrs, 206

Auchinleck, General Sir Claude, 71 n., 77

August 19, 1916, Scheer's sortie on, 140–2, 249 n.

Australia, 213, 214, 215, 225, 228

Bacon, Vice-Admiral Sir Reginald, 60, 151, 158, 186, 196, 203–4, 206, 207, 246, 248

Balfour, A. J., 85–6, 90, 93, 133 and n., 134, 143, 149, 151, 152, 153 and n., 171, 201, 207–9

Battenberg, Prince Louis of, 50, 56, 66, 72 n., 189, 206

Bayly, Vice-Admiral Sir Lewis, 23, 55 n., 84, 91, 171, 256

Beatty, Admiral Sir David, 29, 60, 63, 73, 74–5, 77–82, 84, 86–90, 92–8, 100–2, 103, 109–16, 118, 120, 124–8, 131, 133–6, 138–9, 141, 144, 146–8, 153, 158–9, 168, 171, 173, 178–82, 185–7, 191, 195, 201–2 and n., 206, 210, 212, 228, 232–6, 239 and n., 241, 243, 247–9, 253–4

Beaverbrook, Lord, 181

Benson, Admiral W. S. (U.S. Navy), 194, 197

Berehaven, 21, 41, 49

Beresford, Admiral Lord Charles, 42, 151, 189 n., 190, 200

Bethell, Admiral Sir A., 211

Borden, Sir R., 223, 224

Borkum, 55, 81–2, 192

Boxer Rebellion, 31–5

Boy Scout Movement, Jellicoe's connection with, 251

Bradford, Vice-Admiral Sir Edward, 76, 256

Bridgeman, Admiral Sir Francis, 27, 45, 46

British Expeditionary Force, crossing to France of, 62–3

British Legion, Jellicoe's connection with, 251

Brock, Rear-Admiral Sir Osmond de Beauvoir, 153, 232–3

Brownrigg, Captain Sir Douglas, 154

Burney, Vice-Admiral Sir Cecil, 18–19, 43, 60, 68, 73, 86, 118, 141, 153, 154, 190, 192 and n., 206, 212, 257

Callaghan, Admiral Sir George, 46, 47, 48–9, 53, 56–8, 59, 60
Canada, 213, 214, 215, 223–6, 228, 252
Cape of Good Hope, 18
Carson, Sir Edward, 153, 155, 163, 167, 171, 173, 175, 180, 181 and n., 183–90, 201, 204 n., 207–9; relations with Jellicoe, 156
Cayzer, Sir Charles, 30, 36 and n., 92 n.
Channel Fleet, 38, 60, 62, 68, 72, 73, 80, 86, 257
Chatfield, Captain A. E. M., 124, 137, 138, 232, 233, 236, 237, 241
China, 30–5
Churchill, (Sir) Winston S., 42, 47, 48, 50–3, 55–8, 68–72, 76–8, 80–1, 84, 85, 97 n., 104, 119, 155, 192, 205, 210, 212, 253; his *The World Crisis*, 50 n., 77, 247–8
Close blockade, abandonment of, 55
Colville, Admiral Sir Stanley, 29–30, 31, 65, 206
Conference, Inter-Allied Naval, 4–5 Sept, 1917, 195
Convoy system: discussed, 152; adoption of, 165–76, 192, 250; American attitude to, 175
Corbett, Sir Julian S., 99, 103, 235, 237 n., 240–2
Coronel, Battle of, 72 and n., 75 n.
Cromarty, 60, 65, 66, 76, 78
Culme-Seymour, Admiral Sir Michael, 27, 28, 29
Cunningham, Admiral of the Fleet Lord, 77, 120, 253
Curzon, Lord, 188

Daily Mail, 199–200
Daily Telegraph, 246–7
Daniel, Colonel E. Y., 241
Dannreuther, Commander H. E., 136
Dardanelles, 19, 82
Der Krieg zur See, 247
Devonport, 157; Devonport Command, 211
Dewar, Captain A. C., 235–7

Dewar, Captain K. G. B., 165, 172 n., 184, 185 n., 235–7
Director firing system, 49–50, 137
Dogger Bank, 147, 149; Battle of, 79, 80, 82, 133
Dover, 60, 158, 186, 249; Barrage, 158 and n., 203; Patrol, 60, 111, 211, 257; Straits, 62, 157, 158, 196
Dreyer, Captain F. C., 39, 119, 137, 138, 154, 155, 214, 228
Duff, Rear-Admiral A. L., 154, 155, 159, 167, 172, 201, 207–9, 249, 250; conversion to adoption of convoy system, 173–4
Dutch East Indies, 218

Empire Mission, 211, 212–29; origins, 212–14; Jellicoe's instructions, 213–14; report on India, 215–16; on Australia, 216–22; section on the Capital Ship, 216–17, 226; report on New Zealand, 222–3; on Canada, 224–6; reaction to Jellicoe's report, 226–7; assessment of the Mission, 227
Esquimalt, 225
Evan-Thomas, Rear-Admiral Sir Hugh, 113, 118, 120, 239–40, 242
Excellent, H.M.S. (gunnery training establishment), 21, 22, 24, 27, 36

Falkland Islands, 18, 72 n.
Fawkes, Rear-Admiral W., 36–7
Field, Rear-Admiral Sir Frederick, 241
First (afterwards Grand) Fleet, 47 n., 55
Firth of Forth, 60, 76, 103
Fisher, Admiral of the Fleet Lord, 21, 24, 37–9, 44–7, 49, 50, 69, 72 and n., 73–4, 78, 80–1, 84–6, 93, 94, 134, 151, 153, 155, 177, 190; reforms of, 37–8; paper 'On the Oil Engine and the Submarine', 53–5; correspondence with Jellicoe, 76–7, 85, 86, 94, 96; resignation, 85
Fisher, Captain W. W., 155
France, 62, 150, 157, 168, 182
Frewen, Commander O., 238

Gallipoli, 19

Gamble, Vice-Admiral Sir Douglas, 86, 256

Geddes, Sir Eric, 181–2, 187–8, 189, 190, 191, 194 n., 201–5, 206–9; his reorganisation of the Admiralty, 197–9, 211–12

George V, 189, 204, 206, 253

Germany, naval rivalry with, 39, 41, 42–3, 52

Gibraltar, 17, 18, 22, 41 n., 174, 175

Goodenough, Commodore W. E., 16, 41, 60 and n., 78 n., 113–14, 115, 123, 140

Grand Fleet; composition of, 60; provision of recreation for, 91–2; change in strategy of, after August 19, 1916, 147–8

Grand Fleet Battle Orders, 103–6; revision of, 138–9

Gunnery practice, problems of, 65–6, 97–8

Haggard, Rear-Admiral W. H., 236, 237, 241

Haig, Field-Marshal Sir Douglas, 162, 164, 171, 182, 187–8, 251

Haldane, Lord, 47

Halifax (Nova Scotia), 158, 225

Hall, Captain Reginald, 138

Halsey, Rear-Admiral L., 91, 154, 182, 188, 204, 207–9

Hamilton, Vice-Admiral Sir Frederick, 56, 58, 82, 86, 90 n., 94, 173, 191 n.

Hankey, Colonel Sir Maurice, 16 n., 85, 99, 171, 174, 177, 181, 184–5, 188; advocacy of convoy system, 167–8

Harper, Captain J. E. T., 230–2, 234–5, 237, 248; Harper Record, 230–5, 238, 248

Harwich, 60, 103 n., 186; Harwich Force, 63, 66, 67, 76, 78, 110–11, 140, 141–2, 149, 211, 257

Hawksley, Commodore J. R. P., 106, 123, 128

Heath, Vice-Admiral Sir Herbert, 191, 207–9

Heligoland, 62, 64, 83, 129, 179, 192, 243, 244; Heligoland Bight, 55, 64, 78, 88, 89, 111, 159, 194, 195; Battle of, 63, 75 n., 133, 196, 201

Henry, Prince, of Prussia, 31, 46

High Seas Fleet, 45, 61–2, 64, 66, 68, 72–4, 76, 78, 80, 88, 90, 97, 100–4, 106, 115–33, 141–2, 147, 149, 151, 152, 192, 236, 241, 244, 247, 249

Hipper, Vice-Admiral F., 78, 107, 111–14, 116, 124, 125, 132

History of the War: Naval Operations, 235, 240–2, 248–9

Holtzendorff, Admiral H. von, 35 n., 160, 161

Hong Kong, 217, 218, 219

Hood, Rear-Admiral the Hon. Horace, 199

Hope, Rear-Admiral G. P. W., 199

Hornby, Vice-Admiral Sir Geoffrey Phipps, 19, 21

Horns Reef, 62, 111, 129–31, 147, 236, 240, 243, 244

Humber River, 60, 80–1

Hurd, Alexander, 242

Imperial War Conference of 1918, 212–14

India, 213, 214, 215–16

Ingenohl, Admiral F. von, 64, 78, 80

Invasion, danger of, 62, 68, 97

Jackson, Admiral Sir Henry, 39 n., 85–6, 87, 90, 94, 96, 100, 103, 136, 140, 143–7, 148, 152–3, 166

Jackson, Captain Thomas, 109 and n., 133 n.

Japan, 31, 214–15, 216, 217–19, 225, 227

Jellicoe, Adam, 14

Jellicoe, Edmond, 15 n., 27

Jellicoe, Rev. Frederick, 15 and n., 16

Jellicoe, George (second Earl), 211 and n.

Jellicoe, Captain J. H., 15

Jellicoe, John Rushworth: ancestry, 14–15; boyhood, 15–16; cadet in *Britannia,* 16–17; skill at games, 16, 17, 21, 28, 31; sea service, in *Newcastle,* 17–18; *Agincourt,* 18–19 and 20–1; *Cruiser,* 19; *Alexandra,* 19; *Monarch,* 22–3; *Colossus,* 23–4; *Sans Pareil* (Commander), 25; *Victoria* (Commander), 26–7; *Ramillies* (Commander), 27–30; *Centurion* (Flag-

Jellicoe—*cont.*

Captain), 30–5; *Drake* (Captain), 36–7; Rear-Admiral second-in-command of Atlantic Fleet, 41; Vice-Admiral commanding Atlantic Fleet, 44–6; commanding Second Division of Home Fleet, 46–50; Admiral and Commander-in-Chief, Grand Fleet, 58–152; courses at Greenwich and Portsmouth, 19, 21; specialisation in gunnery, 20, 21, 24; service in H.M.S. *Excellent*, 21–2, 24, 36; *protégé* of Fisher, 21–2, 41, 44–5, 46–7; life-saving exploits, 23–4; kindness to R.N.R. officer, 25; service at Admiralty: as Assistant Director of Naval Ordnance, 24–25; Assistant Controller, 35–6; Director of Naval Ordnance, 39–40; Controller, 41–4; Second Sea Lord, 50–6; First Sea Lord, 152–205; member of Ordnance Committee, 30; service during Boxer Rebellion, 32–5; K.C.V.O., 41; effects of strain on, 42, 44, 53, 59, 82, 177, 179, 193, 200; knowledge of German Navy, 14, 42–3, 68; dislike of night-fighting, 45 and n., 128; tactical ideas, 49, 67–8, 103–6; brilliant part in naval manœuvres of 1913, 53; character, 59; anxieties and caution, 66–74, 76–7, 88–9, 92–7, 104, 106; health, 82, 92, 140, 147, 177, 252; his dissatisfaction with the Admiralty, 93–4; criticism of, 99–100, 110, 119–20, 124, 142, 199–200, 247–8; difficulties at Jutland, 115–18; deployment at Jutland, 118–20, 247; Beatty's changed opinion of him, 135–6; post-Jutland reforms, 137–40; his changed opinion of Beatty, 148; his reorganisation of the Admiralty War Staff, 155–6; proposes abandonment of 'side-shows', 162–4; attitude to convoy system, 165–8, 173; relations with American admirals, 197; dismissal from First Sea Lordship, 203–5; Viscount, 205; offered Governor-Generalship of Australia, 212; forecasts war with Japan, 214–19; Admiral of the Fleet, 228; Governor-General of New Zealand, 234, 244–6; Earl, 246; closing years, 251–3; writings: *The Grand Fleet*, 210, 242, 244; *The Crisis of the Naval War*, 211, 250; *The Submarine Peril*, 174, 250

Jellicoe, Lady, 36, 37, 58, 140, 205, 211, 214, 228, 229, 246, 252

Jellicoe, Mrs Lucy, 15

Jellicoe, Samuel, 14–15

Jerram, Sir Thomas, 87, 109, 125–6, 127–8, 153

Jutland, Battle of: references to, 26, 43, 50, 67, 76, 80, 88, 91 n., 101, 143, 148, 180, 230, 242, 247, 249, 253, 256; battle-cruiser action, 111–15; gunnery of battle-cruisers at, 76, 98, 114, 233, 247; signalling shortcomings at, 115; first battlefleet action, 121; second battlefleet action, 123–4, 247; night operations, 130–1, 244; losses in, 132; assessment of result, 132–3; reactions to: British public's, 133–4; Jellicoe's, 134–135; the Navy's, 135; Beatty's, 135–6

'Jutland Controversy', 137, 181, 230–244, 246–8

Jutland Despatches, 234

Kattegat, 107, 116, 129, 192, 194

Keyes, Rear-Admiral Roger, 191, 199, 203, 236, 237, 241

Kiel, 43, 192; Kiel Canal, 64, 98

Kinpurnie Castle, 92, 140

Kitchener, Field-Marshal Lord, 29, 162; his death, 134

Lambert, Captain C. F. (Fourth Sea Lord), 143, 145–6

Lloyd George, D., 42, 50, 52, 94, 153, 156, 166, 167, 171, 173–4, 178, 181, 182–8, 189–90, 194, 204 and n., 205, 207, 209, 249

Long, Walter (Lord), 224, 226, 232, 234, 238 and n.

Lowestoft, 102

Maclay, Sir Joseph (Controller of Shipping), 189

Madden, Admiral Sir Charles, 37, 39 n., 60, 144–6, 147, 153, 179, 195, 206, 210, 248, 249

Malta, 19, 20

Manisty, Paymaster Rear-Admiral Sir Eldon, 248–9

Marder, Professor Arthur J., 103 n., 106, 113 n., 124, 237

Massey, W. F., 246

May, Admiral Sir William, 35, 104

Mayo, Admiral H. T. (U.S. Navy), 194, 195–7

McKenna, Reginald, 41–2, 47, 50, 242

Mediterranean, 20–1, 28, 37, 89, 143, 150, 175, 183, 191, 211, 253; Mediterranean Fleet, 19, 28

Merchant shipping losses, 159–60, 161, 169 and n., 176

Milner, Lord, 188–9

Mines, 64, 66 n., 67, 69–70, 83, 87–9, 100, 104, 121, 159 and n., 179 and n., 216

Moore, Rear-Admiral Sir Gordon, 79

Moray Firth, 66, 89, 98

Murray, Sir Oswin, 194 n.

Napier, Vice-Admiral Sir Trevelyan, 127, 201, 226

Naval Staff, lack of a, 93

Naval Staff Appreciation of the Battle of Jutland, 235–7, 238, 247

Nelson, Lord, 13, 47, 96 and n., 104, 119 n., 153, 206, 253

New Guinea, 218, 219

New York, 158, 175

New Zealand, 212, 213, 214, 215, 223, 228–9, 250

Newbolt, Sir Henry, 248–9

Northcliffe, Lord, 156, 199, 204 and n.

North Sea Barrage, 194–6

Oil fuel, 52–3

Oliver, Vice-Admiral Sir Henry, 133 n., 143, 147, 152, 155, 166, 167, 177, 183, 190, 191 and n., 198, 199, 207–9, 241

Orkney Islands, 63, 65, 110, 134, 168

Ostend, 83, 186, 196

Page, Walter H. (American Ambassador), 171

Paine, Commodore G., 207–9

Pakenham, Rear-Admiral W. C., 137

Patton, Admiral Philip, 15

Pelly, Captain H. B., 79

Pentland Firth, 66, 89, 98

Pohl, Admiral H. von, 35 n., 80, 83, 100

Poore, Admiral Sir Richard, 51

Port Said, 20–1

Portsmouth, 19, 21, 43, 157

Pound, Captain Dudley, 241

'Q-ships', 150, 159

Queen Elizabeth class of battleships, 48, 256

Queenstown, 84

Richmond, Captain Herbert, 99, 104, 183, 184, 185 and n., 190, 232 n., 240, 241

Robeck, Vice-Admiral Sir John de, 153

Robertson, General Sir William, 162, 164, 171, 182

Roberts-West, Midshipman, 27 and n.

Rodman, Rear-Admiral H. (U.S. Navy), 196

'Room 40', 109, 129–30, 138, 141

Roskill, Captain S. W., 193, 240–1 and n.

Rosyth, 44, 73, 74, 76, 78, 80–1, 103, 120, 135, 139, 143, 145, 147, 180, 186, 189, 191, 202, 208, 212; dock at, 43, 173

Royal Air Force, establishment of, 193–4

Royal Indian Marine, 215–16

Royal Naval Air Service, 51, 90, 149, 159, 193–4

Royal Naval College, Greenwich, 19, 21

Rushworth, Charles, 18–19

Russia, 21, 134, 218

St Lawrence Hall, 46, 250, 252

Salonika, 143, 157, 160, 162, 164

Scapa Flow, 16, 55, 56, 67, 73, 76, 80–81, 82, 84, 103, 131, 132, 133, 136, 143, 147, 180, 205; defences of, 64–5

Scarborough Raid, 78
Scheer, Admiral R., 102, 107, 110, 114, 116, 118–19, 121, 123–4, 127, 129–30, 132, 134, 140–2, 149, 239 n., 240, 242, 243, 248, 257
Schleswig-Holstein, 82, 100, 129
Scott, Admiral Sir Percy, 36–7, 39, 49, 137
Seaplanes, 90–1, 100; seaplane-carriers, 90–1
Seymour, Admiral Sir Beauchamp, 20
Seymour, Vice-Admiral Sir Edward, 30, 32
Shells: defects of British, 43–4, 113, 233; armour-piercing, 137–8
Shetland Islands, 62, 63, 65, 194, 199
Sims, Rear-Admiral W. S. (U.S. Navy), 39–40, 169–71, 195, 196, **197, 229**
Singapore, 18, 218, 219, 225
Slade, Admiral Sir Edmond, 240
Smith, F. E. (Lord Birkenhead), 135, **200**
Smuts Committee, 193–4
Solomon Islands, 219, 228
South Africa, 213
Spee, Admiral Graf von, 72 and n.
Squadrons:
    British: First Battle Squadron, 86, 91, 153, 256; Second Battle Squadron, 78, 86, 109, 125, 256; Third Battle Squadron, 60, 72, 73, 74, 76, 80, 103, 256; Fourth Battle Squadron, 86, 154, 256; Fifth Battle Squadron, 68, 103, 111–15, 123, 128, 139, 141, 239 and n.; First Battle-Cruiser Squadron, 60, 75–6, 78 and n., 84 n., 256; Third Battle-Cruiser Squadron, 60, 114, 116; Battle-Cruiser Force, 84 and n., 98, 106, 111–15, 135, 136–7, 139–40, 141; First Cruiser Squadron, 109, 120; Second Cruiser Squadron, 60; Third Cruiser Squadron, 60, 80, 103; Tenth Cruiser Squadron, 62, 178–9; First Light Cruiser Squadron, 60; Second Light Cruiser Squadron, 60 n., 113, 128; Third Light Cruiser Squadron, 127;

Fourth Light Cruiser Squadron, 123, 128.
    German: First Battle Squadron, 128; Second Battle Squadron, 107, 127; Fourth Scouting Group, 127
Stirling, Captain A. J. B., 131
Sturdee, Vice-Admiral Sir Doveton, 18, 72 n., 86, 104, 153
Submarines, 54–5, 62: British, 64, 129, 157–8, 219, 255; German, 63, 65, 70, 83–4, 87–8, 100, 104, 107, 109, 121 and n., 141, 149–50, 151, 157–8, 176, 255; unrestricted submarine warfare, 83–84, 160–76
Sunderland, 107, 140
Swilly, Lough, 65
Sylt, 192

Tennyson-d'Eyncourt, Sir Eustace, 138
Third Fleet, 257
Times, The, 149
Tip-and-run raids, German, 73, 97, 102
Tirpitz, Grand Admiral A. von, 78, 90
Tondern, 100, 102, 103
Tothill, Rear-Admiral H. H. D., 207–209
Trafalgar, Battle of, 119 n., 153
Tryon, Admiral Sir George, 26
Tyrwhitt, Commodore, R. Y., 60, 111, 257

United States, 150, 165, 166, 168–9, 170–1, 194, 225, 227, 229
Usedom, Admiral von, 32, 34–5, 43

War Cabinet, 162, 163, 178, 185–6, 187, 188, 194
War Committee, 96 and n., 99, 152
Warrender, Vice-Admiral Sir George, 60, 78, 86–7, 256
Warships:
    British: *Abdiel*, 129; *Aboukir*, 63, 84 n.; *Agincourt*, 18–21, 256; *Albemarle*, 41; *Alexandra*, 19; *Audacious*, 71; *Australia*, 256; *Barfleur*, 31; *Barham*, 113 n., 239 n., 256; *Benbow*, 256; *Birmingham*, 65 n.; *Campania*, 90;

Warships—*cont.*

Camperdown, 26; *Canada*, 256; *Caroline*, 128; *Castor*, 106, 125; *Centurion*, 16 n., 30; *Chatham*, 222; *Colossus*, 23–4; *Commonwealth*, 99; *Cressy*, 63, 84 n.; *Cruiser*, 19; *Defence*, 120; *Dreadnought*, 38, 84; *Emperor of India*, 256; *Erin*, 256; *Exmouth*, 39; *Falmouth*, 142; *Gourkho* (canteen-ship), 91–2; *Hampshire*, 134; *Hawke*, 63; *Hercules*, 44, 48; *Hermes*, 50; *Hogue*, 63, 84 n.; *Hood*, 217; *Illustrious*, 16 n.; *Indefatigable*, 113, 120, 230, 256; *Indomitable*, 256; *Inflexible*, 72 n., 256; *Invincible*, 72 n., 256; *Iron Duke*, 16, 60, 92, 116, 118, 128, 131, 133, 136, 141, 242, 243, 253, 256; *King Edward VII*, 89; *King George V*, 128; *Lion*, 79, 98, 113 and n., 116, 118, 129, 130, 239 n., 242, 243, 256; *Lord Nelson*, 257; *Malaya*, 113, 256; *Marlborough*, 118, 128, 256; *Monarch*, 22–3, 65 n.; *Neptune*, 84; *Newcastle*, 17–18; *New Zealand*, 111, 229, 256; *Nottingham*, 141, 142; *Orion*, 20; *Pathfinder*, 63; *Princess Royal*, 72 and n., 75, 116, 125, 130, 256; *Queen Elizabeth*, 217, 256; *Queen Mary*, 113, 120, 230, 256; *Renown*, 217; *Repulse*, 217; *Revenge*, 256; *Royalist*, 128, 140, 141; *Royal Oak*, 256; *Royal Sovereign*, 217; *Sans Pareil*, 25, 27; *Southampton*, 113, 115, 116, 118, 123; *Tiger*, 75, 79, 98; *Trafalgar*, 29; *Valiant*, 113, 118, 256; *Victoria*, 26–7; *Warrior*, 120; *Warspite*, 113, 120, 256

German: *Blücher*, 72, 79; *Derfflinger*, 75, 127, 132; *Deutschland*, 31; *Friedrich der Grosse*, 109; *Hela*, 64; *Helgoland*, 257; *König Albert*, 257; *Lützow*, 120–1, 231; *Magdeburg*, 78; *Meteor*, 89 and n.; *Moewe*, 167, 178; *Moltke*, 121; *Nassau*, 257; *Pommern*, 131; *Seydlitz*, 79–80, 107, 127, 132; *Von der Tann*, 79; *Westfalen*, 142; *Wiesbaden*, 120

Washington Naval Conference, 227

Wavell, General Sir Archibald, 71 n., 77

Weekly Despatch, 134–5

Wemyss, Vice-Admiral Sir Rosslyn, 183, 189, 190–1, 197, 198–9, 202–203, 204, 206, 207, 208, 226, 230, 231–2, 240

West Indies, 18, 36

Wight, Isle of, 35, 46, 250

Wilhelm II, 46, 61, 133, 254

Wilhelmshaven, 107, 109

Wilson, Admiral of the Fleet Sir A. K., 25, 37, 45, 46, 47, 75, 76, 85, 155

Wilson, President Woodrow, 229

Woods, Commander A. R. W., 119 and n.

Yarmouth, 73, 140, 141

Zeebrugge, 83, 86

Zeppelins, 69, 87, 90–1, 107, 134, 141, 142, 149

"It's no exaggeration to say that no living person has a greater knowledge and understanding of the Jellicoe story than Professor Patterson," writes Captain S. W. Roskill of this first biography to take account of all the newly available sources. "In this book he has produced an admirable condensation from a vast mass of material which cannot be easily assimilated. It is a remarkable feat of careful research and lucid exposition."

As protégé of Lord Fisher, Jellicoe achieved a rapid rise to the highest positions in the Navy before the First World War. Having traced his early career, Professor Patterson describes Jellicoe's problems when, at the outbreak of war, he became commander of the largest fleet the world has ever known—he was, as Winston Churchill said, the only man who could have lost the war in an afternoon.

Professor Patterson sets out the pros and cons of the methods by which, throughout the long vigil of Scapa and at Jutland, Jellicoe preserved the naval superiority over the Germans that was vital to victory—though he disappointed public expectations of a new Trafalgar and his image suffered unfairly by contrast with that of Beatty, his subordinate and successor as Commander-in-Chief.

He goes on to assess Jellicoe's achievements and limitations in the perhaps still more difficult post as First Sea Lord, and seeks by careful analysis to distribute justly the much-disputed credit for the introduction of the convoy system. Finally he follows

Continued on back flap